PRACTICAL FINANCIAL
ECONOMICS

PRACTICAL FINANCIAL ECONOMICS

A New Science

Edited by Austin Murphy

Westport, Connecticut
London

Cau

Library of Congress Cataloging-in-Publication Data

Practical financial economics : a new science / edited by Austin Murphy ; foreword by
  George Frankfurter.
      p.   cm.
  Includes bibliographical references and index.
  ISBN 1–56720–539–9 (alk. paper)
  1. Corporations—Finance.   2. Risk.   I. Murphy, Austin, 1956–
HG4026.P713   2003
332.63'221—dc22   2003057992

British Library Cataloguing in Publication Data is available.

Library of Congress Catalog Card Number: 2003057992
ISBN: 1–56720–539–9

First published in 2003

Praeger Publishers, 88 Post Road West, Westport, CT 06881
An imprint of Greenwood Publishing Group, Inc.
www.praeger.com

Printed in the United States of America

The paper used in this book complies with the
Permanent Paper Standard issued by the National
Information Standards Organization (Z39.48–1984).

10   9   8   7   6   5   4   3   2   1

Professionally dedicated to
a new science of practical financial economics

and

Personally dedicated to my two young children,
who'll learn more than I'll ever know
(and who have already taught me a lot)

Contents

Foreword: Enronomics—
Desperately Seeking Toto

George Frankfurter

We have hardly scratched the surface of the Enron scandal, arguably the biggest corporate failure in the history of American capitalism, and already the case has generated enough heat to qualify as a source of renewable energy. Although the debacle is complex and does not fit easily into sound bites for the thirty-second attention span, the airwaves shimmer (more from heat than light) as both the left and right get in their licks. Even those only remotely connected to the failing firm are chewing the scenery at center stage as they emote their deep consternation and wail for "sweeping reforms" in financial disclosure, client-accountant relations, accountant-management consultant relations, protection of retirement and pension funds, 401(k)s—yada, yada, yada. Why, even the president quipped, "Ken who? I hardly knew the man!"

Public acrimony and scorn are heaped on greedy and ruthless executives, corrupt politicians (always a good target), and even not-so-corrupt politicians (whose only fault was accepting soft-money campaign contributions without which they could not have run for office). Perhaps there were no strings attached; perhaps there were. It is unclear what they did or didn't do to help promote Enron's economic welfare at the expense of the rest of us.

There are other voices as well, usually conservatives who argue that

The name of the game is risk taking, sans which there is no reward, and that if you invested in Enron stock, you should have known that you might lose some or even all your investment.

The market, afterall, did not crash, which redeems investors' confidence in the system.

I especially fancy the second argument. When the market crashed and burned in October 1987, not one of these people said that the system is bad and that it was time to replace it. No, we had the Brady Bunch back then, and they sang us a chorus: program trading and its accomplice—in essence its sine qua non, the computer—were to blame. Felix Rohatyn, a Wall Street high-flyer, opined that the worst thing to happen to the financial industry was an MBA with a laptop. This is where I raise an eyebrow. If anything, the computer makes the market more efficient because it diffuses information faster and more accurately than any other mechanism. But, what do I know?

Now, if hundreds of thousands of investors lose "big time" (to borrow a phrase from Veep Cheney), we do not need to worry if the market itself did not crash. So when exactly should we start worrying about the system? Or should we just concede that this is the only game in town—love it or leave it?

Matters, of course, run much deeper than what we see, hear, or read in the mainstream media. I suspect that what we have is a manifestation of the moral breakdown of the system we cherish and of which we are so proud. What we have, really, is cessation of proper mechanical function, which cannot be readily "fixed" with a pinch of legislation and a dash of regulatory remedies.

Before I go into the crux of my thesis, let me, as the song goes, accentuate the positive. It would appear that there is no longer such a thing as a complete loss or total disaster. If nothing else, at the least the American language has been enriched by the Enron fiasco. Our vocabulary has been broadened by several variants of the word *Enron*, such as "enronization," "enroned me," "enronish," "enron like," and more recently, "enronomics." "'Enroned' a new verb of shame," tisk-tisked the headline of an article by the *New York Times* columnist William Safire.

This, of course, is Safire the etymologist speaking, not William the archconservative. In much the same way that holography uses laser light to produce images by splitting the laser beam into two and recording the interference pattern on a photographic plate, Safire/William produces holograms that, on the surface, reflect his brilliance as a linguist and, when tilted to the light, reveal the darker, underlying image of a single-minded zealot. It was the latter image that surfaced when William, a former speechwriter for Richard Nixon and Spiro Agnew (for whom he coined the unforgettable alliteration, "nattering nabobs of negativism"), attempted to deflect any possibility that the Enron fallout would damage the White House. He congratulated George W.'s cabinet members for not accepting SOS phone calls from Enron after it struck the iceberg of financial disaster and began its *Titanic* plunge. What the conservative William could not—or chose not to—see was evidence of George W.'s chumminess with the man he affectionately called "Kenny Boy," with whom he has exchanged warm, personal correspondence since his gubernatorial campaign in Texas. Though George W. was widely photographed boarding an Enron jet that ferried him from one campaign stop to another on his way to getting appointed as a nondemocratically elected president, the conservative William was apparently blinded to this reality and to the transparent (to everyone else, at least) transmogrification of "Kenny Boy" to "Ken who?"

What we learn from Safire the linguist (the more brilliant half of the hologram) is that originally "the consultants Lippincott & Margulies suggested 'Enteron'" as the name of the firm that resulted from the merger of Houston Natural Gas and InterNorth. When the consultants learned that the medical meaning of the word was "intestines," the name was changed to Enron. Wouldn't you say that was an omen right there?

But unless the GAO's lawsuit against Vice President Cheney is successful, we will never know the exent of Enron's influence on national energy policy or how much of that acquiescence was a payback to Enron for helping put the Bush–Cheney ticket in the White House. Don't hold your breath for speedy disclosure. The vice president has dug in his heels, combatively demanding what right the public has to know how a government official shapes public policy. Executive privilege, after all, is executive privilege.

So far, we know that the Enron executives enronized—and did so precisely when the whole nation was in shock and mourning in the wake of 9/11. During September and October 2001, the top brass cashed in their chips. But greed is good, as we learned from Gordon Gekko (Oliver Stone's paragon of unbridled rapacity in *Wall Street*), and as long as the house of cards did not collapse, both investors and execs did well. Some executives did exceedingly well even as the house of cards tumbled to shambles.

Sadly, if they want to get elected, politicians on both sides of the aisle need the help of corporate America, and Enron was certainly helpful. Three out of every five U.S. senators, in fact, have received contributions from Enron over the years. Let's face it: this is the system we created, and it won't be easy, if possible at all, to undo. In fact, we are so proud of this system that we encourage the whole world to fashion their lives according to American culture, both political and otherwise. Why, President Bush offered this advice even to the Chinese, whose civilization, dating back five thousand years, is among the earliest known advanced cultures and whose art and system of writing are the oldest in the world, having evolved in remote antiquity.

This kind of self-aggrandizement is not what disturbs me most about the Enron scandal. More shocking to me is a third cabal of beneficiaries who shamelessly accepted Enron money, not to be elected as public servants or to maximize wealth for shareholders but to line their own pockets. They call themselves consultants or analysts, but I call this camarilla paid liars, Enron encounters of the third kind. These confidential advisers are neither executives who, however ruthless, had to account to shareholders, nor accountants, who put their reputation and credibility on the line. No, no, no. These people were paid to make Enron look good.

We were told time and again, of course, that markets see through falsehood, nefarious deeds, and tomfoolery. That is one good reason, we are reminded, to leave the markets alone. Go tell this to the multitudes who lost bundles, their pensions, or perhaps their life savings. Even George W.'s *schwieger* lost $8,000. Can't you feel the pain of the president, who now has to deal with an irate mother-in-law? Pleeeeease!

We were told that markets are omnipotent, that they know all and see all. (In fact, now we learn that this was the basic premise of Enron's corporate ethos.) The markets handsomely reward the *fidels* and punish the *infidels* (the manipulators and the cheaters). The markets must rule the world. Indeed, it is the new world order, globalization, the new age, the twenty-first century, the avatar of God. Springtime for Adam Smith and humanity!

Let's pause for a moment and talk about Adam Smith (1723–1790), shall we? Though his major work, *The Wealth of Nations*, earned him glory as a political economist, Smith was also a philosopher (perhaps before he was an economist)—a moralist and a humanitarian of great sensitivity. Strangely, those who co-opted this Scotsman's work as the foundation for what we now call free-market economics picked one statement from Smith's great work: "It is not from the benevolence of the butcher, the brewer, or the baker that we expect our dinner, but from their regard to their own interest" (Smith 1776, Book I, Ch. 2, p. 11).

True, Smith was a radical individualist who objected to the power of king and church. Smith suggested leaving matters in the invisible hands of the market, where buyers and sellers find each other through a "just price." Both the Talmud and medieval Christian scholars had espoused this concept. "Just price" was the agreement between a seller and buyer, under normal, perfectly competitive conditions, by which a good or a service changed hands. Prices were considered unjust if

- There was price discrimination
- Cartels of either buyers and sellers were formed
- The participants took advantage of emergency situations—what we now call price gouging

Operation of the market, it was believed, could also be upset by nefarious or even dishonest activities on the part of either buyer or seller. Smith understood well the perils of such circumstances and was very clear about where a central government should stand: "The government of an exclusive company of merchants is, perhaps, the worst of all governments for any country whatever" (Smith 1776, Book IV, Ch. 7, Part iii, p. 440).

He was also quite explicit about who should receive the lion's share of the economic activity:

Our merchants frequently complain of the high wages of British labour as the cause of their manufacturers being undersold in foreign markets; but they are silent about the high profits of stock. They complain of the extravagant gain of other people; but they say nothing of their own. The high profits of British stock, however, may contribute towards raising the price of British manufactures in many cases as much, and in some perhaps more, than the high wages of British labour. (Smith 1776, Book IV, Ch. 7, Part iii, p. 466)

I have never seen these two quotations in the playbook of today's free marketeers. On the contrary, it seems that most laws favor commerce and industry over the workingman. Still, despite his economic insight and visionary talent, Smith, in the eighteenth century, could not possibly foresee the multinational corporation of the twenty-first century with its practically unlimited power and influence. Matters are much worse than Smith could have ever envisioned.

I am taxing your patience with this commentary on Adam to emphasize how the moral orgone was sucked from his ultimate premise. Unfortunately, without the moral foundations, Smith would have not known from Adam (no pun intended) what became of his theory of a new economic order.

Let's return now to the gallery of the paid liars who labored to turn the sow's ear that was Enron into a public-relations silk purse, for no other purpose than to fatten their own wallets. These holier-than-thou types did not commit any crime for which they can be punished, or even investigated by Congress. They are not the "corrupt" politicians we all love to loathe (so much that we keep reelecting virtually all of them). They are not villainous executives. They are not even co-conspiratorial accountants whose "aggressive" practices helped cook the books. This cabal simply sold out without taking any real risks, something that is contrary to the previously mentioned concept of "there is no reward without risk taking."

Foremost among the moral bankrupts is Ralph Reed, former director of the Christian Coalition and poster boy for Christian video-conservativism. Ralphie Boy (to borrow the president's style) sold his soul to Enron for a mere $380,000. Considering Ralph's arrogance, it was one of Enron's better investments.

According to a *Washington Post* column, Reed proposed a broad political strategy to press Congress for legislation favorable to Enron. Reed suggested to the company that because of his influence with the media and with conservative talk shows, he could promote the interests of Enron, flooding op-ed pages and generating articles in the print media that he would "blast fax" to members of Congress.

Blast fax! I love this. Here is another example of how, in the hands of an opinion terrorist, a seemingly innocent device like a fax machine, much less sophisticated and far less costly than a jet airliner, can be used as a weapon of mass distraction (as in beguilement).

"In public policy it matters less who has the best arguments and more who gets heard—and by whom," Reed told Enron—and ain't that the truth! Although the memo was dated October 27, 2000, Karl Rove, George W.'s Svengali—er, senior adviser—introduced Reed to Enron's top brass. Judicial

Watch, a *conservative* watchdog group, asked for a federal investigation to determine whether the employment of Reed by Enron was a campaign finance violation.

But what about morality, supposedly the unshakable foundation of the moral majority Reed so forcefully represented? How does selling himself for considerably less than thirty pieces of silver sit with the basic Judeo-Christian ethic upon which the whole idea of free markets rests?

How about, indeed! According to the *Washington Post*, Reed wrote in his memo, "Elected officials and regulators will be predisposed to favor greater *market-oriented solutions* [my italics] if they hear from business, civic, and religious leaders in their communities." One must know not what the cookie is but how it crumbles.

Next in line is Mrs. Phil Gramm. In 1993, for example, while working for an oversight commission, the wife of the senior senator from Texas helped exempt Enron from regulation. Five weeks later, she was named to Enron's board of directors. What an unexpected coincidence!

The honor roll goes on and on. Professor Lawrence Lindsey, free market theorist extraordinaire, formerly with Columbia University, now chief economic adviser of the president; Bill Kristol, conservative extraordinaire, editor of the *Weekly Standard*; Paul Krugman, financial columnist and adviser; Larry Kudlow, another financial maven of the television persuasion; U.S. trade representative Robert Zoellick; Marc Racicot, the incoming RNC chair; and the dozen or more financial analysts who still hand-picked Enron as a "strong buy" in the late fall of 2001.

These are only those we know about. Who knows how long the complete list is, how much these people were paid, and for what purpose exactly? I would be interested to know. So would be those who were fleeced by Enron's demise. Wouldn't you be interested to know?

As I write, I learn from my Internet streaming headline that congressional investigators are requesting documents from ten Wall Street investment banking firms. They want to know what was the connection, if any, between these firms' lending money to an already failing Enron while their brokerage operations were pushing Enron stock to their clients. We do not even have to wait for the movie to come out. We already had *Wall Street* and *Boiler Room*, two movies made for those who cannot read, so they also could enjoy moral decay.

And what do you know? For such a "conflict of interest" Merrill Lynch just recently agreed to pay a $100,000,000 fine, which was a real deal for the firm, since it enabled the company to avoid admitting any wrongdoing or having to face criminal charges. A guilty verdict in a trial would have produced for sure a whole slew of civil suits by stockholders, which would have cost the Wall Street giant billions. Apparently there are still bargains "out there."

The most bizarre participant of the "Enron encounters of the third kind" is Allan Greenspan, icon of the fin-de-siècle bull market, who, only nineteen days before Enron declared bankruptcy received the "Enron Prize" from James

Baker's public-policy institute. This is the James Baker, by the way, who served as secretary of state under George H. W. Bush and who, only five months after George H. W. lost the 1992 election, began lobbying Kuwait on Enron's behalf. He is the same James Baker who, when the junior George was desperately wrestling Gore for ballots in the Sunshine State, grabbed the nearest jet (Enron's, perhaps?) to the Land of Oz and took center stage as Dubya's mouthpiece to the national media.

But I digress. Greenspan receive the Enron Prize, but for what—crying out loud? For forecasting erroneously the last twenty nonexistent inflationary cycles and putting, eventually, the economy into a downward spiral? After the techies and the dot.coms wiped out not just the glory but also the daylight from the portfolios of yuppiedom, Greenspan was de-iconed. This was despite Greenspan's discouraging the movers and shakers from "irrational exuberance." Today, Greenspan is all "cautious optimism," but his luster has faded considerably. Perhaps people recall that Herbert Hoover was cautiously optimistic in 1932, when he declared that recovery was just around the corner.

So, what exactly was the Enron Prize? How does the prize Greenspan got compare with the prize those got who now use their Enron stock certificates to paper their bathrooms?

As we arrive in this twenty-first century Oz, which we call free markets, we realize that, during the journey, Dorothy has been gang-raped. Alas, we are reduced to desperately seeking Toto, in need of someone to go behind the curtain and tell us that the wizard's name is enronomics.

REFERENCE

Smith, Adam. 1776. *An Inquiry into the Nature and Causes of the Wealth of Nations (The Wealth of Nations)*. London and New York: George Routledge and Sons.

Preface

Austin Murphy

This book is dedicated to uncovering practical truth in research in finance and such related fields as accounting, economics, and the social sciences. The essential purpose of *Practical Financial Economics* is to disseminate original and rigorous practical research and to publish provocative articles and notes that correct or critique elitist/ideological journal articles, with a view toward positively influencing practical financial discussions and thought. Although thorough mathematical, statistical, behavioral, technological, legal, and interdisciplinary analysis have been strongly encouraged from the contributors, the book emphasizes the usefulness of research implications to the field of finance, as opposed to the "ideology" or complexity of the modeling method. While the book stresses practicality, it does not exclude the development of theories that may be based on practical assumptions and lead to practical implications.

The book is intended to appeal to financial managers, analysts, brokers, bankers, professors, and investors throughout the world. As a result of the targeted general readership, the mathematical and statistical analysis typically necessary for rigorous research is relegated to appendices, so readers can concentrate on the important implications of the research without having to verify and analyze all the complex computations underlying them. The appendices are as complete and long as necessary to allow precise understanding by those desiring in-depth information. Contributors were required to be both practical and rigorous. Our purpose is not to be "pretty" but to develop an objective science that reflects reality and attempts to establish methods to optimize financial behavior in the real world.

We can begin—tongue firmly in cheek—with a set of definitions (by an anonymous author who circulated them on the World Wide Web in 2002) that I think characterizes that "real world" all too well.

CAPITALISM IN THEORY AND CAPITALISM IN PRACTICE

Capitalism in Theory

You have two cows. You sell one and buy a bull. Your herd multiplies, and the economy grows. You sell them and retire on the income.

Capitalism in Practice across the World

Capitalism in the United States: You have two cows. You sell one and force the other to produce the milk of four cows. You are surprised when the cow drops dead.

Capitalism in France: You have two cows. You go on strike because you want three cows.

Capitalism in Japan: You have two cows. You redesign them so they are one tenth the size of ordinary cows and produce twenty times the milk. You then create clever cow cartoon characters called Cowkimon and market them worldwide.

Capitalism in Germany: You have two cows. You reengineer them so that they live one hundred years, eat once a month, and feed themselves.

Capitalism in Britain: You have two cows. They are both mad.

Capitalism in Italy: You have two cows but you don't know where they are. You break for lunch.

Capitalism in Russia: You have two cows. You count them and learn that you have five cows. You count them again and learn that you have forty-two cows. You count them again and learn that you have twelve cows. You stop counting cows and open another bottle of vodka.

Capitalism in Switzerland: You have five thousand cows, none of which belong to you. You charge others for storing them.

Capitalism in China: You have two cows. You have three hundred people milking them. You claim full employment, high bovine productivity, and arrest the newsman who reported the numbers.

The New Economy Capitalism as exemplified by Enron: You have two cows. You sell three of them to your publicly listed company, using letters of credit opened by your brother-in-law at the bank, then execute a debt/equity swap with an associated general offer so that you get all four cows back, with a tax exemption for five cows. The milk rights of the six cows are transferred via an intermediary to a Cayman Island company secretly owned by the majority shareholder who sells the rights to all seven cows back to your listed company. The annual report says the company owns eight cows, with an option on one more. Sell one cow to buy a new President of the

United States, leaving you with nine cows. No balance sheet provided with the release. The public buys your bull!

While the subject matter in the book is somewhat broad, there is a focus on practical valuation analysis—and for a very good reason. One of the most important financial theories, the theory of efficient markets, makes practical valuation analysis virtually useless by assuming that the intrinsic value of any asset is determined by its market price; as a result the subject of practical valuation has been largely neglected in academic research. However, the efficient-markets theory itself, being based on a general assumption that investors properly value securities by their trading, requires the very practical valuation that a belief in market efficiency makes useless. Within this context, it is not surprising that individual stocks, such as Enron, and the entire stock market itself can be effectively mispriced, as this book shows. Numerous chapters are devoted to analyzing the Enron situation.

As editor, I greatly benefited from the assistance and support of an excellent editorial board that included Robert Haugen (professor emeritus, University of California at Irvine) as advising editor, as well as editorial board members (and article reviewers) George Frankfurter, Phillip Gaglio, Orville Lefko, Mike Palazolla, William Margrabe, Stephen O'Byrne, Gene Warren, Hart Will, Joseph Wu, Lutz Kruschwitz, Bartley Madden, Harry Kat, Brian Bruce, David Arnold, Stephen Hawkins, Alexander Bukhvalov, Augustin Fosu, Raymond Cox, Kenneth Lam, Lutz Kruschwitz, and Zoltan Sabov. All chapters were subjected to outside blind review by two referees (a practitioner and an academic) to determine acceptability, as well as to identify necessary improvements to the chapters; their immense help is very gratefully acknowledged. Above all, the writers of the various chapters of the book deserve credit for their outstanding research, as well as for making changes deemed necessary by the reviewers and the editor.

Introduction

Austin Murphy

The collection of chapters in this book represents financial research that is designed to be both rigorous and practical. The absence of constraint by any particular financial ideology (like market efficiency) or testing framework (like the most advanced statistical methods) creates an opportunity for new financial insights.

Because of the timeliness of the Enron fiasco, numerous chapters focus on that situation. The eminent George Frankfurter provides useful editorial perspective on that issue in the foreword. While the book is not restricted to any one area, its major theme is valuation, which is of the utmost importantance in a world that has been indoctrinated with the efficient-markets belief that valuation doesn't matter since one can always value anything at its market price.

The first chapter is my own. Here, I utilize a general valuation analysis within the context of financial history to examine the prospects for the relative long-term performance of stocks and bonds. The analysis flies in the face of most financial theory and advice by showing that it is very likely that bonds will earn more than equities in this century. This conclusion, which would be consistent with a hypothesis that equities were overpriced at the turn of the millennium, has important implications for all investors (who need more than ever to employ valuation analysis and diversity).

The second chapter is by Dusan Mramor, Dejan Joksimovac, and Elton McGoun, who show theoretically that mainstream valuation analysis is a very imprecise science. With investors and their advisers applying imprecise methods of analysis, it should obviously be possible for assets to be mispriced. Although the potential exists to construct ranges of intrinsic value, and although prices should still be forced back within that range by astute investors seeking to profit from excess mispricing, the authors show that the range of possible values can be quite wide. In addition, the uncertainty of those ranges themselves might lead to investors' giving up on trying to value securities rationally, thus leading to greater mispricing of assets. The existence of grossly mispriced assets not only provides the opportunity for abnormal investment profits but also creates a need for more and better valuation analysis that can narrow the range of rational asset values. The next chapter represents a contribution in this area.

The third chapter, my work, conducts a case study analysis of Enron's high stock value in early 2001. I demonstrate that a scientific but straightforward discounted cash flow analysis of Enron indicates its stock to have been grossly overpriced, even using the actual historical financial statements, and even at the maximum possible rational value given those statements. I also show that Enron had effectively financed itself into a situation of extremely probable, if not virtually inevitable, bankruptcy. Only the timing of its bankruptcy was uncertain.

The fourth and fifth chapters are both by Arline Savage and Cynthia Miree, who provide an example of detailed analysis of the strategy and financial statements of the infamous mispriced firm Enron. The purpose of these chapters is to establish the importance of analyzing and understanding strategy as a critical part of financial analysis and to examine the implications of ignoring this mandate. In chapter 4, they essentially demonstrate how aspects of the company's strategy were manipulated to support larger and more pervasive accounting and financial schemes. In chapter 5, they analyze Enron's financial statements in detail to show that the firm's superb reputation for superior financial performance was undeserved.

The sixth chapter is by Usamah A. Uthman, who shows how a special type of financing utilized by Enron can be properly employed to reduce debt costs. This innovative financing involves sale of a forward contract with payment on the contract up front instead of at delivery of the underlying asset; it essentially represents a form of hedged, collateralized debt. Chapter 6 provides an example of the fact that although Enron may have made many mistakes, the company did deserve some of its reputation for innovation, even if some of those innovations contributed to the company's downfall by enabling it to take on excessive financial leverage and risks.

The seventh chapter is by Don Bloomquist and me. Via an analysis of the value of the securities of the company that owned the *Titanic*, this research illustrates the age-old financial incentives for risk taking and unethical behavior that capitalism creates. Chapter 7 also demonstrates some evidence that this behavior almost a hundred years ago took place in markets that were fairly efficient in analyzing complex changes in value related to option-pricing theories of capital structure.

The eighth chapter is by me. In it I provide a simple illustration of how investment value can be created by a simple financial policy that can yield important marketing benefits (especially for consumer products companies) and reduce the incentives for unethical behavior within the framework of the capitalist system. In particular, by allowing consumers to become stockholders easily, with special rights to price discounts on goods/services sold by a company, customer loyalty and satisfaction can be increased at the same time that equity capital is raised, and the goals of corporate management can be unified with those of its customers. The *Titanic* and other corporate scandals (such as the recent tobacco scandals) might be unthinkable in such an environment, where there are fewer incentives for excessive risk-taking.

The ninth chapter is by Ed Maberly and Raylene Pierce, who illustrate some of the serious problems and risks associated with contemporary academic investment analysis, which often merely tries to extrapolate some statistical pattern in the past into the future without considering the fundamental causes of the pattern and its potential to persist. The authors demonstrate inconsistencies and flaws in scholarly investment studies, and they show that conclusions reached from such research can lead to conclusions that are meaningless and even counterproductive for practical investment purposes. Within such an educational environment, the apparent lapses in rational security valuation that occurred in recent years should not be too surprising.

The tenth chapter is also by me. In it I precisely define how currency values are determined utilizing a revolutionary new perspective that takes the point of view of investors, whose trading essentially determines exchanges rates. As explained in the opening chapter, the conclusions of this chapter are useful for generating additional insights on the risk that the U.S. stock market might not perform well over the next century (and may be overpriced). The chapter may also be important for illustrating some of the directions that financial economic theory can take in the future if it is to be more practically useful.

The Outlook for Equity Values: Stocks May Underperform Bonds in the Twenty-First Century

Austin Murphy

EXECUTIVE SUMMARY

Citing prior evidence on foreign markets and on the very long-term history of the U.S. stock market, this research shows that contrary to popular belief, stocks are not necessarily always the best investment over the long haul. Because this century began with extremely high stock prices compared to investment value fundamentals, and because the situation at the beginning of the millennium is similar to that in the past when stocks have performed relatively poorly, there is substantial risk that equities may underperform bonds over this century.

INTRODUCTION

Many financial advisers without an adequate understanding of stock market history say that equities invariably make the best long-term investments, although they typically mention the risks of sizable return variation in the short term.[1] Such statements are generally based on superficial observations of a limited history of U.S. stock returns going back seventy-five years or so and without the context of the factors that drive those returns. The shallow inference generally drawn is that stock returns will beat both inflation and bond returns by at least 5 to 8 percent because they have over the last seventy-five years (Ibbotson & Associates 1999).

A BRIEF REVIEW OF STOCK MARKET HISTORY

To provide greater depth of understanding the risks and prospects for equities, it is necessary only to look farther back into the past. For instance, a very-long-term study of the U.S. securities markets indicates that bond investments outperformed stock investments over two separate intervals of fifty-plus years: between 1802 and 1860 and between 1873 and 1933, as can be seen from graphs of historical returns provided by Siegel (1992) and Jones and Wilson (1987), respectively. This past history is especially important because many of the conditions today are similar to those in the 1800s when bond returns were higher than stock returns. Those conditions include rapid technological change, low inflation, and high real interest rates on bonds.

The rapid technological change exists today because of the information revolution, as opposed to the industrial revolution in the 1800s, but the effect on stocks may very well be the same. In particular, like the stock market of the nineteenth century, the equity market of the twenty-first century may be characterized by some rapidly growing companies, as well as by some declining companies with obsolete technology. In addition, speculative bubbles of over-priced high-tech stocks may result in large stock market losses, with the greatest losses this time on Internet stocks instead of the "high-tech" railroad stocks back then. (While the Internet stock market bubble has already burst since the initial draft of this article was written and posted on the Oakland University Web site in early 2000, that will certainly not be the last burst bubble.)[2]

The environment of low inflation in both the 1800s and the 2000s (0% then versus 2% today) generally represents good times for bonds, as nominal interest rates typically do not have to rise and often even fall under such conditions, resulting in capital gains instead of capital losses on bonds. In addition, the high real interest rates of over 4 percent above inflation (in the 1800s and in 2000) imply fairly high returns that can supplement any capital gains on bonds (Best, Byrne, and Ilmanen 1998).

In particular, one theory indicates that interest rates should approximate economic growth rates, at least in the long term, as average businesses would want to borrow less (more) when the interest cost of borrowing exceeded (was less than) their own profit growth rates, which would tend to approximate that of the aggregate economy long-term (Clements 2001). This theory would therefore imply that the demand for funds would drop when real interest rates exceed real economic growth rates, as average businesses could not pay the debt interest expense out of profit growth. As a result, there would be tendency for relatively high real interest rates to fall, leading to capital appreciation on inflation-indexed bonds.

Given productivity increases of 1 to 2 percent (Associated Press 2001) and population increases of 1 percent in the United States, the U.S. economy could very well grow by less than 3 percent annually in the long term (Murphy 2000a). As a result, it would seem that real interest rates could decline further below 3 percent and create capital gains for investors in inflation-indexed bonds.[3] (Real rate drops of more than 1 percent since 2000 have already produced sizable capital gains for bondholders.)

In addition, since inflation typically does not rise in periods of high real interest rates, because of limited demand, capital gains might also be likely on other bonds that pay only a nominal coupon rate that does not increase with inflation. Note that in comparison to such bonds that are not inflation indexed, stocks are more likely to perform better over long periods in a more inflationary environment (Murphy and Sahu 2001), so the superior performance of such bonds depends on inflation remaining at or below the expected level of about 2 percent implied by the difference between the yields on inflation-indexed bonds and other bonds.[4] Thus, unless stock returns can earn the same 5+ percent above inflation that they did in the 1900s (Siegel 1999), bond returns may very well beat those of stocks in the 2000s, just as they did for much of the 1800s in a similar environment.

The likelihood of U.S. stocks doing as well in the future as they have in the past can be evaluated by examining the context in which those past superior returns were earned. In particular, the United States has been the most successful capitalist country in the world over the last two hundred years. It now dominates the world, and it seems unlikely that it can outperform itself over the next two hundred years, since it cannot go from an unimportant former colony to the most powerful country on earth again.

On the other hand, it is certainly possible that the U.S. capitalist empire can stagnate or even go into decline. To provide some perspective on the risk here, it is necessary only to examine the past long-term performance of stock markets in other countries that did not grow to dominate the world. While there has been a lot of variation in stock market returns across countries (depending at least partially on their relative success in economic strategy and war), the performance of about forty foreign stock markets with sufficient data indicates equity returns that averaged less than the inflation rates in those countries (Jorion and Goetzmann 1999). The implication is that if the performance of the United States is no longer extraordinary but merely average, stock returns may not even match the inflation rate in the long term (and may be substantially less than that if the U.S. economy performs relatively worse).

This conclusion is consistent with an analysis conducted recently indicating that most of stocks' returns above inflation in the twentieth century resulted from far higher dividend yields existing at the beginning of the century than exist today (Chernoff 2000). Stock returns only slightly above inflation rates compare unfavorably with risk-free Treasury bonds guaranteed by the U.S. government to return about 3 percent above the inflation rate over the next thirty years.

BEYOND HISTORY:
CURRENT STOCK MARKET FUNDAMENTALS

Thus, a long and broad view of history (especially based on relative returns in the 1800s and in foreign countries) suggests that there is a reasonably high probability that bond investments will outperform stocks in the future. This conclusion can be drawn even without considering the current high level of stock prices in relation to the earnings and dividend cash flows that determine the intrinsic value of equities. However, an examination of fundamental valuation variables provides an indication of even greater risk that stocks will underperform bonds.

To begin, it should be observed that much of the explosive return in stocks in the second half of the twentieth century stemmed from runups in stock prices that will reduce future stock returns. In particular, the rapid rise in stock values in the last few decades has stemmed at least in part from a reduction in the return on stocks required by investors. This decreased required return, which increased the present value of stocks by lowering the discount rate on future cash flows received from the stocks (i.e., increased the prices investors were willing to pay for a given stream of earnings and dividends), resulted from various factors that reduced the costs and risks associated with stock investments.

For instance, as a result of the imposition of fairer trading rules, there has been a substantial decrease in the transaction costs of trading stocks, especially in the last few years on NASDAQ stocks (Taylor 1996), so investors naturally require a lower premium return to compensate for those reduced costs (Constantinides 1986). In addition, a further reduction in transaction costs and hence required returns may have already been priced into the market prior to the movement toward a decimal pricing system in the next year, which positively affected all stock values (Kelly 2000).

Moreover, effective methods of better meeting the risk preferences of stock investors (such as by reducing risk) have been developed in the last half-century (including via diversification and derivatives), so investors no longer feel the need to require premium returns on stocks (Murphy 2000a). Also contributing to investors requiring lower returns on stocks may be the tendency of the Federal Reserve to loosen monetary policy to counteract any significant downward trend in stock prices, such as by reducing the downside risk of stocks (Balder 2000).

However, there does not appear to be much prospect for further reductions in required stock returns. As a result, further large stock price gains caused by reduced costs and risks of trading stocks are not likely. At the same time, the sharp rise in stock prices resulting from the lower required return in the last few decades has increased investor optimism about future stock returns, and the result is a stock market with prices so high that the future earnings and dividends from those investments may no longer offer any premium returns over bond yields.

In particular, Renshaw (1997) recently reported that U.S. dividend yields and earnings/price ratios to be at their lowest levels in history and that these ratios of current stock yields remain very unattractive (having actually become even lower at the peak of the boom in early 2000 before recently recovering slightly).[5] Lower ratios for these variables imply smaller cash flows supporting inflated valuations. Despite the potential growth in equity cash flows, ratios of low cash flow to prices probably imply lower returns than are offered on fixed-rate bonds that offer higher current yields to maturity.[6]

In fact, the dividend yields and earnings/price ratios in the United States at the turn of the millennium were similar to those in Japan in the late 1980s, just before that stock market fell by more than 50 percent (Peterson 1990); Japanese equity prices have still not recovered ten years later despite 0 percent interest rates (Smithers 1999). Note that the large decline in the Japanese stock market recently was not caused by an economic depression. In particular, that economy continued to grow in the 1990s, although the growth was lower than it had been; in fact, it was similar to, albeit lower than, the normal 2 to 3 percent real growth in the U.S. economy (see, e.g., the IMF's *International Financial Statistics*).

Similarly, a large decline in the overpriced U.S. stock market does not require an economic depression, just more reasonable pricing, as has begun to occur over the first few years of the new millennium. However, such a decline in equity prices themselves would likely reduce economic growth, as it has in Japan (and as a moderate stock market decline in the last year in the United States has already), and lower economic growth would create more room for stock prices to fall farther. While history in Japan does not have to repeat itself in the United States, it certainly could—and lead to an even worse stock market collapse.

THE CONSTRAINTS ON PROFIT GROWTH

There are, of course, more risks for U.S. stocks. Profits have grown much faster than the economy in the last decade (Graja 2000), and profitability levels and profit margins in the United States were at extremely high levels at the turn of the century (see, e.g., the financial statistics on the Value Line Industrial Composite published semiannually by the *Value Line Investment Survey*). This situation exists despite the fact that profits are very small in relation to stock prices.

At least part of the cause of high U.S. profits and past profit growth is welfare reform, which increased the supply of labor, reduced real wage increases despite the U.S. economic boom of the 1990s, and resulted in profits taking a larger share of the economic pie (Cheng 1997). Although rapid growth in the privatization of the prison system could add over a million virtual slaves to the labor force (Wirtz 2000); although millions of single mothers and other poor people have been made desperate for more work at any wage because of the five-year limit on benefits set by the welfare reform law passed in 1996 (Moorehead 2001); although the United States does absorb about three hundred thousand Mexican immigrants (legal and otherwise) annually (Millman 2000); although there are also many illegal migrant workers (Tapinos 1999), with "an all-time high" of between seven and nine million "unauthorized immigrants residing in the U.S." currently (Millman 2002); although there is some limited legal immigration, including about one hundred thousand high-tech workers (Nash 1999); and although there are some political proposals to increase legal immigration work permits an extra hundred thousand per year (Associated Press 2000)—it does not appear likely that much more cheap labor can be squeezed out of the economy, given the current low unemployment rate (and barring a large immigration wave like that of the 1800s). In addition, it is not clear that the political climate can turn much more antilabor without a fight (Strobel and Peterson 1999).[7] In this environment, real wages may indeed rise more rapidly and claim a larger share of the economic pie to the detriment of profit growth.

It is true that rising productivity might create the opportunity for the pie to increase more rapidly than the 2 to 3 percent it has grown in the past and hence lead to more rapid profit growth without increasing profits'. However, there is insufficient evidence of a long-term trend (especially given the slowdown in the last year or two) to support a conclusion that the "new" information revolution economy is raising productivity growth to a higher level than in the past, such as during the industrial revolution. In addition, even if productivity were to increase more rapidly, the effect on stock prices might be negligible if the cause were merely an increase in the rate of savings and reinvestment of earnings. In particular, if an increase in profits is caused by an increase in capital employed without any abnormal rate of return on invested capital, stock values and prices would be unaffected (Murphy 2000b).

THE EFFECT OF THE INTERNATIONAL SITUATION AND CURRENT ACCOUNT DEFICITS

It is also true that corporations' ability to exploit cheap foreign labor with overseas investments can conceivably continue to put downward pressure on domestic wage growth, thus helping to alleviate the problems associated with a continuation of the rapid U.S. profit growth. However, such exploitation requires more foreign production, which in turn exacerbates the international current account deficit (which measures the balance on trade, services, income, and transfers). The U.S. deficit on the international current account is already at an extremely high level, equal to almost 5 percent of gross domestic product (Phillips 2000), and such levels have been repeatedly shown worldwide in the past to create a grave risk for domestic stocks. As shown by Murphy in chapter 10 of this book, such a deficit cannot continue into perpetuity, and it often can be reversed only via a decline in the currency value (which leads to imported inflation, higher interest rates, and a counterproductive inflation-devaluation spiral) or a decline in economic growth (which leads to declining profit growth).

The size of the current U.S. deficit exceeds the level that helped spur the American 1987 stock market crash; is not far below the level in Mexico in

1994 just prior to the collapse of its currency and stock markets; and is similar to that in Southeast Asia just before the market crash in the prices of that region's currencies and equities in 1997. While an immediate currency/stock market crash in the United States does not have to occur to solve the problem, the alternative is a slower decline in the currency value or slower growth in the economy (and hence in profits), with similar negative effects spread over a longer period (as shown again in the concluding chapter of this book). Regardless of whether the current account deficit is solved in a short period or over a long period (or by a currency decline or a drop in real income growth and profits), the effect on stock returns will be very negative in the long term.[8]

CONCLUSION ON THE LONG-TERM OUTLOOK

The long-term outlook for stocks is therefore fairly negative compared to bonds. This forecast may sound counterintuitive compared to what is widely written in the financial press, but it seems to be a conclusion well grounded in history and fundamental theory. A fairly negative outlook in no way implies, however, that a stock market crash is imminent or even that stock returns will be less than the inflation rate. It merely indicates that while stocks could perform in the future as well as they have over the last few decades, it is far more likely that bond investments will earn higher returns than stocks in the long term.

SHORTER-TERM OUTLOOK

In addition to an overall negative long-term outlook for stocks, there are also some negative factors that might negatively influence stock returns in the short run. One such factor is related to demographics. Demographics indicate that the baby boomer generation (i.e., the babies of the 1950s and 1960s) has been in the equity accumulation phase of its life cycle for over a decade, and its members' increasing investments in stocks may have contributed smartly to the stock market boom of the 1980s and 1990s. While this equity accumulation trend may continue a few more years until 2005, the positive flow in this savings variable should soon begin to reverse itself when the large baby boomer section of the population begins to need to draw down on investments for retirement (Chernoff 1998). As a result, the boomers themselves may contribute to an end of inflated stock market prices as they begin to spend some of their invested capital and switch to more conservative bond investments, as is normal for retirees (Erb, Harvey, and Viskanta 1997).

On the other hand, any government transfer of social security funds to the stock market, as some politicians recently proposed for the near future, would contribute positively to the relative near-term performance of stocks (Pullen 1998) and might offset the demographic effect. Some political promises to have more Social Security and retirement funds privatized were made in the 2000 U.S. election campaign (Davis 2000), as well as earlier. However, whereas the demographic effect is probable, a major change in Social Security investment policies does not appear to be very likely, especially since the advantages to the Social Security fund itself are uncertain. For instance, any changes in the allocation of Social Security funds to the stock market would not actually affect the solvency of the fund, as pointed out by Ferguson (2000). In addition, since promises to direct social security funds into the stock market can themselves increase equity values, in anticipation of such money flowing into stocks, it is quite possible that the funds would be invested when the market was at a peak, thereby resulting in lower future returns on the investments. Moreover, the scandal at Enron has virtually eliminated any political backing for putting Social Security funds into the stock market (Cox News Service 2002). Within this context, it could be argued that part of the runup in stock prices in the late 1990s was caused by speculation that Social Security funds would be invested into the stock market, while the rapidity of the recent drop in stock prices may be at least partially attributable to the fact that the initial stock market drop itself (as well as the corporate scandals) caused popular support for the idea to decline, thereby reducing one of the speculative underpinnings of the inflated equity prices themselves.

There also exists another factor that may negatively impact stocks. In particular, commercial banks have already been freed from restrictions on entry into the stock brokerage business, so the increased bank recommendations to individual customers to replace their low-risk savings deposits with stock investments have already had their positive effect on stock prices (*Workers World* 2001). As a result, such continued pushing of equities in the future may not generate much new investment. In fact, the effect of such past recommendations may actually have a negative impact in the future, as any initial stock market losses cause inexperienced investors to lose confidence and sell their stocks permanently (Haugen 1999).

However, there are other technical factors that might still positively influence stock returns over various short-term intervals. In particular, over the last 168 years, stock returns have averaged 10 percent in the six months prior to presidential elections (Whelehan 1997), perhaps at least partly because presidents tend to pump up the economy in preparation for the election campaign (Allvine and O'Neill 1980), and partially because investor optimism may be spurred by political campaign promises (Murphy 2000a). This latter hypothesis is consistent with a finding that Americans tend to believe in and vote for more optimistic candidates (Andrews 2000). Nevertheless, the typically high preelection return is then followed (since 1832) by an approximate 0 percent average return earned on stocks in the full two years after the presidential election (Whelehan 1997). The latter poor performance may be related to postelection blues caused by attempts to slow down the economy after it has been boosted during the election year. Alternatively, this cyclical effect could be caused by investors belatedly figuring out that they have been deceived by political promises once again (Murphy 2000a). Regardless of the cause, this effect may have contributed to the poor performance of the stock market through 2002 and to what appears to be the beginning of a temporary rebound through 2004.

Regardless, betting on stocks to beat bonds over the short term is a speculative gamble. It is largely a bet on investor optimism staying high, and that bet is already starting to appear shaky.[9] In any event, betting on stocks to beat bonds longer-term is an even bigger gamble, with potentially worse odds.[10]

OVERALL CONCLUSION

In conclusion, it is important to repeat the old axiom that only one thing is certain: There is no certainty in forecasting security returns. As a result, diversification into both stocks and bonds (as well as foreign assets and real estate) is always a good idea to reduce risk, especially in the short term. However, the current investment environment provides a great incentive to focus more of one's wealth into fairly risk-free investments like U.S. Treasury inflation-index bonds, which guarantee a return about 3 percent above the inflation rate.[11]

NOTES

1. The original version of this chapter was written in the spring of 2000 and posted on the Oakland University Web site. The subsequent large decline in the NASDAQ supports the conclusions of the chapter, but that decline and other events (including the September 11, 2001, terrorist bombings of New York and Washington, D.C.) have not materially changed the overall outlook.

2. The bubble-bursting of the "high tech" railroad sector of the nineteenth century is similar to the Internet crash today in another respect also, insofar as both crashes were caused by the creation of excess capacity, with too many rail lines and cars then and too many optic fiber cables and business Web sites now (*Workers World* 2002).

3. An example of the importance of bond capital gains is provided by the 1980s, when the longest-term bonds actually earned higher double-digit returns than stocks despite the big bull stock market in that decade.

4. It should be mentioned that real interest rates on U.S. government securities in the 1800s were typically above 5 percent, which might imply some risk of real interest rates rising above the current 3 percent level. However, economic growth rates back then were higher, at least partially because of extremely high levels of immigration, which boosted the size of the work force. The conditions for such rapid real growth and corresponding high real interest rates do not seem to exist today.

5. While payouts to shareholders would be larger if the increased share buybacks were taken into consideration, the overall payout would still remain far below average. In addition, the share buybacks do not explain any portion of the high P/e ratios, which are actually being deflated by much more aggressive accounting policies (Nocera 2002).

6. In comparison to the dividend yields that were often over 5 percent in the 1800s (Clark, Craig, and Wilson 1999), the 1 to 2 percent dividend yields of today seem to be especially low. However, because of low earnings retention ratios, capital gains on equities were very low during the 1800s (Burr 2000), with total returns on equities averaging below 5 percent over one long measured sample of that century between 1832 and 1899 (Huang 1985).

7. In particular, besides general supply-and-demand forces that normally would push up real wages farther when the available labor force is near full employment, pro-union legislation, higher corporate tax rates, and greater business regulation can also decrease profit's share of the economic pie. Although the current trend is favorable to business (as illustrated by the downward movement of corporate tax rates over the last few decades), Strobel and Peterson (1999) believe that workers will become more militant unless this trend reverses itself.

8. While it has been shown that domestic equity prices can be positively impacted in the short term by real currency declines (Kim 2003), chapter 10 implies that addressing a current account problem with a domestic real income decline can be postponed only with devaluations and only as long as currency investors believe in an eventual nondevaluation solution.

9. A conclusion that stock returns may be above average in the short term but below average in the long term has been reached by Asness (2000) who simply examined various components of the relationship between stock returns, dividend yields, and relative stock/bond volatility.

10. Note, however, that despite the finding that bonds may be more likely to outperform stocks over the twenty-first century, the expected value of the return on stocks over that period may be higher, because of the greater positive skewness of stock returns (especially in inflationary environments). In addition, given the sharp drop in both real interest rates (from over 4% to under 3%) and the stock market in the first few years of the century, the relative outlook for bonds vis-à-vis stocks for the rest of the century is not as good as it was at the beginning of the millennium.

11. A totally separate, abridged summary of this conclusion was published prior to this book (Murphy 2002). The dividend tax cuts enacted recently could represent a new positive for stocks, but the temporariness of the cuts would make the effect very minor. Probably more than offsetting is the consumption (instead of growth-enhancing investment), which may exasperate the international balance-of-payments problem that is already extremely critical (see chapter 10).

REFERENCES

Allvine, F., and D. O'Neill. 1980. "Stock Market Returns and the Presidential Election Cycle." *Financial Analysts Journal* 36 (September/October): 49–56.

Andrews V. 2000. "Optimists Rule." http://content.health.msn.com/content/article/1674.50898 (September 19).

Asness, C. 2000. "Stocks versus Bonds: Explaining the Equity Risk Premium." *Financial Analysts Journal* 56 (March/April): 96–113.

Associated Press. 2000. "High-Tech Industry Frets after Dispute Stalls Bills to Boost Visas for Workers." *Oakland Press* (June 15).

———. 2001. "Productivity Decline Surprises Analysts." *Oakland Press* (May 9).

Balder, J. 2000. "A Fed Bias Investors Have Learned to Exploit." *Pensions & Investments* (November 13), 16.

Best, P., A. Byrne, and A. Ilmanen. 1998. "What Really Happened to U.S. Bond Yields." *Financial Analysts Journal* 54 (May/June): 41–49.

Burr, B. 2000. "11 Years of Work Unearths 1815–1925 Returns on Stock." *Pensions & Investments* (June 26), 2, 49.

Cheng, J. 1997. "'Stop Slavery, We Need Real Jobs.'" *Workers World* (January 16), 4.

Chernoff, J. 1998. "12 More Years." *Pensions & Investments* (October 19), 28–31.

———. 2000. "Death of Equity Risk Premium Predicted." *Pensions & Investments* (November 13), 1, 70.

Clark, R., L. Craig, and J. Wilson. 1999. "Managing a Pension Portfolio in the Nineteenth Century." *Business and Economic History* 28 (Fall): 93–104.

Clements, J. 2001. "Stocks over Bonds: A Hollow Victory?" *Wall Street Journal* (May 8), C1.

Constantinides, G. 1986. "Capital Market Equilibrium with Transaction Costs." *Journal of Political Economy* 94: 842-862.

Cox News Service. 2002. "Enron Scandal Will Touch All Americans, Financial Expert Says." *Oakland Press* (February 17), A19.

Davis, B. 2000. "Gore Weights Plans for Retiree Account, Near-Abolition of Social Security Deficit." *Wall Street Journal* (June 9), A20.

Erb, C., C. Harvey, and T. Viskanta. 1997. "Demographics and International Investments." *Financial Analysts Journal* 53 (July/August): 14–28.

Ferguson, R. 2000. "Saving Social Security." *Financial Analysts Journal* 56 (January/February): 13–16.

Graja, C. 2000. "So What's the Connection?" *Bloomberg Personal Finance* (September), 19–20.

Haugen, R. 1999. *The Inefficient Stock Market.* Upper Saddle River, N.J.: Prentice-Hall.

Huang, R. 1985. "Common Stock Returns and Presidential Elections." *Financial Analysts Journal* 41 (March/April): 58–61.

Ibbotson and Associates. 1999. *Stocks, Bonds, Bills, and Inflation: 1999 Yearbook.* Chicago: Ibbotson.

Jones, C., and J. Wilson. 1987. "Stocks, Bonds, Paper, and Inflation: 1870–1985." *Journal of Portfolio Management* (Fall): 20–24.

Jorion, P., and W. Goetzmann. 1999. "Global Stock Markets in the Twentieth Century." *Journal of Finance* 54: 953–980.

Kelly, B. 2000. "NYSE Formulating Plans to Stay Competitive in an Electronic Era." *Pension & Investments* (July 10), 55.

Kim, K. 2003. "Dollar Exchange Rate and Stock Price: Evidence from Multivariate Cointegration and Error Correction Models." *Review of Financial Economics* 12: 301–313.

Millman, J. 2000. "A New Future for Mexico's Work Force." *Wall Street Journal* (April 14), A15.

———. 2002. "Beefed-Up U.S. Border Patrolling Fails to Curb Illegal Immigration." *Wall Street Journal* (July 17), A14.

Moorehead, M. 2001. "Spend Surplus on Saving Poor, Not the Rich." *Workers World* (March 15), 5.

Murphy, A. 2000a. "A Financial Analysis of the Economic Effects of Having to Reverse Current Account Deficits." Working Paper, Oakland University.

———. 2000b. *Scientific Investment Analysis.* Westport, Conn.: Quorum Books.

———. 2000c. "Stock Investments May Earn Less Than Bonds in the 21st Century." *Journal of Investing* 11 (Summer): 23–24.

Murphy, A., and A. Sahu. 2001. "Empirical Evidence of a Positive Inflation Premium Being Incorporated into Stock Prices." *Atlantic Economic Journal* 29: 177–185.

Nash, K. 1999. "H-1B Miscount May Alter '00 Quota." *Computerworld* 33 (October 11), 1, 16.

Nocera, J. 2002. "Who's to Blame?" *Money* (March), 79–81.

Peterson, R. 1990. "Scrutinizing the Inscrutable." *Investment Vision* 1: 25–27.

Phillips, M. 2000. "Key Trade Deficit Measure Sets Record." *Wall Street Journal* (March 16), A2.

Pullen, R. 1998. "Looking at Privatizating Social Security." *Best's Review* (October), 12.

Renshaw, E. 1997. "Will Stocks Continue to Outperform Bonds in the Future?" *Financial Analysts Journal* 53 (March/April): 67–73.

Siegel, J. 1992. "The Equity Premium: Stock and Bond Returns Since 1802." *Financial Analysts Journal* 48 (January/February): 28–38.

———. 1999. "The Shrinking Equity Premium." *Journal of Portfolio Management* 26 (Fall): 10–17.

Smithers, A. 1999. "To the Lifeboats!" *Forbes Global* (June 14), 114–115.

Strobel, F., and W. Peterson. 1999. *The Coming Class War and How to Avoid It*. New York: Sharpe.

Tapinos, G. 1999. "Illegal Immigrants and the Labor Market." *OECD Observer* (December), 35–37.

Taylor, J. 1996. "A Fairer Nasdaq? SEC Approves New Rules." *Wall Street Journal* (August 29), C1.

Whelehan, B. 1997. "Will President Clinton's Reelection Trigger a Market Correction?" *Mutual Funds* (January), 21–22.

Wirtz, R. 2000. "Jobs Wanted: Will Work for (Next to) Nothing." *Fedgazette* 12 (January): 10–12.

Workers World. 2001. "Chained to Debt." (March 22), 10.

———. 2002. "Marx & Tyco." (June 13), 10.

2

How Uncertain Is Firm Valuation?

Dusan Mramor, Dejan Joksimovic,
and Elton McGoun

EXECUTIVE SUMMARY

Valuing firms using discounted cash flow is one of the most useful applications of finance theory, being employed in fundamental analysis, mergers and acquisitions analysis, and the valuation of closely held companies,
and having become an especially important tool in the privatization of
enterprises in formerly planned economies. In general, it is the heart of
equity valuation and thus is of considerable use to practitioners. Nonetheless, it has received relatively little attention in the academic literature,
with the exception of a handful of articles such as Kaplan and Ruback
(1995) and Hickman and Petry (1990).

When we value an enterprise using the DCF-based functions suggested
by finance theory, we are naturally interested in how good the valuation
is. We are well aware that there are errors in our measurements of each of
the variables; however, we hope that our valuation will nonetheless be
fairly accurate. In fact, recent empirical work by Kaplan and Ruback
(1995), Amin and Morton (1994), and Whaley (1982) appears to confirm
this conclusion. But science and engineering can provide us with more
precise statistical methods to address measurement errors, and these confirm for the more general case the conclusion of Hickman and Petry (1990)
for the dividend discount method that we ought to be extremely cautious
about the confidence we place in these valuations.

Using realistic assumptions of our abilities to estimate the variables in
a standard valuation equation, the market value of a firm could be 25 to 30
percent above or below the estimated market value. If we assume that
there is a uniform distribution of variable estimates (in which they are
equally likely to be found anywhere within a given range) rather than a

normal distribution, the confidence interval is a staggering 85 percent. Thus, it should not surprise us that the market value of the firm is quite volatile. As the market estimates of the independent variables that make up the value of the firm move around a little within fairly narrow intervals, the overall valuation of the firm can vary significantly. The problem is likely to be compounded, rather than reduced, by the use of many different valuation models by market participants.

DCF valuation equations may give us a somewhat false sense of the accuracy of our calculations. Even with almost unattainably precise input, we still end up with quite imprecise output. While this may be known among many professional appraisers and investment analysts, it is not quite so obvious to many academicians that the same phenomenon also affects the market prices for stocks.

INTRODUCTION

Valuing firms using discounted cash flow (DCF) is one of the most useful applications of finance theory, being used in fundamental analysis, mergers and acquisitons analysis, and the valuation of closely held companies, and having become an especially important tool in the privatization of enterprises in formerly planned economies. In general, it is the heart of equity valuation and thus is of considerable use to practitioners. Nonetheless, it has received relatively little attention in the academic literature, with the exception of a handful of articles, such as Kaplan and Ruback (1995) and Hickman and Petry (1990).

When we are valuing an enterprise using the DCF-based functions suggested by finance theory, we are naturally interested in how good the valuation is.[1] We are well aware that there are errors in our measurements of each of the variables; however, we hope that our valuation will nonetheless be fairly accurate. In fact, recent empirical work by Kaplan and Ruback (1995), Amin and Morton (1994), and Whaley (1982) appears to confirm this conclusion. Despite the existence of these tests indicating reasonable accuracy for DCF valuation, however, others intuitively believe that DCF valuation errors are considerable.

Science and engineering can provide us with more precise statistical methods to address measurement errors and resolve these conflicting beliefs. Such methods confirm for the more general case the conclusion of Hickman and Petry (1990) for the dividend discount method that we ought to be extremely cautious about the confidence we place in these valuations.

The next section, Measurement in Science and Engineering, describes the scientific analysis of measurement error. The following section, Measurement in Finance, describes the measurement of firm value using a standard discounted cash flow formulation that is widely accepted and applied by professional appraisers. The next section applies the techniques of the second section to the equation of the third section using conservative estimates of our ability to estimate the variables that enter into the firm valuation equation. The chapter concludes with a critique of recent papers, most of which, contrary to the findings of this chapter, appear to show that firm valuation using discounted cash flow is a fairly accurate procedure.

MEASUREMENT IN SCIENCE AND ENGINEERING

Error has long been a concern of scientists and engineers. There are *real* objects out there in the *real* world having *real* attributes, and an important task of scientists and engineers is to measure the values of those attributes or to compute them from measurements of the values of other attributes. Unfortunately, we can never make perfect measurements; all measurements are in error. In astronomy, for example, we know that a star is really out there somewhere, and we need a method for determining where it really is, but, in fact we have only imperfect measurements of its position as we observe it. In fluid dynamics, we know that a fluid has a flow, and we need a method for determining what this flow really is, but we must compute it from imperfect measurements of the fluid's frequency, pressure, and temperature.

With statistical methods, we can address measurement error. We can take imperfect measurements and make useful statements about what the value of an attribute really is. However, statistical methods were developed to work under very specific conditions:

- Objects have real attributes with real values.
- Measurements are subject to random errors.
- There are a large number of measurements.
- Measurements are independent of each other.

Determining the location of stars is a classical application of statistics to measurement. Astronomers can compute the mean and standard deviation of a distribution of a large number of independent measurements and make statements about the most likely position of a star and how likely the star is to be within a certain distance of that position.

Matters are similar, but more complicated, for the flow of a fluid, which is a function of frequency, pressure, and temperature. Scientists and engineers can compute the means and standard deviations of the distributions of independent measurements of each of the variables frequency, pressure, and temperature. To make statements regarding the most likely flow of a fluid and how likely the real flow is to be within a certain range of that computed flow, it is necessary to compute a mean and standard deviation for the fluid flow from the means and standard deviations of the frequency, temperature, and pressure. Computing the uncertainty of a dependent variable is very common in science and engineering, and there is a very common formula making the computation, which is explained in appendix 2.1.

In finance, we encounter problems that appear similar to the problems in science and engineering described in this section. Is it possible to apply this formula for the confidence interval of a physical variable to a financial variable, such as the value of a firm?

MEASUREMENT IN FINANCE

There are several models in the finance literature based on the discounted cash flow method, where the value of a firm is expressed as a continuous function of a number of variables. The best known is Gordon's model, the accuracy of which is addressed by Hickman and Petry (1990). However we will use another variation of DCF, proposed by Copeland et al. (1994, 283), which is much more frequently used by practitioners.[2] In this model the value of firm's total capital can be expressed as equation (1).

$$V = \frac{NOPLAT_1}{WACC_t - g}\left(1 - \frac{g}{r}\right) \tag{1}$$

where

V = value of the firm's capital
$NOPLAT_1$ = net operating profit less adjusted taxes
$WACC_t$ = target value of weighted average cost of capital[3]
g = growth of NOPLAT[4]
r = return on new invested capital[5]

When talking about the valuation of the firm, we mean the valuation of the firm's common equity (S).[6] Assuming that the firm has only two sources of capital—common equity and interest-bearing debt—we get the value of firm's common equity by subtracting the value of the debt from the value of the total capital. In addition we adjust for a discount for minority interests and a discount for lack of marketability. Use of these discounts is frequently necessary;[7] however, they can be subject to large errors since they are difficult to estimate. Making these and other refinements, we are left with equation (2) for the value of a firm and equation (3) for the errors in equation (2). The explanation of these equations and the descriptions of all the variables in them may be found in appendix 2.2.

$$S = \left[\frac{MAR \times REV \times (1-T)}{x_s\left(k_{RF} + k_{MP}\beta\right) + (1-x_s)k_b(1-T) - g}\left(1 - \frac{g}{r}\right) - B\right]\frac{1}{D_M D_{MA}}. \tag{2}$$

$$RU_S^2 = \left(\frac{\frac{\partial S}{\partial REV}}{\frac{S}{REV}}\right)^2 RU_{REV}^2 + \left(\frac{\frac{\partial S}{\partial MAR}}{\frac{S}{MAR}}\right)^2 RU_{MAR}^2 + \ldots + \left(\frac{\frac{\partial S}{\partial D_{MA}}}{\frac{S}{D_{MA}}}\right)^2 RU_{D_{MA}}^2 \tag{3}$$

As complex as equation (2) appears to be, it is in fact commonly used by appraisers to value businesses. Also, while finance has not yet acknowledged it, the still more complex equation (3) is necessary to estimate just how good our valuations are.

THE VALUE OF A FIRM: AN EXAMPLE

Let us analyze equation (3) using an example with real numbers. Even though the result of this exercise will be valid only for our example, it will enable us to illustrate the uncertainty associated with discounted cash flow valuation.

The data for our example are shown in table 2.1.[8]

Inserting the values from this list into equation (3), we obtain equation (4).

$$RU_S^2 = 1.8034RU_{REV}^2 + 1.8034RU_{MAR}^2 + 0.0624RU_T^2 + 5.3880RU_g^2 +$$
$$+ 0.8014RU_r^2 + 4.1059RU_{x_s}^2 + 3.8813RU_{k_{RF}}^2 + 3.3463RU_{k_{MP}}^2 + \qquad (4)$$
$$+ 3.3463RU_\beta^2 + 0.5774RU_{k_b}^2 + 0.1176RU_B^2 + RU_{D_M}^2 + RU_{D_{MA}}^2 .$$

As discussed in the first section, one of the assumptions of the analysis was the same desired level of confidence $(1 - \alpha)$ for all of the variables—for all the independent variables, as well as for the dependent variable, the value of the firm's common equity. Unfortunately, there is no sufficiently detailed empirical data concerning the values of all of these variables that different analysts might use when valuing firms. There are no distributions, mean values, and

Table 2.1
Example Values of Independent Variables

$REV = 77,867$	Net revenues
$MAR = 12\%$	Operating margin
$T = 30\%$	Corporate income tax rate
$g = 8\%$	NOPLAT growth rate
$r = 20\%$	Return on new invested capital
$x_s = 70\%$	Proportion of common equity in firm's capital structure
$k_{RF} = 7\%$	Risk free rate of return
$k_{MP} = 5\%$	Market risk premium
$k_b = 9\%$	Cost of interest-earing debt
$[beta] = 1.3$	Systematic risk of common equity
$B = 30,000$	Market value of interest-bearing debt
$D_M = 1$	Discount factor for minority interests
$D_{MA} = 1.25$	Discount factor for lack of marketability

standard deviations for samples of the independent variables. Therefore, we must make some estimates of the ranges within which we can be (1-a) percent confident (in this example, we will say 95%) of finding the market's estimate of the value of that variable. The estimates in table 2.2 are likely to be on the optimistic side regarding the ability of analysts to agree, thereby resulting in a narrower confidence interval.

Consider, for example, the variables that are found in the capital asset pricing model. Some authorities recommend using the ten-year,[9] some twenty-year,[10] and some even thirty-year government bond yield as the risk-free rate, because the duration is comparable to that of firms' free cash flows and for other reasons.[11] Other authorities, however, recommend short-term government bonds with maturities from three to twelve months. On September 12, 1995, the yield on one-year U.S. Treasury securities was 5.67 percent, on ten-year treasuries 6.24 percent, and on thirty-year treasuries 6.60 percent.[12] The difference between these rates, of course, depends on the specific shape yield curve at a given point in time.

As with the risk-free rate, authorities also do not agree on which market risk premium is the right one. Copeland recommends a 5 to 6 percent market risk premium, based on the premium of the return on the S&P 500 versus the return on long-term government bonds from 1926 to 1993.[13] However, the market risk premium has clearly changed over time, as can be seen in table 2.3.

As with all other variables in the capital asset pricing model, the value of a firm's systematic risk is also problematic. Different institutions in the United States determine company betas using different methods. Merrill Lynch, for

Table 2.2
Example Confidence Intervals of Independent Variables under Normal Assumptions

$RU_{REV} = \pm 5\ \%$	$73{,}974 < REV < 81{,}760$
$RU_{MAR} = \pm 5\ \%$	$11.4\ \% < MAR < 12.6\ \%$
$RU_T = \pm 5\ \%$	$28.5\ \% < T < 31.5\ \%$
$RU_g = \pm 5\ \%,$	$7.6\ \% < g < 8.4\ \%$
$RU_r = \pm 5\ \%$	$19.0\ \% < r < 21.0\ \%$
$RU_{x_s} = \pm 2\ \%$	$68.6\ \% < x_s < 71.4\ \%$
$RU_{k_{RF}} = \pm 3\ \%$	$6.79\ \% < k_{RF} < 7.21\ \%$
$RU_{k_{MP}} = \pm 8\ \%$	$4.60\ \% < k_{MP} < 5.40\ \%$
$RU_\beta = \pm 7\ \%$	$1.209 < \beta < 1.391$
$RU_{k_b} = \pm 2\ \%$	$8.82\ \% < k_b < 9.18\ \%$
$RU_B = \pm 1\ \%$	$29{,}700 < B < 30{,}300$
$RU_{D_M} = \pm 10\ \%$	$0.90 < D_M < 1.10$
$RU_{D_{MA}} = \pm 5\ \%$	$1.19 < D_{MA} < 1.31$

Table 2.3
Historical Market Risk Premium

	1926-1993	1962-1993
Arithmetic average returns	6.9 %	4.2 %
Geometric average returns	5.0 %	3.6 %

Source: Copeland et al. 1994. *Valuation*. New York: John Wiley & Sons, 261.

example, uses the S&P 500 as the market index and five years of monthly returns. *Value Line* takes a different approach by using the New York Stock Exchange Composite Index and five years of weekly returns and also adjusts the regression result. One analysis has shown on average a 5.4 percent difference between *Value Line* and Merrill Lynch betas, excluding extreme data.[14] We observe that the beta of the S&P 500 itself is 0.94, calculated against a broader stock market index.[15]

The discount factors are equally difficult to estimate. The discount for minority interests is one of the biggest puzzles of the DCF method of business valuation. The opinions of valuation authorities differ on whether a discounted cash flow analysis gives the value of a minority interest or the value of a controlling interest.[16] If the result of valuation is the minority interest value, then there should be a premium for the controlling interest. From 1985 to 1994 the average premium paid over the market price five business days prior to the announcement of the company buyout amounted to 39.5 percent, which implies a discount for a minority interest of 28.3 percent.[17]

The discount for lack of marketability is less controversial from a theoretical point of view. All other things being equal, less liquid assets are riskier than more liquid ones. The bigger problem is to define the appropriate discount. Pratt et al. (1996) summarize a number of studies that show a discount for lack of the marketability under different market conditions ranging, on average, between 40 and 63 percent.

Using these data for the confidence intervals for the independent variables, we obtain

$$RU_S = 28.34\%.$$

The value of common equity, calculated from the mean values of the independent variables is 70,000; therefore, we can be 95 percent certain of finding the market value of the firm's equity between 50,159 and 89,841.

Suppose we assume that there is no uncertainty in the following variables: risk-free rate, market risk premium, company beta, cost of interest-bearing debt, market value of interest-bearing debt, and capital structure. Still, half the width of the confidence interval for the firm's common equity value is

$$RU_S = 19.23\%.$$

Even using the very conservative intervals given in table 2.4, the value of RU_S is still

$$RU_S = 11.56\%.$$

This translates into a range between 61,909 and 78,091.

These confidence intervals are still quite large. What happens to them if we change some of the assumptions on which the analysis so far has been based? Thus far, we have assumed that the analysts' estimates of each of the variables are normally distributed. For a relatively small group having similar training and using similar data, this is probably not a bad assumption. The assumption may not be so good, however, if we consider anyone in the market to be an analyst. In engineering, it is common in situations in which we know nothing of distributions to assume a uniform distribution—that is, that the value for a variable is equally likely to be found anywhere within a given range of values. Assuming a uniform distribution rather than a normal distribution for the in-

Table 2.4
Example Confidence Intervals of Independent Variables under Very Conservative Assumptions

$RU_{REV} = \pm2.5\%$	$75{,}920 < REV < 79{,}814$
$RU_{MAR} = \pm2.5\%$	$11.70\% < MAR < 12.30\%$
$RU_T = \pm1.0\%$	$29.7\% < T < 30.3\%$
$RU_g = \pm2.5\%$,	$7.80\% < g < 8.20\%$
$RU_r = \pm2.5\%$	$19.5\% < r < 20.5\%$
$RU_{x_s} = \pm1.0\%$	$69.3\% < x_s < 70.7\%$
$RU_{k_{RF}} = \pm2.0\%$	$6.86\% < k_{RF} < 7.14\%$
$RU_{k_{MP}} = \pm3.0\%$	$4.85\% < k_{MP} < 5.15\%$
$RU_\beta = \pm2.0\%$	$1.274 < \beta < 1.326$
$RU_{k_b} = \pm0.5\%$	$8.96\% < k_b < 9.05\%$
$RU_B = \pm0.5\%$	$29.850 < B < 30.150$
$RU_{D_M} = \pm3.0\%$	$0.97 < D_M < 1.03$
$RU_{D_{MA}} = \pm0.0\%$	$1.25 < D_{MA} < 1.25$

dependent variables (and consequently for the dependent variable, common equity value, as well), equation (4) becomes equation (5):

$$RU_{S,U} = [1.3429RU_{REV} + 1.3429RU_{MAR} + 0.2498RU_I + 2.3212RU_g +$$
$$+ 0.8952RU_r + 2.0263RU_{x_s} + +1.9701RU_{k_{RF}} + 1.8293RU_{k_{MP}} + \quad (5)$$
$$+ 1.8293RU_\beta + 0.7599RU_{k_h} + 0.3429RU_B + RU_{D_M} + RU_{D_{MI}}]$$

Using this equation and the assumptions given in table 2.2, we get a confidence interval of

$$RU_{SU} = 85.03\%.$$

which translates into a firm value between 10,482 and 129,517. Using this equation and the more conservative assumptions given in table 2.4, we get a somewhat smaller, but still quite large, confidence interval, since

$$RU_{SU} = 33.67\%.$$

which translates into a firm value between 46,431 and 93,569.

In our model, there is linear relationship between the value of the common equity and net revenues, operating margin, and the market value of interest-bearing debt. The relationship between the common equity value and all of the other independent variables, however, is nonlinear. We have checked the reliability of our calculations, in which the nonlinear relationships were substituted for linear approximations, by performing a computer simulation. After generating five thousand examples of values of the independent variables with normally distributed errors around their means with the parameters from table 2.2, the standard deviation of the value *S* was 13.60 percent. Half of the relative width of the confidence interval was therefore $RU_s = 26.66$ percent. This is fairly close to the predicted value of 28.34 percent, which justifies the a linear approximation of the function *S* from equation (A2.1-1). The values of *S* obtained in the simulation are also very close to normally distributed, providing an additional justification for the approximation.[18]

These results are also consistent with those of Hickman and Petry (1990), who tested the accuracy of another DCF model, the Gordon model of discounted dividends. Using estimates of the variables in two versions of that particular model, they found errors of 88 percent and 69 percent of the actual average prices of firms. Most other recent studies, however, have been much more optimistic concerning valuation models.

DISCUSSION

Using realistic assumptions of our abilities to estimate the variables in a standard valuation equation (as in table 2.2), we have shown that the market value of a firm could be 25 to 30 percent above or below the estimated market value. Obviously, we ought not to place too much reliance on any one analyst's estimate, and we ought not to be surprised that different analysts' estimates can differ by quite a lot.

Kaplan and Ruback (1995) provide some empirical tests on the accuracy of firm valuation, and their results seem to contradict these conclusions. They favorably report, "Our median estimates of discounted cash flows for 51 HLTs [highly leveraged transactions] are within 10% of the market values of the complete transactions" (p. 1091). If we take a closer look at their methods however, we might question their conclusion of valuation accuracy.

First, they are concerned with the median error of the estimates of values of a number of firms. Of more practical significance is the confidence one can place in a single estimate of a single firm—the task with which this chapter has been concerned. There is a far broader interval than 10 percent surrounding a single estimate within which the so-called true value is likely to be found. Kaplan and Ruback's means of the absolute errors, which are likely to mean more to practitioners concerned with valuation accuracy, are from 16.7 percent to 21.1 percent, and the histograms accompanying the article (Kaplan and Ruback 1995, 1075) show confidence intervals that appear to be on the order of ±50 percent for the discounted cash flow method of valuation.

Second, Kaplan and Ruback estimate the mean error of estimates of market value of the firm—that is, the sum of the market values of both debt and equity. Because there is less uncertainty regarding the value of debt than of equity, the mean error of estimates of the value of equity will be higher than that of the market value of debt and equity together, and it is the value of equity that is more likely to be of interest to analysts. Third, the 10 percent refers to differences in the logs of the valuation and the market value of the transaction, "because it assumes a more reasonable multiplicative error structure" (p. 1080). Since the result of their computation is a positive mean error and the histograms show high positive individual errors, the result is underestimated. Fourth, the "market value" of the transaction is not what most would regard as a true *market* value. Out of a sample of fifty-one highly leveraged transactions (forty-three management buyouts and eight recapitalizations), there was no "overt outside pressure" in twenty-seven. There were competing bids in only eighteen and "hostile pressure" in the remaining six. Furthermore, the cash flows used in the valuation were the cash flow forecasts published in conjunction with the transaction.

When we consider that the 16.7 percent to 21.1 percent is a *mean* error (not a 95 percent confidence interval) of total market value under circumstances highly biased toward accurate valuation, we are forced to disagree with Kaplan and Ruback and to conclude on the basis of their own data that discounted cash flow valuation is not very precise at all. Furthermore, while they note that the valuation accuracy they found is comparable to that of Whaley (1982) for stock option pricing (mean errors of 1.1% to 2.2% with standard deviations of

23.8% to 25.2%) and to that of Amin and Morton (1994) for Eurodollar futures option pricing (mean errors of 15.2% to 21.1%), this is poor accuracy as well.[19]

A more difficult issue is the relationship of the market value to the "true value."[20] If we look at the market value of a firm as a sample of estimates of the true value of the firm, the confidence interval for the true value of the firm about the market value is still 25 to 30 percent. If we assume that there is a uniform distribution of variable estimates rather than a normal distribution, the confidence interval is a staggering 85 percent. Thus, it should not surprise us that the market value of a firm is quite volatile. As the market estimates of the independent variables that make up the value of a firm move around a little within fairly narrow intervals such as those in table 2.2, the overall valuation of the firm can vary significantly. The problem is likely to be compounded, rather than reduced, by the use of many different valuation models by market participants.

Thus, valuation equations such as (2) may give us a somewhat false sense of the accuracy of our calculations. Even with almost unattainably precise input, we still end up with quite imprecise output. This is well known among experienced professional appraisers, who prefer to use a guideline company approach employing different multiples (e.g., market to book ratio, price/earnings ratio, etc.).[21] It is not quite so obvious that the same phenomenon also affects the market for stocks, and it may be the source of much of the volatility we observe in prices.

APPENDIX 2.1:
UNCERTAINTY OF A DEPENDENT VARIABLE

Let r be dependent on n measurable variables:

$$r = r(X_1, X_2, ..., X_n) \qquad \text{(A2.1-1)}$$

and assume the following:

- The function (A2.1-1) is continuous over the domain of interest and has continuous derivatives with respect to variables X_i.
- Variables X_i are normally distributed around their (unknown) real values. We can estimate the means of these variables from samples having a *Student's* distribution.

The error in the value of r is often computed with the help of a linear function that depends on the errors of the independent variables and that is a good approximation for the value of r as long as the errors are relatively small—that is, within a range where the function r is close to being linear. A first-order Taylor approximation around the expected values is used to create this linear function:

$$r(X_1, X_2, ..., X_n) \approx r(E_{X_1}, E_{X_2}, ..., E_{X_n}) + \sum_{i=1}^{n} \frac{\partial r}{\partial X_i}(X_i - E_{X_i}) \quad \text{(A2.1-2)}$$

where E_{X_i} is the expected value of variable X_i.

This approximated value of r also has normally distributed errors; therefore, common statistical techniques can be applied to their analysis. When the variables X_i are not independent of one another, the variance of variable r is given by the following expression:[22]

$$\sigma_r^2 = \sum_{i=1}^{n} \sum_{j=1}^{n} \frac{\partial r}{\partial X_i} \frac{\partial r}{\partial X_j} \rho_{X_i, X_j} \sigma_{X_i} \sigma_{X_j}$$

(A2.1-3)

$$= \sum_{i=1}^{n} \left[\left(\frac{\partial r}{\partial X_i} \right)^2 \sigma_{X_i}^2 + \sum_{\substack{j=1 \\ j \neq i}}^{n} \frac{\partial r}{\partial X_i} \frac{\partial r}{\partial X_j} \rho_{X_i, X_j} \sigma_{X_i} \sigma_{X_j} \right]$$

where

σ_r^2 = variable r variance

$\rho_{X_i X_j}$ = correlation coefficient between variables X_i and X_j

$\sigma_{X_i}^2$ = variable X_i variance.

If the variables X_i are independent of one another, their correlation coefficients are zero. Thus, equation (A2.1-3) becomes much simpler:

$$\sigma_r^2 = \sum_{i=1}^{n} \left(\frac{\partial r}{\partial X_i} \right)^2 \sigma_{X_i}^2. \quad \text{(A2.1-4)}$$

In practice, the variances σ_{X_i} are not known, and variances of a sample of measurements that have been made are used instead. Considering this, equation (A2.1-4) becomes:

$$s_r^2 = \sum_{i=1}^{n} \left(\frac{\partial r}{\partial X_i} \right)^2 s_{X_i}^2 \quad \text{(A2.1-5)}$$

where

s_r^2 = sample variance of variable r
$s_{X_i}^2$ = sample variance of variable X_i.

The sample variance of variable X_i is defined as:

$$s_{X_i}^2 = \frac{1}{n-1}\sum_{i=1}^{n}\left(x_{ji} - \overline{X}_i\right)^2 \tag{A2.1-6}$$

where

n = number of observations in the sample of values of variable X_i,
X_i = arithmetic mean of variable X_i, of the sample.

Half the width of the confidence interval within which the true value of variable X_i lies with probability $(1 - \alpha)$ is then

$$U_{X_i} = t_{\frac{\alpha}{2}} \cdot s_{X_i} \tag{A2.1-7}$$

where

U_{x_i} = half of the width of the confidence interval
t = value of the desired confidence level $1 - \alpha$. (i.e., 90%, 95%, 99%, etc.).

Assuming the same desired confidence level $(1 - \alpha)$ for all the variables and multiplying both sides of equation (A2.1-5) by the square of the *Student's* distribution t value, we get

$$\left(t \cdot s_r\right)^2 = \sum_{i=1}^{n}\left(\frac{\partial r}{\partial X_i}\right)^2 \left(t \cdot s_{X_i}\right). \tag{A2.1-8}$$

Substituting (A2.1-7) into (A2.1-8), we get the following expression for the square of half the width of the confidence interval of variable r:

$$U_r^2 = \sum_{i=1}^{n}\left(\frac{\partial r}{\partial X_i}\right)^2 U_{X_i}^2. \tag{A2.1-9}$$

The square of the relative value of Ur , expressed in terms of the relative values of the confidence interval widths of the independent variables, is

$$RU_r^2 = \left(\frac{\frac{\partial r}{\partial X_1}}{\frac{r}{X_2}}\right)^2 RU_{X_1}^2 + \left(\frac{\frac{\partial r}{\partial X_2}}{\frac{r}{X_2}}\right)^2 RU_{X_1}^2 + \dots + \left(\frac{\frac{\partial r}{\partial X_n}}{\frac{R}{X_n}}\right)^2 RU_{X_n}^2 \tag{A2.1-10}$$

where

$$RU_{X_i} = \frac{U_{X_i}}{X_i} \quad \text{and} \quad RU_r = \frac{U_r}{r}.$$

APPENDIX 2.2:
ERROR ANALYSIS AND THE VALUATION EQUATION

From equation (1) we thus obtain

$$S = \left[\frac{NOPLAT_1}{WACC_t - g}\left(1 - \frac{g}{r}\right) - B \right]\frac{1}{D_M D_{MA}} , \qquad (A2.2\text{-}1)$$

where

S = value of the firm's common equity
B = market value of firm's interest-bearing debt
D_M = discount factor for minority interests
D_{MA} = discount factor for lack of marketability.

The discount factor for lack of marketability has a value greater than 1 if there is a problem with marketability. Due to controversy regarding the discount factor for minority interests, it can be either larger than 1, when it is considered as the discount for a minority interest, or less than 1, when it is considered as the premium for a controlling interest.

In equation (A2.2-1) *NOPLAT* and *WACC* are computed as shown in equations (A2.2-2) and (A2.2-3).

$$NOPLAT = REV \times MAR \times (1 - T) \qquad (A2.2\text{-}2)$$

$$WACC_t = x_s k_s + (1 - x_s)k_b(1 - T) \qquad (A2.2\text{-}3)$$

where
REV = net revenues
MAR = operating margin
T = corporate income tax rate[23]
x_s = fraction of common equity in the target capital structure
k_s = opportunity cost of common equity
k_b = opportunity cost of debt.

Further, assuming that the opportunity cost of the firm's common equity can be determined using the capital asset pricing model, we obtain

$$k_s = k_{RF} + k_{MP}\beta \qquad (A2.2\text{-}4)$$

where

k_{RF} = risk free rate of return

k_{MP} = market risk premium

β = beta or systematic risk of firm's common equity.

Making all the substitutions into equation (A2.2-1), we can finally obtain the value of the firm's common equity as the following rather complicated, but still commonly used, function of thirteen variables:

$$S = \left[\frac{MAR \times REV \times (1-T)}{x_s \left(k_{RF} + k_{MP}\beta\right) + (1-x_s)k_b(1-T) - g} \left(1 - \frac{g}{r}\right) - B \right] \frac{1}{D_M D_{MA}}. \qquad (2)$$

The key questions at this point concern the statistical methods developed in the previous section for the evaluation of errors in equations such as this. Can we use them to estimate the possible error in the value of the firm's common equity if we can determine the ranges within which the values of independent variables can vary?

The four specific conditions under which statistical methods were developed to work are problematic for the valuation of a firm, since the variables from which it is computed are not the same as readings on scientific instruments. Let us therefore take a somewhat different approach. Assume that the purpose of firm valuation is to "measure" the consensus that a group would arrive at if set to the task, which group consensus we might refer to as the "market." Accordingly, the variables are the values the members of this group use to make their estimates of firm value. While these estimates cannot be said to be imperfect, there is indeed a mean from which they can deviate. There can be large numbers of estimates, and estimates can be independent (although it is doubtful in practice that they are). Thus, we can apply the statistical method of error analysis, and we can compute a mean and standard deviation for the consensus a group of analysts would arrive at for the valuation of the firm.[24]

Applying equation (A2.1-10) to equation (2), we obtain:

$$RU_S^2 = \left(\frac{\frac{\partial S}{\partial REV}}{\frac{S}{REV}} \right)^2 RU_{REV}^2 + \left(\frac{\frac{\partial S}{\partial MAR}}{\frac{S}{MAR}} \right)^2 RU_{MAR}^2 + \ldots + \left(\frac{\frac{\partial S}{\partial D_{MA}}}{\frac{S}{D_{MA}}} \right)^2 RU_{D_{MA}}^2 \quad (3)$$

The coefficients in equation (3) can be described as the squares of the elasticities of the value of the firm with respect to the individual independent variables. These individual elasticities are

$$\frac{\frac{\partial S}{\partial REV}}{\frac{S}{REV}} = \frac{REV \ MAR(1-T)\left(1-\frac{g}{r}\right)}{REV \ MAR(1-T)\left(1-\frac{g}{r}\right) - B(WACC_c - g)}$$

$$\frac{\frac{\partial S}{\partial MAR}}{\frac{S}{MAR}} = \frac{MAR \ \ REV(1-T)\left(1-\frac{g}{r}\right)}{REV \ \ MAR(1-T)\left(1-\frac{g}{r}\right) - B(WACC_c - g)}$$

$$\frac{\frac{\partial S}{\partial T}}{\frac{S}{T}} = \frac{T \ \ REV \ \ MAR[g - x_s(k_{RF} + k_{MP}\beta)]}{REV \ \ MAR(1-T)\left(1-\frac{g}{r}\right) - B(WACC_c - g)} \cdot \frac{1-\frac{g}{r}}{WACC_c - g}$$

$$\frac{\frac{\partial S}{\partial g}}{\frac{S}{g}} = \frac{g \ \ REV \ \ MAR(1-T)}{REV \ \ MAR(1-T)\left(1-\frac{g}{r}\right) - B(WACC_c - g)} \cdot \frac{1-\frac{WACC_c}{r}}{WACC_c - g}$$

$$\frac{\frac{\partial S}{\partial r}}{\frac{S}{r}} = \frac{REV \ \ MAR(1-T)\frac{g}{r}}{REV \ \ MAR(1-T)\left(1-\frac{g}{r}\right) - B(WACC_c - g)}$$

$$\frac{\frac{\partial S}{\partial x_s}}{\frac{S}{x_s}} = \frac{x_s \ \ REV \ \ MAR(1-T)\left(1-\frac{g}{r}\right)}{REV \ \ MAR(1-T)\left(1-\frac{g}{r}\right) - B(WACC_c - g)} \cdot \frac{k_{RF} + k_{MP}\beta - k_b(1-T)}{WACC_c - g}$$

$$\frac{\frac{\partial S}{\partial k_{RF}}}{\frac{S}{k_{RF}}} = \frac{k_{RF} \ \ REV \ \ MAR(1-T)\left(1-\frac{g}{r}\right)}{REV \ \ MAR(1-T)\left(1-\frac{g}{r}\right) - B(WACC_c - g)} \cdot \frac{x_s}{WACC_c - g}$$

$$\frac{\frac{\partial S}{\partial k_{MP}}}{\frac{S}{k_{MP}}} = \frac{k_{MP} \ \ REV \ \ MAR(1-T)\left(1-\frac{g}{r}\right)}{REV \ \ MAR(1-T)\left(1-\frac{g}{r}\right) - B(WACC_c - g)} \cdot \frac{\beta \ x_s}{WACC_c - g}$$

$$\frac{\frac{\partial S}{\partial \beta}}{\frac{S}{\beta}} = \frac{\beta \ \ REV \ \ MAR(1-T)\left(1-\frac{g}{r}\right)}{REV \ \ MAR(1-T)\left(1-\frac{g}{r}\right) - B(WACC_c - g)} \cdot \frac{x_s k_{MP}}{WACC_c - g}$$

$$\frac{\frac{\partial S}{\partial k_b}}{\frac{S}{k_b}} = \frac{k_b \quad REV \quad MAR(1-T)\left(1-\frac{g}{r}\right)}{REV \quad MAR\left(1-T\right)\left(1-\frac{g}{r}\right) - B(WACC_c - g)} \cdot \frac{(1-x_s)(1-T)}{WACC_c - g}$$

$$\frac{\frac{\partial S}{\partial B}}{\frac{S}{B}} = \frac{B \quad (WACC_c - g)}{REV \quad MAR(1-T)\left(1-\frac{g}{r}\right) - B(WACC_c - g)}$$

$$\frac{\frac{\partial S}{\partial D_M}}{\frac{S}{D_M}} = 1$$

$$\frac{\frac{\partial S}{\partial D_{MA}}}{\frac{S}{D_{MA}}} = 1$$

NOTES

The authors would like to acknowledge the generous assistance of Neza Mramor-Kosta in the preparation of this paper and the helpful comments of Shannon Pratt.

1. In developed economies there are other methods of valuation based on the guideline company approach which some consider to be preferable (Fishman et al. 1994). More recently, however, DCF has become an important tool in the privatization of enterprises in formerly planned economies, because in these economies it is almost always the only applicable valuation method (Mramor 1992). Market inefficiency in emerging markets (Gordon and Rittenberg 1995; Murphy and Sabov 1992) can make price comparisons problematic. The prices at which socially owned firms are sold to private owners not only have important microeconomic and macroeconomic consequences, but also important social consequences. (Ribnikar 1994).

2. This is a popular text used for valuation in many countries.

3. Among practitioners there is considerable controversy over the appropriate discount rate to use for a discounted cash flow valuation. There is no concensus that WACC is that discount rate, and there is no concensus on how to compute the components of WACC if it is used (Wilson 1996).

4. Of course g must be less than *WACC*, and g/r must be less than 1 in this equation. Because of these limits, g cannot be normally distributed; however, in the examples

used in this paper to illustrate the effects of measurement errors, the mean of g is so much less than *WACC* that any deviations from a normal distribution are insignificant.

5. This equation is simply a variation on the formula for the present value of an infinite stream of cash flows growing at a constant rate g discounted at $WACC_r$. The first cash flow to capital in the stream is the net operating profit less adjusted taxes (*NOPLAT*) multiplied by the fraction of operating profit paid out to capital $(1 - K)$ by the firm. Here, we assume that the growth rate of *NOPLAT* (g) is equal to the fraction of operating profit retained by the firm (K) multiplied by the return on new invested capital (r).

6. The expressions "valuation of the firm" and "valuation of a firm's common equity" are used interchangeably.

7. See Amihud and Mendelson (1986) concerning marketability and Schilt (1996), Becker (1997), and Taub (1998) concerning minority interests.

8. This example is based on the actual valuation of a closely held Slovenian company with most of the actual numbers rounded off. In this particular case, the value of the firm was disputed, so a number of licensed and highly qualified independent professional appraisers were consulted. The results of their appraisals differed substantially.

9. Copeland et al. (1994), 259.

10. Pratt et al. (1996), Brigham et al. (1999), 155.

11. Brigham et al. (1999), 154–155.

12. *Financial Times*, September, 12, 1995, 28.

13. Copeland et al. (1994), 260. The common equity value calculated with a 5 percent market risk premium is approximately 8 percent higher than the one calculated with 6 percent market risk premium, all other things being equal.

14. Brigham and Gapensky (1993), 190.

15. Radcliffe (1994), 233.

16. Cornell (1993), 247. However, there is certain consensus that the value is estimated for minority interest if my minority cash flows are utilized and vice versa.

17. Pratt et al. (1996) 317.

18. This simulation was repeated several times, and the results were the same within the limits of computational precision.

19. Over the past few years, "real options" have become an important consideration in equity valuation (Trigeorgis 1996). If there are errors of this size in the valuation of financial options, consider the potential errors in the valution of real options, for which the parameters of the option pricing formula are difficult if not impossible to obtain.

20. "True value" is a term frequently encountered in finance, but infrequently explained. Perhaps the best definition is that it is the value given perfect foresight. For a more complete discussion of the concept, see McGoun (1997).

21. "The discounted economic income methods are extremely sensitive to changes in the input variables" (Pratt et al. 1996, 191).

22. Coleman and Steele (1989), 188–189.

23. This equation omits taxes on interest income and the tax shield for interest paid; however, this is not important, as we are interested in the uncertainty of the value and not in the value itself.

24. We will assume that all thirteen variables from equation (2) are independent of one another for each analyst. This assumption is likely to result in a smaller confidence interval for firm value, since estimates of several of the independent variables

are more likely to be positively than negatively correlated, thereby increasing the uncertainty of the dependent variable, firm value.

REFERENCES

Amihud, Yakov, and Haim Mendelson. 1986. "Asset Pricing and the Bid Ask Spread." *Journal of Financial Economics* 17: 223–249.

Amin, Kaushik, and Andrew Morton. 1994. "Implied Volatility in Term Structure Models." *Journal of Financial Economics* 35: 141–180.

Becker, Brian C. 1997. "Minority Interests in Market Valuation: An Adjustment Procedure." *Business Valuation Review* 16, No. 1 (March): 27–31.

Brigham, E. F., and L. C. Gapenski. 1993. *Intermediate Financial Management.* Fort Worth, Tex.: The Dryden Press.

Brigham, E. F., L. C. Gapenski, and P. R. Dasves. 1999. *Intermediate Financial Management.* Fort Worth, Tex.: The Dryden Press.

Coleman, H. W., and W. G. Steele, Jr. 1989. *Experimentation and Uncertainty Analysis for Engineers.* New York: John Wiley and Sons.

Copeland, T. E., T. Coller, and J. Murrin. 1994. *Valuation: Measuring and Managing the Value of Companies.* New York: John Wiley and Sons.

Cornell B. 1993. *Corporate Valuation: Tools for Effective Appraisal and Decision Making.* Homewood, Ill.: Business One Irwin.

Fishman, Jay E., Shannon P. Pratt, J. Clifford Griffith, and D. Keith Wilson. 1994. *Guide to Business Valuation.* 4th ed. Fort Worth, Tex.: Practitioners.

Gordon, B., and L. Rittenberg. 1995. "The Warsaw Stock Exchange: A Test of Market Efficiency." *Comparative Economic Studies* 37: 1–27.

Hickman, Kent, and Glenn H. Petry. 1990. "A Comparison of Stock Price Predictions Using Court Accepted Formulas, Dividend Discount, and P/E Models." *Financial Management* 19, No. 4 (Summer): 76–87.

Kaplan, S. N., and R. S. Ruback. 1995. "The Valuation of Cash Flow Forecasts: An Empirical Analysis." *The Journal of Finance* 50, No. 4 (September): 1059–1093.

McGoun, Elton G. 1997. "Hyperreal Finance." *Critical Perspectives on Accounting* 8: 97–122.

Mramor, Dusan. 1992. "Business Appraisal for Privatization: The Case of a Slovenian Company." *Central and East European Privatization Network Workshop Series Number 2*, 89–99.

Murphy, A., and Z. Sabov. 1992. "Empirical Analysis of Pricing Efficiency in the Hungarian Capital Markets." *Applied Financial Economics* 2: 63–78.

Pratt, S. P., R. F. Reilly, and R. P. Schweihs. 1996. *Valuing a Business: The Analysis and Appraisal of Closely Held Companies.* Homewood, Ill.: Irwin.

Radcliffe, R. C. 1994. *Investment.* New York: HarperCollins College.

Ribnikar, Ivan. 1994. "The Financial System of a Small, Emerging Market Economy." *International Review of Financial Analysis* 3, No. 2: 137–148.

Schilt, James H. 1996. "Discounts for Minority Interests." *Business Valuation Review* 15, No. 4 (December): 161–166.

Taub, Maxwell J. 1998. "Valuing a Minority Interest: Whether to Adjust Elements of a Financial Statement over Which the Minority Shareholder Has No Control." *Business Valuation Review* 17, No. 1 (March): 7–9.

Trigeorgis, Lenos. 1996. *Real Options: Managerial Flexibility and Strategy in Re-source Allocation*. Cambridge: MIT Press.
Whaley, Robert E. 1982. "Valuation of American Call Options on Dividend Paying Stock: Empirical Tests." *Journal of Financial Economics* 10: 29–58.
Wilson, L. Deane. 1996. "The Discount Rate: Fiction or Nonfiction?" *Valuation* 40, No. 1 (June): 14–22.

3

Valuation: A Case Study of Scientifically Valuing Enron Using the Historical Financial Statements

Austin Murphy

EXECUTIVE SUMMARY

This chapter illustrates how to scientifically value equities and conduct credit analysis. On the basis of Enron a half-year prior to bankruptcy as a case study, a scientific analysis of the company's financial statements shows that the overvaluation of Enron's equity and the enormous credit risk of the company could have been seen quite easily before the collapse. In particular, Enron's business fundamentals in its low growth industry could not justify its high stock prices. In addition, its low debt-coverage ratios, combined with low liquidity and substantial volatility in recurring income, could not justify an investment grade credit rating. The company's high risk of bankruptcy implied that the company's demise was really only a matter of time, and this fact itself made the company's stock virtually worthless long before the actual collapse.

INTRODUCTION

Because security valuation is a somewhat subjective process that requires the use of substantial judgment, estimates of the true intrinsic value of a security may vary. However, it is possible to utilize financial logic to greatly narrow down the range of possible values. This chapter illustrates one method of scientific valuation using the case of Enron a half-year prior to its bankruptcy.

Enron is a particularly important case study to examine, because its bankruptcy was the largest in history and the company had long been voted the "most innovative company in the U.S." (Romaine 2001). The company represents an especially useful example from a valuation standpoint, because its stock price dropped so rapidly and because its bankruptcy caught so many people by surprise. Investment analysts claimed to have been deceived by the company into continuing "buy" recommendations almost until Enron's bankruptcy filing (Associated Press 2002). The company's own employees assert that Enron officials misled them into buying the stock just before its collapse (*Los Angeles Times* 2002).

While much of the criticism of Enron in the mainstream press has focused on the accounting and financial irregularities associated with the company,[1] a large share of the actual blame for the disastrous price performance of the stock lies with the apparent inability of the market of investors to value equity securities. In particular, despite some deceptive accounting practices (ISDA 2002) and some questionable stock recommendations by investment banks that were affected by Enron's investment banking business relationships (Smith 2002), it should have been possible for competent investors and analysts to see that the stock had long been overpriced (and to avoid the catastrophic investment).

STOCK VALUATION

In particular, a discounted cash flow model of stock value based on forecasted pro forma financial statements should optimally be applied to the valuation of any equity (Murphy 2000). Such a model requires forecasts on future unit volume increases, future price increases, future operating profit margins, future tax rates, future dividend payout ratios, future leverage ratios, and future asset turnover ratios (Murphy 1989). Such forecasts, combined with thirty-seven items from the current financial statements (including footnote details), permit prediction of income statements and balance sheets far into the future and thereby enable computation of future dividends and the summed present value thereof (Callaghan and Murphy 1999). A brief outline of the procedure is provided in table 3.1.

The model forecasts financial statements and dividends out seventy-five years, at which time a liquidation value for the stock is estimated based on the model-forecasted earnings of the company between sixty-five and seventy-five years in the future (Murphy, 1989). In particular, assuming no abnormal growth/reinvestment opportunities after sixty-five years, and assuming a 100 percent dividend payout between sixty-five and seventy-five years in the future, the average earnings over that 10-year span is divided by the required return on the stock to compute the stock value in seventy-five years. Then the present value of this figure is added to the present value of all the seventy-five years of dividends forecasted to compute the value of the stock.

Table 3.1
Forecasting Future Dividends with Pro Forma Financial Statements

Computation Each Year	Source of Estimate
Sales	Unit sales, inflation, market share
x Operating margin	Forecasted operating margin
Operating income before adjustments	
- Current cost adjustment	Financial statement data
- Pension expense adjustment	Financial statement data
Operating income	
- Depreciation	Financial statements, sales, turnover
- Interest	Financial statements, sales, turnover, leverage
Profit before tax	
x (1 – tax rate)	Forecasted tax rate
Profit after tax from old businesses	
+Profit from other businesses	Prior fund surplus, required return
-Other equity claims	Financial statements
Net profit to common shareholders divided by number of common shares	Financial statements; fund shortage
Earnings per common share	
x dividend payout ratio	Forecasted dividend payout ratio
Dividend per common share discounted at the required return	T-yields, beta, leverage changes
Present value of dividend	

Source: Reprinted with permission from Austin Murphy, *Scientific Investment Analysis*, Westport, Conn.: Quorum Books, 2000.

A HISTORICAL VALUATION OF ENRON STOCK

Application of the framework in table 3.1 to the valuation of Enron equity shows the stock to have been overvalued on almost any day. Take for instance, the date upon which the company filed its 2000 10-K annual report with the SEC. On that day, April 2, 2001, the company's stock price was at $56.57. The following analysis is undertaken using only public information that was available on that date.

Since Enron largely sells energy, which is likely to experience price increases in line with the economy, it seems reasonable to assume that the prices at which the company sells its products will rise over the long term with inflation. An economic forecast of inflation can be gathered from the *Wall Street Journal* by subtracting the yield on a long-term inflation-indexed Treasury bond from the yield on a long-term T-bond that is not inflation indexed. This computation indicated an industry inflation rate of 5.63 percent to 3.50 percent = 2.13 percent. This forecast seems to be reasonably conservative, especially since April 2, 2001, futures prices for crude oil, heating oil, and natural gas all indicated an expected drop in energy prices over the next few years.

Since energy is not really a high-technology industry with above-average growth potential, it seems reasonable to assume that unit sales growth for the company's energy industry will equal that of the economy. Murphy (2000) suggests assuming that the economy will grow in the long term at about 3 percent as it has in the long-term past. There is little reason to believe that Enron has or can maintain any particular advantage (or disadvantage) in this commodity industry to achieve any market shares gains (or losses).

Similarly, there is little reason to believe that Enron's operating profit margins will increase in the future. Given that Enron had been successfully exploiting the deregulation of energy markets in places like California with questionable and possibly illegal, but very profitable, wholesale energy trading activities that would likely be prohibited by future government actions (Kranhold, Lee, and Benson 2002), it would actually seem probable that the company's operating margin would decline in the future. In addition, while the most recent *Value Line Investment Survey* page analysis of Enron available on April 2, 2001, indicated that "sustained high gas prices . . . , which we expect, augur well for ENE's energy intermediation businesses" (Schwartzman 2001), the April 2, 2001, futures prices indicated a forecast of a major drop in natural gas prices (by 15% in the next year alone) that would likely cause a decline in the company's profitability. Note that although *Value Line* at that time also forecast that Enron would profit from a forecast of "considerable price volatility in the power markets," it was questionable to assume that Enron's traders would be able to consistently generate arbitrage profits from volatility in markets that would likely become more efficient (offering fewer opportunities to profit from volatility or any other factor) rather than less efficient.[2] Besides considering the possibility of lower profitability from its energy business, it should also be mentioned that Enron ran a hedge fund that had generated extremely profitable trades (Zuckerman 2002), which might not be expected to continue forever in an efficient market. While a decline in the operating margin might appear likely under these circumstances, the possibility always exists that, at least long-term, the company will be able to maintain its profit margins, and so it is optimistically forecast that Enron's profit margin will remain the same as in the prior year.

Assuming a constant leverage ratio, constant asset turnover ratios and a constant dividend payout ratio also seem reasonable. In order not to rely on subjective or outside estimates, an average beta (of 1.0) and an average risk of bankruptcy (implying a safety rank of 3) are assumed.

Enron's income tax rate can also be assumed to remain long-term at the statutory 35 percent. Footnote 5 of the company's 2000 financial statements indicates that it had lower tax rates in prior years related to special items, such as the sale of stock, that would not be expected to continue. (In fact, the tax rate might be expected to be above 35%, as that footnote indicates state income taxes increased the effective rate by 2.5%, while the nondeductibility of goodwill expenses increased it by 1.6%, which leads to a net recurring increase of 1.7% to 36.7%, after factoring out a reduction in the tax rate by 2.4% because of lower taxes on the company's overseas operations.)

Entering these data along with the current financial statement information, it is possible to estimate the value of the company almost instantaneously with a software package, such as SIA, that can feed in Compustat data. The value of Enron under these assumptions is found to be $14.17. Given Callaghan and Murphy's (1999) finding that stock prices tend to eventually move toward their values estimated using such models, it should not be surprising that Enron's stock price collapsed.

Note that the only parameters that might reasonably be changed to improve the stock value were the stock's beta and the company's future tax rate. In early 2001, the *Value Line Investment Survey* estimated the beta of the company to be 0.9 (Schwartzman 2001), which would increase the value of the stock computed under the other prior assumptions to $15.77 (from $14.17). With respect to taxes, the company's tax footnote indicated that a large portion of its actual expensed income tax (about half) was deferred. If that deferral could be continued for a significant amount of time (such as perpetually), the company's effective tax rate might very well have been less than the statutory 35 percent. Enron was reputed to utilize very effective means to reduce its cash tax liability (McKinnon 2002), such as selling future oil deliveries to investment banks (receiving cash up front so that the oil sale represented more of a loan collateralized by hedged oil deliveries, as explained in chapter 6 of this book) and then postponing delivery until a loss needed to be realized for tax purposes (Sapsford and Raghavan 2002). If it were assumed that the company could maintain only a 15 percent tax rate perpetually (and assuming the more favorable beta of 0.9 estimated by Value Line), the value of the company would be $24.17. An alternative parameter that was often suggested to be much higher than assumed here was the company's market share (Cruver 2002), which if increased by 1 percent each year for the next twenty years (to 30% from about 10% in 2000) would alone increase the stock value to $27.84.

Note that all these stock values are based on an assumption that the company's trading activities could continue to exploit inefficient market prices at the same rate as it had in the past. This assumption is very questionable, when the very arbitrage pursued by Enron (and other investors who copy Enron) would tend to drive out the inefficiency over time, resulting eventually in lower profit margins, not reflected in these forecasts. The company had indeed grown revenues over the past few years at a very rapid clip (increasing by over 100% in 2000), but sustainable high growth in earnings per share could not be attained by the company, with a return on equity (ROE) reported to be only 9.2

percent in 2000,[3] the outlook of which indicated no change in its profitability, at best.

Much of Enron's increase in revenues in the prior year had been financed by a large increase in its liabilities/assets ratio, which increased from 71.4 percent in 1999 to 82.1 percent in 2000. Although its debt/equity ratio only increased from 0.96 in 1999 to 0.97 in 2000, its total liabilities incorporated some camouflaged debt items, making it the more reliable measure of financial leverage. As explained in the next section, the company's high level of financial leverage could not be maintained indefinitely.

STOCK VALUES, THE BANKRUPTCY OF ENRON, AND CREDIT ANALYSIS

While Enron's stock price eventually fell much farther than the level estimated by the computer model, it did so only after the company went bankrupt, and astute financial analysts should have also been able to see the high risk of bankruptcy for the firm. Entering the high risk of bankruptcy into the stock valuation model would have greatly reduced the present value of the expected cash flows from the stock, because the stock valuation model correctly multiplies each forecasted cash flow by one minus the cumulative probability of bankruptcy until the cash flow is received.

The Murphy (2000) model of credit analysis is utilized to estimate the probability of bankruptcy for Enron. This model, which has been shown to be an accurate forecaster of default risk (Callaghan and Murphy 1999), indicates that Enron was existing on the very edge of financial failure on April 2, 2001.

The Murphy (2000) model utilizes 6 steps to determine a company's chance of bankruptcy. The first step is to compute the company's times interest earned (TIE) ratio and compare it to the TIEs of groups of companies with specific credit ratings. A listing of TIEs and credit ratings is provided in columns 1 and 6 of table 3.2, which is largely compiled from 1997 data provided by Standard & Poors, although columns (4) and (8) represent rough estimates provided by Murphy (1988).

A HISTORICAL CREDIT ANALYSIS OF ENRON

Enron's TIE had been at the level of 2.5 in 2000, 2.5 in 1999, and 2.4 in 1998, yielding an average TIE of 2.5, which approximates that of the average Ba2 company. (Factoring out the company's interest expense owed to its shell subsidiary, which had issued preferred stock to collect the payments, would only increase the TIE to 2.7 and would be inappropriate at any rate, since the interest, while deferrable in cash for up to five years, is legally owed to outside investors.) While the extreme stability of the TIE (and the nonnegative trend in that ratio) would imply that Enron should have a higher credit rating than

Table 3.2
Default Risk Parameter Estimates

(1)	(2)	(3)	(4)	(5)	(6)	(7)	(8)
	Default	Default	Estimated	Estimated	Default	Debt/	
Agency	Rate	Rate	Recovery		TIE	Capital	
Rating	1900-43	1997	1988	Losses	1994-6	1994-6	Beta
INVESTMENT GRADE:							
Aaa	0.52%	0.10%	60%	0.04%	16.1	23.6%	.03
Aa	0.62%	0.15%	52%	0.07%	11.1	29.7%	.09
A	1.38%	0.23%	42%	0.13%	6.3	38.7%	.18
Baa	2.09%	0.50%	34%	0.33%	4.1	46.8%	.27
JUNK:	5.21%	34%	.				
Ba	1.95%	1.29%			2.3	55.8%	.36
B	2.83%	1.87%			1.2	68.9%	.45
Caa		3.96%		2.61%			.51
Ca		10%		6.60%			.54
C		20+%		13.20+%			.57

Source: Reprinted with permission from Austin Murphy, *Scientific Investment Analysis*, Westport, Conn.: Quorum Books, 2000.

the typical company with such an average TIE, there was evidence in the financial statements that the TIE stability was artificial and not likely to recur.

In particular, the company reported special gains of $371 million in 2000, $1,297 million in 1999, and $684 million in 1998. Factoring out these gains, the company's TIE would have been 2.1 in 2000, 0.8 in 1999, and 1.3 in 1998, for an average of 1.4. This lower average and higher volatility provide some evidence for the likelihood of the company's TIE falling below the magic level of 1.0. At such a level, the company would be unable to cover its interest expense out of operating income (as it indeed failed to do in one of the three years). The adjusted TIE average of 1.4 itself would imply a B1 rating from table 3.2, while the volatility would imply the rating should probably be lowered to at least B3.

While there were also some special write-offs in two of the three years ($326 million in 2000 and $441 million in 1999) that would have raised the TIE back up to 2.5 in 2000 and 1.4 in 1999 if factored out, a significant amount of volatility remains. It should also be mentioned that the special write-offs were stated to be "impairment of long-lived assets" and may have reflected a continuous understatement of depreciation and amortization expenses.[4] Dividing those write-offs over the three years indicates a TIE of 2.4 in 2000, 1.1

in 1999, and 0.9 in 1998, indicating even more risk that the company's interest would not be payable out of income. Although these new ratios indicate some positive trend in the TIEs (with a significant improvement in 2000), the lack of any apparent trend implied from the previous TIE ratios, the questionable ability of the company to maintain its past level of operating profitability (as explained in a prior section) and the increase in the company's leverage in 2000 (with the liabilities/assets ratio rising from 71.3% to 82.5% in 2000 and the debt/capital ratio rising from 46% to 50%) would imply that the trend is likely not to continue. A Caa1 rating might be easily justified (especially since there is other evidence of volatility, such as the account "other income" ranging between $181 million and –$37 million).

If interest is not payable out of income, it must be financed from outside funding or the company's own internal liquidity. Given that the company's debt/capital ratio of 50 percent implies from column 7 of table 3.2 a rating that borders on junk, it cannot be assumed that outside funding would be available if the company could not finance its interest expenses from internal liquidity.

A pro forma cash budget for the firm indicates that it had insufficient internal liquidity to survive even a minor deterioration in its profitability levels. In particular, the 2000 financial statements indicate cash of $1.374 billion, up to $11.043 billion in cash available from factoring receivables (90% of $12.270 billion in total current receivables), $3.930 billion in unused lines of credit ($3.8 – 0.29 = $3.51 billion in unused committed and $0.42 billion in uncommitted lines), and $2.153 billion in pretax cash flow (from $979 million in net income, plus $434 million in income taxes, plus $855 million in depreciation, less $115 million in net nonrecurring gains), for total gross cash resources of $18.500 billion if there were no change in 2001 compared to 2000. That cash would be needed to pay off $2.982 billion in short-term debt ($1.679 billion listed as current and $1.303 billion listed as long-term because of committed long-term credit lines): $9.777 billion accounts payable due within one year, $4.277 billion in short-term customer deposits (which represent collateral for the companies' derivative operations and don't appear to be something that automatically refinances, given the mere $44 million size of this account in 1999),[5] and $2.178 billion in other current liabilities, for a total of $19.214 billion. The excess current liabilities over cash resources indicates a cash shortage of $0.714 billion, which is certainly a sign of inadequate internal liquidity.

While trade creditors might be willing to roll over their credit as long as the company was profitable, a single reported loss might very well cause them to ask for payment in cash, given the aforementioned analysis of the riskiness of the firm, and force the company into bankruptcy. That would imply that a $2.153/$100.789 = 2.14 percent drop in revenues without a corresponding drop in costs would cause the company to run out of cash. Alternatively, a $2.153/$94.517 = 2.3 percent rise in costs without a corresponding increase in revenues would cause the company to run out of cash. Another scenario that would cause the company to run out of cash would be for unit sales to drop by

$$\$2.153/(\$100.789 - \$94.517) = 34.3 \text{ percent.}$$

Despite the company's hedging activities, the risk of such events happening appears to be very significant (especially since it appears from the net gains reported from its merchant activities that it may utilize its hedging operations as a profit center that undertakes significant risk).

Given that the company has been unable to cover its interest expense from recurring income in one of the last three years even when it had less financial leverage, and given that the company has inadequate internal liquidity to finance a loss, the annual risk of bankruptcy might be as high as 33 percent even if the situation stays the same as it has over the prior three years. Since the outlook for the company's operations with lower energy prices may be worse than it was before, the probability of bankruptcy may well be above 33 percent.

Such a large risk exists even without considering the $2.513 billion in liabilities of unconsolidated affiliates that Enron reported in footnote 15 of its 2000 financial statements as being guaranteed by the parent company (but not reported on the balance sheet). In addition, the large chance of bankruptcy is apparent even without considering the separate risk associated with several billion dollars in contingent liabilities related to forward contracts into which Enron had entered to buy 54.8 million shares of its own stock for an average price of $67.92 per share (reported in footnote 11 of Enron's 2000 financial statements). Moreover, another factor not incorporated into the foregoing analysis is the fact that there were sizable additional liabilities (totaling a maximum of about $2 billion) that would be triggered if the company's stock price were to decline below a specified level ($48.55 for about half these additional liabilities) or if the company's credit rating fell below the investment-grade level (as reported in footnote 10 of the company's 2000 financial statements). Both of these latter two events would seem to be quite likely (as explained in the prior section and here, respectively), further increasing the chance of bankruptcy.

Although the fact that some of these liabilities could be paid with stock reduces the probability of them being a drain on cash, the risk of such dilution along with the high risk of bankruptcy increase the chance both of the liabilities being triggered and of the company not being able to pay for them with authorized shares of stock, which would be worthless in bankruptcy or with excessive dilution. The very triggering of those liabilities would undoubtedly hasten the fall in the value of the stock at the same time that it increased the company's chance of bankruptcy, which in turn would cause the stock to fall farther and even faster at the same time that it would further increase the chance of bankruptcy (and so on, until bankruptcy was indeed declared). The fact that Enron's operations relied heavily on its business customers believing in its creditworthiness greatly magnified this additional risk (Fusaro and Miller 2002).

In conclusion, although Enron's public credit rating in April 2001 was Baa1 by Moody's (and equivalently at BBB+ by S&P), it appears to have had a probability of bankruptcy like that of a very poor C-rated company.[6] The firm was essentially living on the edge of a cliff, and it was less a question of whether the company would go bankrupt than of when.

THE EFFECT OF THE PROBABILITY
ON THE STOCK VALUE

With such a large chance of bankruptcy, the safety rank in the stock valuation input should have been changed from the average level of 3 (which is the midpoint of the *Value Line* Safety Rank range of 1–5) to a much higher level. Although the foregoing analysis has been made after the fact, it is difficult to see how a credit rating much higher than C could be justified in this situation.

To provide some verification for that statement, in October 2002 I gave my undergraduate students in an introductory investments course a surprise quiz (after just two weeks of credit analysis education) that required them to determine the credit rating of an anonymous company. Without their knowledge, I listed Enron's recurring TIEs over the past three years, the percentages that sales prices and unit sales would have to fall for the company to run out of cash, and the percentage that costs would have to rise for Enron to run out of cash. I also indicated that the futures market was forecasting a 15 percent drop in the price of both the commodities the firm sells and the commodities that make up the company's cost of goods sold. All of the responding students gave the company a junk credit rating, with over 80 percent giving the firm a rating of Ca or C (the average estimated probability of bankruptcy for the firm was estimated to be 31%).[7]

Even assuming a Ca rating, the company would have a probability of bankruptcy of 10 percent per year according to table 3.2. Translating that figure into a new safety rank (which happens to be 10) utilizing a conversion formula employed by SIA software (Murphy 1994), it is possible to evaluate the effect of such a high chance of ruin on the expected value of the cash flows from the stock (which are reduced by the compounded probability of bankruptcy). The result of such a high probability of bankruptcy is that Enron's stock was worth only $1.56 on April 2, 2001.

As mentioned in the previous section, the annual probability of bankruptcy for Enron was probably closer to 40 percent (which converts to a safety rank of 90 in the conversion model). Effectively inputing such a high chance of bankruptcy yields a stock value of just $0.09.

In effect, given the fact that the company's bankruptcy was extremely likely in the next few years, there was little probability that the company would exist long enough for the expected value of future dividends to be significant. In addition, the model takes into consideration the fact that there was a high likelihood that creditors would soon realize the riskiness of the company and require much higher interest rates on debt rolled over in the future, thereby reducing expected income significantly even without a downturn in its operating profitability (and eventually resulting in losses). By 2000, the company had essentially financed itself into worthlessness, but it took a single reported loss on its income statement in the fall of 2001 before the market realized that.[8]

THE IMPLICATION FOR MARKET EFFICIENCY

Markets are only as efficient as the investors who determine market prices. When analysts and investors do not utilize rational valuation models to make investment decisions, the possibility of prices deviating enormously from value can occur. Such a possibility creates the opportunity for large losses for the ignorant (and large gains for the educated). Enron is just one example where analysts and investors may have greatly overestimated a firm's prospects and may have greatly underestimated the risk of bankruptcy for a firm.[9] While this chapter has been written in hindsight, its use of strictly historical information does illustrate how application of rational models and expectations can potentially lead to greater efficiency in asset valuation in ways that may potentially help investors avoid disastrous investments like Enron.

NOTES

1. For instance, Enron was able to have many losses go unreported because they occurred in the companies' myriad of nonconsolidated affiliates, and because write-downs of investments in those partnerships were underreported (Schroeder 2002a). Enron had actually contingently guaranteed some of the liabilities of these affiliates, with the contingent guarantee being contracted to be triggered by a drop in the company's stock price or credit rating (Henry, Timmons, Rosenbush, and Arndt 2002). Some of these transactions were reflected in questionable accounting practices that have led to a criminal investigation of Enron's auditor, Arthur Andersen LLP (Barrionuevo and Weil 2002). In addition, many of these transactions might have been prohibited by the Securities and Exchange Commission (SEC) if that commission had not granted the company a waiver in 1993 from registering under the Public Utility Holding Company Act (Schroeder 2002a). Enron had apparently used its influence on politicians to avoid regulatory oversight by both the Commodity Futures Trading Commission (CFTC) as well as the SEC (Kuttner 2002).

2. Energy prices actually fell farther than the futures market forecast indicated, with natural gas prices falling from $5.10/MMBtu on April 2, 2001, to a price of $2.10 by September 21, 2001, at the same time that the implied volatility in natural gas futures option prices rose slightly. Nevertheless, *Value Line* persisted in its belief that Enron trading profits were positively correlated with the volatility of energy prices (regardless of the direction) and predicted at the later date (on September 21, 2001) that Enron's profits would decline with *Value Line*'s own forecast of a future decline in "commodity price volatility" (Romaine 2001a). Note that, as before with respect to the direction of energy prices, *Value Line*'s forecast of the volatility of energy prices was at odds with the forecast implied in futures prices.

Note also that *Value Line*'s colored analysis could not be attributed to any investment banking business with Enron.

3. As explained in the following section, a sizable portion of Enron's income was in the form of nonrecurring gains, so that the recurring ROE was only 6.8 percent.

4. Subsequently, it has been discovered that Enron's reported write-downs themselves grossly and knowingly underestimated the actual write-downs that should have been reported (Smith and Kranhold 2002).

5. Some of these deposits may have actually been effective loans not included in their formal debt accounts and ratios because they were considered "hedges for commodities trades" as opposed to "new financing" (*New York Times* 2002). As explained earlier, some of these loans were used to manipulate the company's tax liability.

6. The company's overall credit rating would be a function not only of its probability of bankruptcy but also the expected recovery rate on debt in bankruptcy (Callaghan and Murphy 1999). However, with such a high probability of bankruptcy, almost any expected reasonable payoff on the firm's assets (Murphy 2000) would lead to a recovery on the debt that would still yield default losses in table 3.2 that indicate a very poor C-rated debt. The fact that Moody's rated the company's subordinated debt home grades lower (at Baa3) than its senior debt would be consistent with a relatively low payoff in default being expected (Murphy 2001).

7. In a separate problem that was stated to be independent, I gave the same students the ROE, beta, and P/e ratio of Enron and the S&P500 index on April 2, 2001, and asked them to write down which investment they thought was better as an addition to a diversified portfolio. All chose the S&P 500 (as did all students in an MBA investments course I was also teaching).

8. Some have asserted that one of the reasons for Enron's high stock valuation was its broadband operations (Bruner and Bodily 2002), which had assets of $1.3 billion in 2000, had revenues of under $500 million, and yielded a pretax loss of $60 million (according to the company's 2000 financial statements). These high-technology revenues represented less than 0.5 percent of the company's overall sales (equal to about a half-dollar per share); the loss had a negligible impact on the company's income statement (dropping it by less than a dime per share), and the assets represented only 2 percent of the company's total assets (implying less than two dollars per share invested into those operations). The absurd overvaluation of such assets by the stock market in early 2000 had already led to an enormous bust in high-technology stocks, so that by early 2001 those types of assets were no longer valued at many times revenues and book value. As a result, the market's inefficient valuation of high-technology assets in early 2000 cannot explain the overvaluation of Enron's stock in early 2001. Moreover, even if Enron's high-technology assets were expected to yield enormous profits in the future, the credit analysis of the company indicated that the firm would likely not last long enough for such profits to materialize (making them virtually worthless anyway). Thus, the excuse of investment analysts that they "were misled by Enron" (Associated Press 2002) does not appear to justify their positive recommendations on the stock, recommendations that continued almost up until the company's bankruptcy filing.

9. This overestimation of firms' prospects may have led to the market overvaluation of stocks in general at the turn of the millenium. Another interpretation of the high market values at that time may have been a low premium being required for bearing

risk (Murphy 2000). For instance, if the premium expected return for a unit of beta risk were merely 1 percent instead of the 5 percent assumed in the model, and if Enron had really had average bankruptcy risk, Enron's stock would have been worth over $46.93 on April 2, 2001. However, as shown in this chapter, Enron really did have significant bankruptcy risk, and even utilizing a 1 percent premium for bearing a unit of beta risk raised the firm's stock value to only $1.77 when the safety rank was estimated to be 10 (and did not raise the company's equity value to over $.10 when the safety rank was estimated to be 90). It is interesting to observe that the belief of some investor analysts that Enron could continue to exist and grow rapidly by exploiting inefficiencies in market prices assumes permanence in the very inefficient markets that allowed Enron to have an incredibly overpriced stock. It is more likely that market prices would eventually become more efficient and rational, thereby greatly reducing the company's stock price, which would be further reduced in value in an efficient market by the reduction in trading profitability that would exist if all market prices were efficient.

REFERENCES

Associated Press. 2002. "Financial Analysts Testify about Their Role in Enron Debacle." *Oakland Press* (February 28), A18.

Barrionuevo, A., and J. Weil. 2002. "Partner Warned Arthur Andersen on Enron Audit." *Wall Street Journal* (May 9), C1.

Bruner, R., and S. Bodily. 2002. *Enron Case Study, 1986–2001*. Darden: University of Virginia.

Callaghan, J., and A. Murphy. 1999. "An Empirical Evaluation of the Forecasting Power of Fundamental Stock Analysis Models over Time." *Journal of Research in Finance* 2: 138–157.

Cruver, B. 2002. *Anatomy of Greed*. New York: Carroll and Graf.

Fusaro, P., and R. Miller. 2002. *What Went Wrong at Enron*. Hoboken, N.J.: John Wiley and Sons.

Henry, D., H. Timmons, S. Rosenbush, and M. Arndt. 2002. "Who Else is Hiding Debt." *Business Week* (January 28), 37.

ISDA. 2002. "Enron: Corporate Failure, Market Success." *Financial Engineering News* (June/July), 1, 4, 5, 7, 24, 25, 30.

Kranhold, K., B. Lee, and M. Benson. 2002. "Enron Rigged Power Market in California, Documents Say." *Wall Street Journal* (May 7), A1.

Kuttner, R. 2002. "Enron: A Powerful Blow to Market Fundamentalists." *Business Week* (February 4), 20.

Los Angeles Times. 2002. "Letter: Enron Workers Deceived." *Oakland Press* (January 13), A20.

McKinnon, J. 2002. "Congressional Probe to Examine Enron's Tax-Avoidance Strategies." *Wall Street Journal* (February 19), A6.

Murphy, A. 1988. "A Discounted Cash-Flow Model of Fixed-Income Securities Subject to Multiple Calls." *Southern Economic Journal* 55: 21–36.

———. 1989. "A Mechanical Procedure for Incorporating Detailed Forecasts and Accounting Data into the Stock Price Model." *Midwestern Journal of Business and Economics* 4 (Fall): 15–30.

———. 1994. *Scientific Investment Analysis*. Alexandria, Va.: Orchises.

————. 2000. *Scientific Investment Analysis*. Westport, Conn.: Quorum Books.

————. 2001. "A Comparison of Taxable and Tax-Deductible Preferred Yields." *Research in Finance* 18: 169–193.

New York Times. 2002. Shady Partnerships Only a Part of Enron Debt Story." Oakland Press (February 17), A15.

Romaine, S. 2001a. "Enron Corp." *Value Line Investment Survey* (September 21), 449.

————. 2001b. "Enron Corp." *Value Line Investment Survey* (December 21), 447.

Sapsford, J., and A. Raghavan. 2002. "Lawsuit Spotlights J. P. Morgan's Ties to the Enron Debacle." *Wall Street Journal* (January 25), A1, A4.

Schroeder, M. 2002a. "SEC Feels Heat over Exemptions to Enron." *Wall Street Journal* (January 21), A8.

————. 2002b. "As Enron's Derivatives Trading Comes into Focus, Gap in Oversight Is Spotlighted." *Wall Street Journal* (January 28), C1.

Schwartzman, T. 2001. "Enron Corp." *Value Line Investment Survey* (March 23), 454.

Smith, R. 2002. "The Analyst Who Warned about Enron." *Wall Street Journal* (January 29), C1.

Smith, R., and K. Kranhold. 2002. "Enron Knew Foreign Portfolio Had Lost Value." *Wall Street Journal* (May 6), C1.

Zuckerman, G. 2002. "Enron Quietly Ran a Risky Hedge Fund That Did Well." Wall Street Journal (April 11), C1.

4

Was the Writing on the Wall for Enron? The Importance of Strategy Analysis to Financial Analysts

Cynthia Miree and Arline Savage

EXECUTIVE SUMMARY

The recent crisis associated with Enron Corporation has shaken the general public's confidence in financial professionals and has called into question the methods that they use to assess a firm's financial viability. Because accounting standards allow managers to use discretion in making accounting policy choices and using estimates in financial reporting, it is incumbent upon external auditors, financial analysts, the financial news media and the SEC to act as watchdogs to connect business realities with accounting rules and guard against insider manipulation of the numbers, thus forming a layer of protection for stakeholders outside of the firm. The collapse of such a widely admired company came as a surprise to many. Also disturbing was that only a few perceptive analysts were able to see through the firm's strategic rhetoric and call into question Enron's financial stability, given the "vagueness" of their business model. Since a firm's business model provides the framework through which the logic of value creation is articulated, financial analysts need to analyze a firm's strategy as a part of their regular practice. A solid understanding of a firm's strategy provides financial analysts with a framework for understanding the root of its financial performance and enables them to discern and appropriately interpret possible negative deviations from that strategy.

In this chapter we analyze Enron's self-described external business environment, business strategy, and strategic management, based on information contained in its Security and Exchange Commission filings and annual and quarterly reports available prior to the firm's collapse. We then compare this information with their strategic moves and accounting data and identify a number of strategy-related "red flags." We use the term "red flag" throughout this paper to identify statements, disclosures, or other pieces of financial data that should have merited further scrutiny by financial analysts because they represent evidence of possible negative deviations from optimal execution of the company's management strategy.

In summary, Enron was able to sustain its operations and build a faux advantage by leveraging the several key elements of its corporate and competitive strategies. Vertical integration allowed Enron to control more than one stage of the industry's transactions. This, coupled with the industry's information imperfection, enabled it to gain a strong position, as the firm had access to strategically important information that others participating in transactions with Enron did not. Enron's size and scope permitted a low-cost structure, and the brand equity associated with the Enron name created an atmosphere of trust. This trust was buoyed by the perpetual climb in its stock price and implied ability to fulfill its contractual arrangement, thereby permitting continued access to new capital. Lower costs and increased control over transactions was also facilitated through the use of the EnronOnline trading technology. In sum, Enron's critical success factors were to capitalize on unregulated gaps existing in the marketplace while maintaining investor and lender confidence.

This strategy, even during its peak, was not without risks, and we identify key risk areas to focus on for accounting analysis purposes. These are (1) management's strategic decision to move away from highly successful core businesses into higher-risk dealer activities, (2) management's self-declared and intense focus on earnings per share, and (3) the firm's international high-risk and asset-heavy ventures and complex partnership structures, which put tremendous strain on its capital budgeting and capital management systems. The inconsistency between the company's need to maintrain creditworthiness for operating purposes and the company's financial strategy that effectively increased credit risk proved to be a recipe for disaster.

INTRODUCTION

The 1990s ushered in a new era in information access. Never before has so much financial and competitive information been available to those interested in investing or those who advise on investment decisions. Access to information is an important first step, but an understanding of how to use appropriate frameworks to deal with the complexities associated with competitive and financial data is equally critical. The recent crisis associated with Enron Corporation has shaken the general public's confidence in many financial professionals and called into question the methods used to assess a firm's financial viability. In the aftermath of this crisis, several questions remain unanswered. Should financial analysts have seen the evidence of possible negative deviations from an optimal execution of their management strategy? Should they have warned investors of the Houston-based energy-trading giant's precarious financial situation? Further, were there actionable danger signals apparent in the financial statements and mandated Securities and Exchange Commission filings that any analyst could have discerned?

In an effort to offer a substantiated opinion on these questions, we begin by explaining the importance of strategy analysis and linking this type of analysis to accounting and financial analyses. We then explore Enron's annual reports and its Form 10-K and 10-Q SEC filings. Form 10-K is the annual report containing audited financial statements that most public companies file with the SEC. It provides a comprehensive overview of the firm's business. The Form 10-Q is a report filed quarterly by these companies. It includes unaudited financial statements and provides a cumulative view of the company's financial results and financial position during the fiscal year. Enron filed all these forms, which were available to investors and analysts prior to November 8, 2001, the day on which Enron filed an 8-K form informing the SEC that it intended to restate its financial statements and reduce its previously reported net income retroactive to 1997 by $591 million.

In arriving at the outcome of our investigation of Enron's publicly available documents, we systematically employ three of the Palepu et al. (2000)[1] components for effective business analysis using financial statements: business strategy analysis (covered in this chapter), accounting analysis, and financial analysis (the latter two performed in the next chapter), to evaluate Enron's Form 10-K and 10-Q SEC filings for the 1996 to 2000 fiscal years, as well as the firm's 1998 to 2000 annual reports. A business strategy analysis is done first because it gives subsequent analysis a grounding in business reality. The overall business strategy analysis contains an industry analysis and also a strategy analysis that includes the identification of profit drivers and critical risks facing the firm. In chapter 5 we do the accounting analysis, which involves examining how well Enron's accounting rules and practices reflect its business economics and business strategy. Then, after restating reported accounting amounts to undo the distortions that we believe are justifiable, we perform financial analysis. This involves analyzing financial ratio and cash flow measures for financing, investing, and operating activities to evaluate the effectiveness of the firm's strategy (Palepu et al. 2000, iv–v).

WHY STRATEGY ANALYSIS?

Financial analysts need to analyze the firm's strategy as a part of their regular practice. At the heart of strategic management is the assertion that competitive advantage is built on a firm's ability to create a unique and valuable competitive position (Porter 1996). This unique position results from the effective interplay of a firm's business model and its competitive strategy. Business models describe how the company intends to make money over the long term and should be able to answer the following four questions: Who is the customer? What does the customer value? How does this business make its money? What is the underlying economic logic that explains how the firm can deliver value to customers at an appropriate cost? (Eisenmann 2002; Magretta 2002). In other words, the business model provides the framework through which the logic of value creation is articulated. Competitive strategy, in contrast, explains how the firm is able to outcompete its rivals (Magretta 2002).

The sustainability of a firm's advantage derives from the organization's capacity to develop and exploit differences between itself and other companies (Porter 1996). These differences stem from the choice to perform a set of activities that are completely different from competitors or by choosing to perform common activities in different ways (Porter 1996). In either case, these differences provide the cornerstone for strategy formulation and, if successful, should enable the firm to generate economic returns above those of its competitors (Porter 1996). These returns, or lack thereof, are reflected in the firm's financial statements, which provide stakeholders with various measures of performance.

While the importance of closely examining the symbiotic relationship between firm strategy and the choice and use of recorded financial performance measures has not historically received much attention in the literature, significant efforts to reverse this trend are emerging in the works of Palepu et al. (2000) and Kaplan and Norton (2000). Both these sets of authors encourage strategic and financial analysts to consider the causal and predictive links between the two. A solid understanding of a firm's strategy provides financial analysts with a framework for comprehending the root of the firm's financial performance, and such an understanding enables them to discern and appropriately interpret possible negative deviations from an optimal execution of the strategy (Kaplan and Norton 2000). We define evidence of such negative deviations from the management strategy as "red flags" (i.e., statements, disclosures, or other pieces of financial data that should have merited further scrutiny by financial analysts because they represent evidence of possible negative deviations away from optimal execution of the company's management strategy).

Equally important is the need for analysts to consider the viability of a firm's strategy (i.e., the scope of the business, competitive positioning, critical success factors and risks) based on conditions that exist in the external business environment (i.e., capital markets, labor markets, product markets, and business regulations) (Palepu et al. 2000, 1–4). An analysis of the firm's external environment, as a part of strategy analysis, is vital to the financial analysis function, as it provides opportunities in the form of resources and constraints in the form of regulations, thus impacting a firm's ability to implement its strategy through its financing, investing, and operating business activities. For example, the deregulation of the U.S. energy industry post-1992 and exemptions in the commodity-trading law allowed online energy-trading firms to operate without government oversight (Morgan 2001; Lee 2002). In this regard, Enron, a trailblazing first-mover in energy-related securities trading, managed to successfully lobby Congress to escape the regulation that applies to other types of security trading (Schroeder and Ip 2001).

The firm's accounting information system measures and reports on the economic consequences of three types of business activities (financing, investing, and operating). The intention is to fairly and accurately reflect the firm's financial results and its underlying financial condition to stakeholders. The firm's accounting system is, in turn, affected by its external accounting environment (e.g., capital market structure, corporate governance, accounting regulations and conventions, taxation, independent auditing, legal system), which flows from the external business environment; and management's accounting strategies (choice of accounting policies, estimates, reporting format, voluntary disclosures), which stem from the firm's business strategy (see Palepu et al. 2000).

Since accounting standards allow managers, who have superior knowledge about the inner workings of their firm, to use their discretion in making choices and using estimates in financial reporting, it is incumbent upon external auditors, financial analysts, the financial news media and the SEC to act as watchdogs to connect business reality with accounting rules and to guard against insider manipulation of the numbers, thus forming a layer of protection for stakeholders outside of the firm. Based on the foregoing, it is essential for financial analysts to understand the firm's business model and strategy before forming an opinion as to the fairness of a firm's financial reports. Finally, by putting a firm's critical success factors and risk areas under the microscope, an analyst can "zoom in" on particular accounting disclosures that reflect the economic consequences of the firm's most crucial business activities and examine them very closely without becoming distracted by the plethora of other financial information available.

Because of the critical importance of business strategy analysis, we first analyze Enron's self-described external business environment and business strategy, based on information contained in its SEC filings and those annual and quarterly reports that were available prior to the firm's collapse. Our intention is to look for red flags pointing to deviations from the optimal execution of their management strategy. One particulart problem that has been pointed out previously for Enron's strategy was the company's strategic risk taking at the same time that its strategic operations required a high level of creditworthiness and low risk taking (Fusario and Miller 2002).

ENRON'S ACCOUNT OF THE EXTERNAL ENVIRONMENT AND ITS STRATEGY

Industry-Related Information

On the first page of its 10-K and 10-Q filings for the 1996 to 1999 fiscal years ending on December 31, as well as for the first three quarters of the 2000 fiscal year, Enron discloses its standard industrial classification (SIC) as "Petroleum and Petroleum Products Wholesalers, Except Bulk Stations and Terminals" (SIC 5172). According to the U.S. Census Bureau (2002), SIC

5172 comprises establishments primarily engaged in wholesaling petroleum and petroleum products (except from bulk liquid storage facilities). At the end of the *fourth quarter* in its 2000 10-K filing, Enron's industrial classification is suddenly changed to that of "Security Brokers, Dealers, and Flotation Companies" (coded as SIC 6211). SIC 6211 comprises establishments primarily engaged in acting as principals (excluding investment bankers, securities dealers, and commodity contracts dealers) in buying or selling of financial contracts, generally on a spread basis. "Principals" are investors who buy or sell for their own account (U.S. Census Bureau 2002). This disclosure alone, made on the very first page of the 2000 Form 10-K, should at the very least have inspired analysts to ask why. In particular, why has Enron chosen a classification different from that of the analysts? *Value Line Investment Survey*, for example, categorizes Enron in the "Natural Gas (Diversified)" industry throughout the period of investigation. Further, *Moody's Public Utility Manual* (1997–2000) consistently describes Enron as "an integrated natural gas and utility company." This inconsistency leads us to search for further disclosures to explain the discrepancy.

A search of both the 2000 fiscal year annual report and Form 10-K for an explanation for this major change in, and confusion about, appropriate industrial classification during the last quarter of the 2000 fiscal year produces nothing. This raises the first red flag and leads us to take a closer look at the business strategy and operating business segment disclosures in the 10-K and annual reports in an attempt to gain more insight into Enron's change of direction and primary business activities. A change from a "tried and tested" core of highly successful natural gas operating activities to derivative trading activities would increase risk substantially. In an effort to ascertain exactly which industry classification is most appropriate, we look at Enron's business operations disclosures.

Form 10-K General Business Disclosures

Enron makes the following formal disclosures about the business it engages in as part of its required SEC 10-K filings (under the prescribed section Part 1, Item 1—Business, General).

Fiscal Year 2000

Enron describes itself as an Oregon corporation, headquartered in Houston, that provides products and services related to natural gas, electricity, and communications to wholesale and retail customers. This does not fit with Enron's new self-reported SIC 5172 code used for the first three-quarters of the year or with its new SIC 6211 code used during the last quarter. Enron states that its operations are conducted through its subsidiaries and affiliates, which are principally engaged in six types of operating activities:

1. Transportation of natural gas through pipelines to markets throughout the United States

2. Generation, transmission, and distribution of electricity in the northwestern United States

3. Marketing of natural gas, electricity, and other commodities and related risk-management and finance services worldwide

4. Development, construction, and operation of power plants, pipelines, and other energy related assets worldwide

5. Delivery and management of energy commodities and capabilities to end-use retail customers in the industrial and commercial business sectors

6. Development of an intelligent network platform to provide bandwidth-management services and the delivery of high-bandwidth communication applications.

Fiscal Year 1999

Enron describes itself as an energy and communications company. Here too, no mention is made of petroleum and petroleum products. However, the fifth operating activity disclosure listed in 2000, "Delivery and management of energy commodities and capabilities to end-use retail customers in the industrial and commercial business sectors," does not appear in the 1999 10-K report. While this fifth activity was the only addition to the operating activities in the 2000 disclosure, it is not clear whether this represents a dramatic change in its main business focus. Thus, we need to raise the red flag even higher. This inconsistency could be an attempt to obscure an important shift in focus; if not, Enron management is confused or unsure about the core of its operations. Neither scenario inspires our confidence.

Fiscal Year 1998

The company describes itself as being "principally engaged in the exploration for and production of natural gas and crude oil." In 1998, there is no mention of "communications," as there is for 1999 and 2000. Enron discloses that its subsidiaries and affiliates are engaged in five types of operating activities:

1. Exploration for and production of natural gas and crude oil in the United States and internationally (listed first here, but completely disappears in 1999)

2. Transportation of natural gas through pipelines throughout the United States

3. Generation and transmission of electricity to the northwestern United States

4. Marketing of natural gas, electricity, and other commodities and related risk-management and finance services worldwide

5. Development, construction, and operation of power plants, pipelines, and other energy-related assets worldwide

The last operating activity mentioned in 1999 and 2000, "Development of an intelligent network platform to provide bandwidth management services and the delivery of high bandwidth communication applications," does not appear separately in the 1998 disclosure. Consequently, there appears to be a major shift of focus beginning in 1999, away from oil and gas exploration and production and toward bandwidth communications systems and services—a second red flag, because this is an emerging and hence high-risk industry.

Fiscal Year 1997

The disclosure is essentially the same as that for 1998, but it does mention a "realignment of Enron's operations" in 1997.

Fiscal Year 1996

As in 1997 and 1998, Enron is described as a natural gas and electricity company. Its five primary operating activities are

1. Transportation and wholesale marketing of natural gas throughout the United States and internationally, through natural gas pipelines
2. Exploration for and production of natural gas and crude oil in the United States and internationally
3. Production, purchase, transportation, and worldwide marketing of natural gas liquids and refined petroleum products
4. Independent development, promotion, construction, and operation of power plants, natural gas liquids facilities, and pipelines in the United States and internationally
5. Purchasing and marketing of electricity and other energy-related commitments

The only discernible change between 1996 and 1997 appears to be the 1997 reference to "the marketing of . . . and other commodities and related risk management and finance services worldwide." This may imply a move toward derivatives trading, but it is not very specific; it should raise a red flag for analysts and lead them to keep a particular eye on this aspect of the business. This could be the "realignment of operations" mentioned in 1997, but we were unable to find conclusive information to substantiate that conjecture.

In summary, it appears that important changes in business activities began to emerge in 1997, even though Enron consistently described itself as a natural gas and electricity company throughout the period from 1996 to 1998. This is in contradiction to its self-declared SIC code. In 1999, however, Enron described itself as an energy and communications company, in what seems to be a major shift in focus, by which the company appeared to move away from oil and gas exploration and production, toward bandwidth communications systems and services. A once-key operating activity, exploration for and production of natural gas and crude oil in the United States, disappears from the scene, and a new operating activity appears—the development of an intelligent network platform to provide bandwidth-management services and the delivery of high-bandwidth communication applications. Enron's profit mix does not seem to support this change in direction, a point that requires further investigation. Between 1997 and 2000, Enron derived most of its profits from its Wholesale Services business (50%, 56%, 66%, and 91%, respectively) (*Value Line* 1997, 1998, 1999, 2000, 2001). Its Gas Pipeline Group, with respective profit contributions of 27 percent, 20 percent, 34 percent, and 29 percent, followed (*Value Line* 1997, 1998, 1999, 2000, 2001). Finally, according to the U.S. Census Bureau (2002), the new bandwidth industry is still being defined by the North America Industry Classification System and is therefore high risk, because of the limited availability of information. The company's self-declared standard industrial classification changes in conjunction with this new operating activity, from "Petroleum and Petroleum Products Wholesalers" to "Security Brokers, Dealers, and Flotation Companies," while in 2000, *Value Line* still classifies Enron as a "Natural Gas (Diversified) Industry." We can only wonder why analysts would not question this difference in perception—a fourth red flag.

To gain additional insight into these changes, we continue the analysis by looking at each of the company's operating business segments and selected financial disclosures to see whether the aforementioned inconsistencies were addressed or clarified. We also take a closer look at the "realignment of operations" briefly mentioned in the 1997 10-K report.

Operating Business Segment Disclosures

The business segments from the 10-K reports and annual reports for 1996 to 2000 were defined as follows:

Exploration and Production: natural gas and crude oil exploration and production (consistent from 1996, discontinued after August 16, 1999).

Broadband Services: construction and management of a nationwide fiber-optic network, marketing and management of bandwidth, delivery of high-bandwidth content (this classification appears in a separate category for the first time in 2000, moves from number six in 1998, to number four in 1999, and to number two in 2000).

Transportation and Distribution: interstate transmission of natural gas, management and operation of pipelines, electric utility operations.

Wholesale Services: commodity sales and services; risk management products and financial services; development, acquisition, and operation of power plants, natural gas pipelines, and other energy-related assets.

Retail Energy Services: sales of natural gas and electricity and related products directly to end-users, particularly in the commercial and industrial sectors; outsourcing of energy-related activities.

Corporate and Other: includes operation of water businesses (1998 to 2000), renewable energy businesses and clean fuels plants (1996–2000), communications businesses (1998), and overall corporate activities (2000).

In 1996, before the realignment of operations, natural gas featured in all four of the business segments, listed as Transportation and Operation, Domestic Gas and Power Services, International Operations and Development, and Exploration and Production. From 1997 onward, there is a major shift in the focus of the business, from natural gas, crude oil, and electricity distribution toward trading in other industries, such as bandwidth and water. While that may partly explain the change in the standard industrial classification, there is certainly not enough evidence to convince us of the validity of or the need for the change. In fact, forays into these new non-core areas raise additional red flags, due to increased risk in (for Enron) untested waters. Further, these new ventures appear, on the surface, to be generating operating losses (see table 4.1). As a result, our level of discomfort at the change in industrial classification is elevated, rather than abated. Moreover, a cursory analysis of table 4.1 raises the following concerns:

The "realignment of activities" year (1997) indicates operating profitability problems. The "Corporate and Other" business segment generates massive operating profits. Forays into the operation of water, renewable energy, and clean fuel businesses warrant closer scrutiny. This category has a severe negative impact on Enron's overall 1999 profitability. Losses exceeded revenues. *Concern 1*: What is the explanation for this, and are these new ventures high risk?

So-called unaffiliated sales include sales to unconsolidated equity affiliates (see 2000 annual report footnote on page 50). *Concern 2*: Unaffiliated sales to affiliates? This doesn't make sense.

The company ventured into a new industry, far removed from its area of expertise— broadband communication services. Broadband is mentioned as an activity in 1999 but is lumped together in the Wholesale Services business segment. It appears in its own segment in 2000 but generates a 3 percent operating loss. *Concern 3*: Can this be a profitable venture in the long term? Why is Enron moving away from its very successful core businesses into unknown and untested waters?

Wholesale Services, which includes commodity sales and services, generates the bulk of the firm's revenues (between 86% and 93%) and profits (85% in 2000). Revenues leap from $35,501 million in 1999 to $93,278 million in 2000, a 163 percent increase, while operating profits increased from $887 million to $1,668 million, an 88 percent increase. *Concern 4*: Are revenue recognition policies appropriate? This leap in revenue is especially important in light of the "unaffiliated" sales to equity affiliates.

Next, we will search the remainder of the business section of the 10-K reports, in the hope that we may find management explanations for these discrepancies and questions.

Table 4.1
Enron: Operating Business Segments and Selected Financial Information
(millions of U.S. dollars)

Segment Description	Year	Unaffiliated revenues*	Operating income (loss)	Total assets
Transportation and Distribution	1996	702 (5%)	337 (49%)	2,879 (18%)
(regulated industries; interstate	1997	1,402 (7%)	398 (2653%)	7,636 (34%)
transmission of natural gas; management	1998	1,833 (6%)	562 (41%)	7,616 (26%)
and operation of pipelines; electric utility	1999	2,013 (5%)	551 (69%)	7,959 (24%)
operations)	2000	2,742 (3%)	565 (29%)	8,283 (13%)
Wholesale Services (commodity sales	1996	11,413 (86%)	287 (42%)	9,884 (61%)
and services; risk management products	1997	17,344 (86%)	376 (2507%)	10,593 (47%)
and financial services; development,	1998	27,220 (87%)	880 (64%)	14,837 (51%)
acquisition and operation of power	1999	35,501 (89%)	889 (111%)	21,185 (63%)
plants, natural gas pipelines and other	2000	93,278 (93%)	1,668 (85%)	47,934 (73%)
energy-related assets)				
Retail Energy Services (sales of natural	1996	513 (4%)	0	0
gas and electricity and related products	1997	683 (3%)	(105) (-700%)	322 (1%)
directly to end-users, particularly in the	1998	1,072 (3%)	(124) (-9%)	747 (3%)
commercial and industrial sectors;	1999	1,518 (4%)	(81) (- 10%)	956 (3%)
outsourcing of energy-related activities)	2000	3,824 (4%)	58 (3%)	4,370 (7%)
Broadband Services (construction and	1996	N/A	N/A	N/A
management of a nation-wide fiber-optic	1997	N/A	N/A	N/A
network; marketing and management of	1998	N/A	N/A	N/A
bandwidth; delivery of high-bandwidth	1999	N/A	N/A	N/A
content; since 2000)	2000	408 (0%)	(64) (-3%)	1,337 (2%)
Exploration and Production (natural gas	1996	647 (5%)	205 (30%)	2,371 (15%)
and crude oil exploration and production;	1997	789 (4%)	185 (1233%)	2,668 (12%)
until August 16, 1999)	1998	750 (2%)	133 (10%)	3,001 (10%)
	1999	429 (1%)	66 (8%)	0
	2000	N/A	N/A	N/A
Corporate and Other (includes operation	1996	14 (0%)	(139) (-20%)	1,003 (6%)
of water, renewable energy businesses	1997	55 (0%)	(839)(-5593%)	1,333 (6%)
and clean fuels plants, as well as overall	1998	385 (1%)	(73) (-5%)	3,149 (11%)
corporate activities)	1999	651 (2%)	(623) (-78%)	3,281 (10%)
	2000	537 (1%)	(274) (14%)	3,579 (5%)
Totals	1996	13,289	690	16,137
	1997	20,273	15	22,552
	1998	31,260	1,378	29,350
	1999	40,112	802	33,381
	2000	100,789	1,953	65,503

*Unaffiliated sales, includes sales to unconsolidated affiliates.

Further Disclosures from Form 10-K

The 1996 "International" business segment, which contains some high-risk ventures (see disclosure on Dabhol Power in India, where the government attempted to renege on the agreement for a power plant after development had begun). Strangely, this segment disappears in 1997 and international business thereafter is spread across other segments. This raises another red flag. *Concern 5*: Does this change in segment classification effectively hide future segment losses arising from high-risk ventures in developing countries and emerging markets that Enron is now pursuing?

The 1998 Form 10-K states (under the "Other Enron Businesses" subtitle) that the company is pursuing opportunities in the global water business and that it is building a long-haul fiber-optic network in an emerging marketplace, clearly affirming some degree of movement away from its traditional core business activities.

The 1999 and 2000 Form 10-K filings show an increased propensity toward trading in commodities other than natural gas and oil. Enron's wholesale business segment dominates and includes other worldwide dealings in established and newly deregulated and developing markets. Its wholesale operations includes commodity trading via EnronOnline, and Enron is engaged in the creation of networks involving selective asset ownership, contractual access to third-party assets and market-making activities (Preston 2001).

While many of Enron's 10-K form statements can be likened to "strategic mumbling," two things are fairly transparent. First, between 1996 and 2000, Enron transformed itself into something that is difficult to define accurately, thus making an appropriate industry classification problematic. Second, competent financial analysts should have been highly suspicious of these murky self-statements and numerous red flags (see table 4.2). Enron originally developed a very successful business strategy within the natural gas industry and developed the resources and capabilities to support this strategy. Increasingly from 1997 onward, however, it appears to have applied its knowledge and skills to the redefinition of its business environment, and its strategy becomes unclear. By 1998, Enron appears to be principal, agent, and market maker in deals involving a wide range of commodities. This is untested territory, and Enron seems to be the innovative first-mover. But this type of innovation substantially increases investment risk. Additionally, technological advances have allowed markets to mature very rapidly, quickly eroding Enron's advantage, and can result in rapidly declining profit potential from each new market that is created. Analysts need to bear this in mind when reviewing financial statements. In a final attempt to understand Enron's business operations, based on management's self-statements, we look for clarity and direction in the 1998 to 2000 annual reports.

The purpose of a firm's mission statement is to set direction, establish a basis for resource allocation and other strategic decision making, and provide for unanimity of purpose within the organization (David 2001). One should be able to read a company's mission statement and walk away with a fairly clear understanding of the firm's key customers, products/services, key markets, self-concept, and business philosophy, as well as the core resources and competencies it uses to compete in the marketplace (David 2001). Despite their length, Enron's 10-K filings do not provide us with a clear understanding of its business. Consequently, in a final effort to alleviate our concerns, we

Table 4.2
Enron's Red Flags

Red Flags		Nature of Concern	Source
Number One A	Sudden change of Standard Industry Classification (SIC) code in the last quarter of 2000	Classification seems inconsistent with primary business activities.	SEC 10-K 2000 Filing
Number One B	Addition of 5th operating activity "delivery and management of energy commodities and capabilities to end-use retail customers in the industrial and commercial business sectors," which appears to be the only change resulting in new SIC code.	This unobtrusive addition could either be an attempt to minimize this important shift in focus, or else Enron is confused or unsure about the type of business that is core to its operations.	SEC 10-K 2000 Filing and SEC 10-K 1999 Filing
Number Two	The last operating activity mentioned in 1999 and 2000, "development of an intelligent network platform to provide bandwidth management services and the delivery of high bandwidth communication applications," *does not appear separately* in the 1998 disclosure.	There appears to be a shift of focus beginning in 1999, towards the high- risk bandwidth communications systems and services.	SEC 10-K 1998 Filing
Number Three	The inclusion of the statement "the marketing of …and other commodities and related risk management and finance services worldwide." In the description of their business activities	This may imply a move towards high-risk derivatives trading, but it is not very specific.	SEC 10-K 1997 Filing
Number Four	Risks associated with new business ventures	There is a major shift in the focus of the business, from natural gas, crude oil and electricity distribution towards trading in other industries such as bandwidth and water. There is an increased risk in untested (for Enron) waters. Further, these new ventures appear, on the surface, to be generating operating losses.	SEC 10-K 1996 Filing
Number Five	Concealing high risk ventures in other categories	This change in segment classification may effectively hide future segment losses arising from high-risk ventures in developing countries and emerging markets.	SEC 10-K 1996 Filing

turn to the annual reports as a means of understanding Enron's core business and strategic direction.

Annual Report Disclosures on Corporate Mission

Unfortunately, Enron's annual reports further confirm our misgivings. The wording of the annual report disclosures moves from that of a fairly clear view of the industry and its corporate mission in 1998 to a lack of industry-specific focus and a convoluted emphasis on intangibles in 1999 and 2000. For example, in 1998, the very first sentence on the inside of the front cover of the annual report describes a very clear mission, with a clear industry emphasis: "Enron uses its global network of people, assets, products and services to dispatch electricity and natural gas around the world." The first two sentences of the letter to shareholders, signed by Ken Lay (Chairman and CEO) and Jeff Skilling (President and COO), confirm this direction with the following company description: "Global energy franchise. We believe our unparalleled ability to deliver on these three words will propel Enron to become THE 'blue-chip' electricity and natural gas company of the 21st century" (p.3).

The 1999 annual report, however, paints a new picture of a knowledge-based communication business, with no specific mention of the previous core products, mainly natural gas and electricity.

Enron operates networks throughout the world to develop and enhance energy and broadband communication services. Networks, unlike vertically integrated business structures, facilitate the flow of information and expertise. We can spot market signals faster and respond more quickly. Networks empower individuals, freeing them to craft innovative and substantive solutions to customer problems. Networks are the foundation of our knowledge-based businesses. (inside front cover)

In the first two sentences of the letter to shareholders, we find, "Enron is moving so fast that sometimes others have trouble defining us." Based on our analysis so far, we have to agree. The paragraph continues: "We are clearly a knowledge-based company, and the skills and resources we used to transform the energy business are proving to be equally valuable in other businesses. Yes, we will remain the world's leading energy company, but we also will use our skills and talents to gain leadership in fields where the right opportunities beckon" (p. 2).

The remainder of the letter to shareholders raises a number of issues that merit further investigation by analysts. First, it deemphasizes the importance of owning hard assets and places continual emphasis on creative employees as the most important corporate asset. The following quotes are representative of this new direction:

To reap greater growth and value in our traditional energy businesses without a parallel increase in capital spending, we have evolved into a series of global networks. (p.2)

What you own is not as important as what you know. Hard-wired businesses, such as energy and communications, have turned into knowledge-based industries that place a premium on creativity. (p. 2)

It is our intellectual capital—not only our physical assets—that makes us Enron. (p. 2)

[Our] strength comes from knowledge, not just from physical assets. (p. 2)

The fluidity of knowledge and skills throughout Enron increasingly enables us to capture value in the New Economy. (p. 2)

Physical assets play a strategic, but not central, role in the way we earn our money, and this reduced emphasis on merely earning a return on physical assets allows us to divest non-strategic assets. (p. 2)

The report then specifically mentions a sale and exchange of Enron's interest in Enron Oil and Gas Company, which generated "approximately $1 billion in cash" (p. 2), and the pending sale of Portland General Electric to Sierra Pacific Resources, expected to generate around $2 billion in cash (p. 4).

Creativity is a fragile commodity. (p. 5)

Our culture of innovation is difficult to duplicate. Our philosophy is not to stand in the way of our employees, so we don't insist on hierarchical approval. (p. 5)

We recognize that our intellectual capital is our most important asset. (p. 5)

Enron's self-proclaimed decreased focus on hard assets and increased focus on human resource assets leads to the following additional concerns: Did Enron sell important physical assets? If employees are its most important assets, how does it retain this very fluid and intangible asset? Unlike physical assets, intangible assets can evaporate overnight, as evidenced by the recent dotcom meltdown. At the beginning of the 2000 annual report we are told:

Enron manages efficient, flexible networks to reliably deliver physical products at predictable prices. In 2000 Enron used its networks to deliver a record amount of physical natural gas, electricity, bandwidth capacity and other products. With our networks, we can significantly expand our existing businesses while extending our services to new markets with enormous potential for growth.

From the letter to shareholders (pp. 2–5), additional red flags emerge:

Enron is laser-focused on earnings per share.

Enron hardly resembles the company we were in the early days.

We have metamorphosed from an asset-based pipeline and power generating company to a marketing and logistics company whose biggest assets are its well-established business approach and its innovative people.

Our growth rates are rising in areas such as metals, forest products, weather derivatives and coal.

And last but not least,

Our performance and capabilities cannot be compared to a traditional energy peer group.

OUR ACCOUNT OF ENRON'S EXTERNAL ENVIRONMENT AND STRATEGY

In the first part of this analysis we considered Enron's public disclosures and identified a number of red flags. We will now perform a more formal industry and strategy analysis to reaffirm and possibly add to the red flags that we have thus far identified. Enron's disclosures contain a certain amount of mystification. Their numerous inconsistencies and vague statements make analysis difficult at best. We apply the framework suggested in Palepu et al. (2000) to overcome this barrier in an attempt to better understand Enron's strategy and external environment.

Palepu et al. (2000, 2–1 to 2–9) build on the work of Porter (1980) and identify the following competitive forces that influence industry profitability and should be considered by financial analysts when assessing a firm's industry environment:

Intensity of actual and potential competition determines the potential for earning profits by the firms in the industry. Three competitive forces—*rivalry among existing firms, threat of new entrants,* and *threat of substitute products*—influence the intensity of competition.

Bargaining power in input and output markets determines whether the profits can be maintained within the industry. Two other competitive forces—*bargaining power of buyers* and *bargaining power of sellers*—influence this category.

To begin, we should determine an appropriate industry classification for Enron. We are in agreement with *Value Line* and *Moody's* in seeing Enron as a diversified company with primary operations in the natural gas industry; by its own admission, Enron's "most developed business" is still natural gas (2000 annual report, 3).

Industry Profile and Analysis

The Natural Gas Production and Distribution industry (SIC 492) comprises of four key segments: natural gas transmission (4922), gas transmission and distribution (4923), natural gas distribution (4924), and gas production and/or distribution (4925). Firms operating in this industry are characterized as producers (for example, owners of the wells), pipeline companies (those that transport the gas along a network of pipeline to distributors or end-users), distribution companies (local vendors that distribute gas), and gas marketers (firms that sell gas or other energy solutions to end-users). Companies that combine a subset of these operations are known as "integrated companies." Competition among distribution companies is regionalized, and many natural gas organizations are integrated players competing in multiple segments of the industry.

As previously discussed, the five main forces that influence profitability are rivalry among existing firms, the threat of new entrants, the threat of substitute products, bargaining power of buyers, and bargaining power of suppliers. We will review each of these within the natural gas industry to uncover some of the factors influencing the economics and competitive conditions of this industry.

Competitive Force 1: Rivalry among Existing Firms

The greater the competition between firms in an industry, the lower the average profitability is likely to be. Factors influencing firm rivalry within the natural gas industry include growth, economies of scale, concentration and balance of competitors, degree of differentiation, excess capacity, switching costs, and exit barriers. Each of these is considered separately to gain an overall feel for the profitability of the industry.

Growth Rate. The natural gas–transmission segment experienced a peak in growth during the 1990s. This was a welcome growth spurt, as natural gas consumption finally exceeded 1974 consumption levels. Growth in the natural gas market was influenced by the Clean Air Act of 1990, which promoted natural gas as a desirable alternative to gas and coal, and by a number of regulatory changes designed to increase competition and level the playing field (Bellenir 1994). Several regulations have also sparked growth. Specifically, FERC Orders 636 and 636A of 1992 forced gas transmission companies to "unbundle" their services. Pipeline companies were required to their separate their gas services and to price and sell each component (gas sales, gas transportation, or gas storage) individually (Bellenir 1998; McCann 1997). As a consequence, local distribution companies and large industrial customers were able to directly enter purchase agreements with pipeline companies, thereby exercising more choice and influence over prices. A second result of this legislation was that many pipeline companies refocused their attention toward gas transportation services and leasing storage capacity and away from buying and selling gas (Bellenir 1994). This function, the buying and selling of gas, was in turn transferred to gas producers (who acted as brokers) and gas distributors (end-users) (Bellenir 1998). Continued demand for natural gas is influenced by the weather, economic activity, the use of gas for cooling, and to a lesser extent, the commercialization of natural gas vehicles.

Concentration and Balance of Competitors. Natural gas transmission is a concentrated industry. Through its subsidiaries, Enron was the largest buyer and seller of gas in North America, the largest supplier of natural gas to

America's electric generation industry, as well as the operator of the largest transmission system in the Western Hemisphere and the second largest in the world. During the 1990s Enron alone handled approximately 20 percent of America's consumed natural gas (Belliner 1998). Other key competitors in this industry include Dynegy Corporation, Reliant Energy, and Duke Energy.

Degree of Differentiation. Natural gas is a standardized product. There are very few opportunities for differentiation or the premium prices associated with this strategy.

Capacity and Storage. Capacity is an important issue in the natural gas industry. Fluctuating demand can put a tremendous strain on both natural gas producers and end-users. Low demand brings down gas prices and creates a disincentive for firms to produce natural gas. Sudden peaks in demand (based on changes in weather patterns or other types of economic activity) can cause gas shortages and interrupt industrial activity. Although natural gas can be stored for a period of time, many firms respond to these fluctuations in supply by entering into contracts with natural gas producers and pipeline firms that guarantee natural gas delivery.

Switching Costs. Switching costs can be high based on contractual arrangements and pressures to maintain supply.

Consolidation among Industry Players. After deregulation, there was consolidation within the natural gas industry. Many of these mergers were motivated by the firms' desire to achieve economies of scale, cut costs (by reducing duplication), or protect market share (McCann 1997). In addition to consolidation among industry players, a number of mergers took place between natural gas firms and electric utility firms. These newly merged "energy" firms are able to meet all of the customer's energy needs by combining electric and gas power products and services (McCann 1997).

Exit Barriers. The presence of exit barriers such as large capital investment in facilities and transmission equipment and service contracts make it costly to exit this industry.

Competitive Forces 2 and 3:
Threat of New Entrants and Substitutes

The threat of new entrants is mitigated by the presence of economies of scale, first-mover advantages, greater access to distribution channels and existing customers, and legal barriers to entry. While the presence of economies of scale and high capital requirements limit the number of new entrants, they do not eliminate the threat. Deregulation opened a pathway for electricity companies to enter the industry through mergers with natural gas firms. These mergers intensified competition within the industry and enabled electricity firms to bundle energy products and services to suit customer needs. Oil is also a substitute within this industry. Fluctuations in demand and capacity increase the threat of substitution and strengthen the position of these broader energy firms.

Competitive Force 4: Bargaining Power of Buyers

Natural gas firms can have many different customers, depending on where they compete in the industry. Buyers attempt to influence the prices at which an industry's goods are sold. Greater bargaining power for buyers translates into lower profits for the firms competing in the industry. The bargaining power of buyers is dependent on their price sensitivity and their importance to the selling firm. A number of factors can increase the bargaining power of buyers. Historically, pipeline firms were the primary customers for gas producers, and local distribution firms were the key customers for pipeline organizations. Consequently, local distribution companies and large industrial customers were able to directly enter into purchase agreements with pipeline companies, thereby exercising more choice and influence over prices, and disrupting the historical value chain by increasing the bargaining power of buyers. In addition, purchasers typically buy natural gas product in large volume, further increasing the power that buyers wield over prices.

There are also a number of factors that decrease buyer's power. First, regional competition and concentration in the industry limits the number of choices of potential natural gas suppliers. Second, the large capital investments required to produce or transmit natural gas significantly reduce the likelihood of backward vertical integration by local distribution firms and companies that provide pipeline services (and increase buyer dependence). Finally, the switching costs of moving from one energy firm to another can be high, based on contractual relationship, thereby reducing buyer bargaining power.

Competitive Force 5: Bargaining Power of Suppliers

As previously stated, many of the firms in this industry compete in more than one segment of the industry. The presence of integration, particularly backward vertical integration into natural gas exploration and production, reduces the bargaining power of suppliers to those firms. For players not pursuing this type of vertical integration, the supplier's ability to dictate the price of inputs can be much higher, especially for those firms competing in downstream activities when the industry is experiencing capacity shortages. The greater the suppliers' bargaining power, the lower the industry's profitability.

Overall Assessment

Deregulation sparked growth and increased competition in the natural gas industry as natural firms consolidated to gain market scope and power, and as electric firms continued to enter the industry through mergers with natural gas companies, keeping competition among key players fairly strong. Thin profit margins make this industry relatively unattractive and demand that firms not only maintain market share but also pursue aggressive growth strategies to remain profitable. The capital investments needed to either enter or grow within this industry make the nature and timing of investment decisions critical. Continued access to capital is therefore a strategically important variable if firms are to remain competitive in this industry. Empowered buyers seeking cost-effective energy solutions look to electricity firms and other substitute products to consistently meet their energy needs. Firm profitability is contingent upon profitable growth, maintaining current market share, and developing secure revenue streams. Fluctuations in capacity can induce industry participants to develop contractual mechanisms to stabilize profit margins.

In the next section, we analyze Enron's corporate level and competitive strategy, and we identify risk factors associated with their competitive position.

Corporate Level and Competitive Strategy

Corporate-level strategy is guided by a vision of how the firm, as a whole, can create value (Collis and Montgomery 1998) by positioning itself to compete across multiple industries, thereby creating opportunities for cost savings or the transfer of knowledge (Thompson and Strickland 2001). Decisions about which industries to include within the corporate portfolio are not haphazard. Organizations are able to create value and build a corporate level advantage when they effectively apply their resources across a set of related businesses (Collis and Montgomery 1998).

Palepu et al. (2000) identifies five areas that can help analysts to understand a firm's corporate level strategy: significant imperfections in the industries within which the firm competes (and the associated impact on transaction costs); ownership of special or unique resources; the presence of strategic fits among the firm's business units; decision-making authority and the presence of internal management and information and incentive systems to reduce agency costs and increase coordination. We review each of these in depth.

Enron's Overall Strategy

Until very recently, Enron was best described as a "vertically integrated natural gas and electricity company with operations conducted through subsidiaries and affiliates engaged in the international exploration and production of natural gas and crude oil, the transportation of natural gas through pipelines to markets within the US, the generation and transmission of electricity and the marketing of natural gas, electricity and other commodities" (*Moody's Public Utility Manual*, 2000). Enron also pursued a related diversification strategy through its holding in broadband services and other utilities.

Enron's activities were conducted though five key business units: Transportation and Distribution, Wholesales Services, Retail Energy Services, Broadband Services, and Other. Transportation and Distribution comprised the firm's natural gas and electricity transmission services within the United States.

Wholesale Services operated through two lines of business, Commodity Sales, and Service and Assets and Investments. This division uses a network strategy that includes the selective ownership of assets, contractual access to third-party assets, and market-making activities. Retail Energy Services sells natural gas, electricity, liquids, other commodities, and energy management services directly to commercial and industrial customers. Finally, Broadband Services provides bandwidth services though a high-capacity global fiber optic network (*Yahoo Market Guide* 2002).

Table 4.3 highlights the company's profit mix between 1996 and 2000 (*Value Line* 1997, 1998, 1999, 2000, 2001). Before 1997, the majority of Enron's

Table 4.3
Enron's Profit Mix

Year	Divisional Contributions
2000 Profit Mix	Wholesale Services 91% Transportation and Distribution (formerly Gas Pipeline Group) 29% Retail Energy Services 7% Broadband services -2% Corporate and Other -25%
1999 Profit Mix	Exploration and Production 3% Gas Pipeline Group 34% Wholesale Energy Operations 66% Retail Energy Services -3%
1998 Profit Mix	Exploration and Production 7% Gas Pipeline Group 20% Portland General (acquired 7/1/97) 17% Wholesale Energy Services 56%
1997 Profit Mix	Exploration and Production 14% Gas Pipeline Group 27% Portland General 9% Wholesale Energy Services 50%
1996 Profit Mix	Enron Operations (construct, manage pipelines, operate power plants) 47% Energy Capital and Trade (purchase, market, finance gas and liquids, manage intrastate pipelines, domestic power plants) 23% Enron International (develop, acquire overseas gas power and liquids plants, pipelines), 13% Exploration and Production, 17%

profits stemmed from its asset-intensive Operations division. Between 1997 and 1999, Wholesale Energy Services made the largest contributions to profit. As the primary cash generator, this business played a pivotal role in financial new projects and other business endeavors (McLean 2001).

Profit mix for the year 2000 raises a red flag, as the firm experienced significant losses in its "Broadband" and "Other" categories. This, coupled with the vague disclosures in its 2000 10-K filing, should have caused analysts to questions Enron's strategic direction. Since relatedness is a key underpinning of corporate-level advantage (Collis and Montgomery 1998), movement into these new areas should cause concern. Attempts to appropriate the intellect of Enron's human resources, its self-described "most important asset" (*Enron Annual Report* 1999), for achieving an advantage would demand that these managers have knowledge or skills that can be readily applied to the new industries, as opposed to intellect in and of itself. This lack of true managerial fit should raise questions about these individuals' ability to succeed in these new areas. Nevertheless, Enron's corporate holding facilitated the creation of value and the perpetuation of its business model based on the following dimensions:

Industry Imperfections. Deregulation in the natural gas industry provided an "opportunistic" advantage for Enron. Without proper controls, Enron was able to act as both a buyer and a seller of natural energy commodities gas. This created a significant imperfection in the financial markets because Enron (the market maker and largest player) had complete information while those entering into contracts with them had only partial information (Schonfeld 2001). According to a recent article questioning Enron's stock price, "Enron uses derivatives (like swaps, options and forwards) to create contracts for third parties and hedge its exposure to credit risks and other variables" (McLean 2001). The danger of this type of imperfection is highlighted by the following quotes from the popular press:

Enron acted as both seller and buyer, providing a liquid market for commodities by guaranteeing every trade. (Schonfeld 2001)

Normal brokers arrange contracts between buyer and sellers for a particular good. Enron entered into separate contracts with both the buyers and the sellers, making a profit on the difference between the quotes. Enron also used more complex contracts— derivatives aimed at hedging risks arising from uncertainty in interest rates, currency fluctuations, uncertainty about the weather or a customer's ability to settle a contract. (Sridhar 2002)

Buyers and sellers were prevented from having info on the quotes in the market, which gave Enron, the market maker, access to privileged information at the costs of the other participants in the energy-trading contracts. (Sridhar 2002)

This gap in regulation created a significant risk factor for Enron because it allowed the firm to enter into high-risk behaviors without proper checks and balances.

Ownership of Unique Assets. In the natural gas business, perhaps the greatest asset a firm can possess is the integrity and reliability associated with its name. Enron pursued a differentiation strategy based on trust and reliability associated with its name. This brand equity is based on the firm's ability to deliver the product and can significantly impact the firm's ability to access capital. The Enron name became the "brand" that signaled "creditworthiness and ability to execute trades." "Enron then used its expertise, networked relationships and reputation to make guarantees" (Preston 2001). In other words, the equity associated with the Enron name provided access to capital and continuity in credit rating. The decision to leverage this equity was critical to Enron's strategy. Without access to capital, Enron would not have been able to finance its growth and international expansion. Indeed, Enron CFO Andrew Fasto is quoted in 1999 as saying, "My credit rating is strategically critical" (Fink 1999). This great need for capital was another risk factor, as it placed the company under tremendous pressure to obtain capital. The decision to raise this capital with an ever-increasing amount of debt eventually caused a deterioration of the company's creditworthiness, which in turn negatively impacted operations that required a high level of creditworthiness. The negative impact on operating profits caused a further deterioration in creditworthiness, in a rapid and vicious circle that led to bankruptcy.

Presence of Strategic Fits and Internal Coordination (through Information Systems). Enron's corporate level strategies were facilitated through the use of extensive domestic and international partnerships. Enron was able to leverage supply chain, distribution, managerial, and administrative support strategic fits between itself and its network of partnerships. Strategic fits exist when the value chains of different businesses can be combined or leveraged to provide the firm with opportunities for transferring competitively valuable expertise or technological know-how; combining the related activities of separate businesses into a single operation to reduce costs; and exploiting common use of a well-known brand name or cross-business collaboration to create resource strengths and capabilities (Porter 1980; Thompson and Strickland 2001). Partnerships were used to enter new markets and acquire additional debt (Sridhar 2002). The company backed these debts by issuing its own stock or promising to issue its own stock in value terms rather than in terms of numbers of shares. These partnerships (more than three thousand partnerships; eight hundred were in tax havens) played a key role in Enron's strategy, because debts had to be kept off the balance sheet to preserve the firm's credit rating and access to capital (Sridhar 2002).

The spider web of organizational structure resulting from these partnerships was another risk factor for Enron, as there was little or no clear justification for these arrangements and no rational explanation of their role in the firm's overall strategy. Enron was able to create a technological strategic fit between its separate business units through the development and use of Enron Online (a virtual trading company). It traded contracts for electricity and natural gas, high-speed telecommunications networks, and financial hedges against changes in the weather (Altman 2002). Atlman further describes Enron as using "a sophisticated on-line platform backed by a financial apparatus meant to hedge the company's bets." A recent article in the BBC News describes EnronOnline as

an internet-based global transaction system which allowed Enron's customers to view real-time prices from Enron's traders and transact instantly online. . . . No commission and no subscription fee. . . . 2100 different products were offered to traders across four continents and in 15 different countries. . . . One catch, Enron made itself the trading partner in every deal. . . . Enron Online worked by matching itself with every potential buyer and seller rather than commanding the means of production and distribution. (Hale 2002)

This would not have been possible without linking the different aspects of its business through information technology. Enron was also able to achieve strategic market fits, and as a result, customize products and services to match consumer needs. The following typifies this ability:

[Enron Gas Services] could engineer virtually any type of financial contract its users demanded, and it often bundled physical and financial contracts together for ease in marketing. The . . . family of products represented an attempt to create a handful of brand name, standardized products that would be simple to understand and communicate to users (and their regulators). These products offered users a menu of choices by which they could modify their exposure to quantity or price risk.[2]

As a vertically integrated firm, Enron significantly strengthened its competitive position in the industry by reducing the uncertainty associated with capacity fluctuations, by leveraging its brand equity to different stages of the industry's value chain, and by generating tremendous costs savings through its use of Enron Online and economies of scale.

Key Elements of Enron's Strategy and Key Risks

Enron was able to sustain its operations and build a faux advantage by leveraging several key elements of its corporate and competitive strategies. Vertical integration allowed Enron to control more than one stage of the industry's transactions. This, coupled with the industry's information imperfection, enabled it to gain a strong position, as the firm had access to strategically important information that others participating in transactions with it did not. Enron's size and scope permitted a low cost structure, and the brand equity associated with the Enron name created an atmosphere of trust. This trust was buoyed by the perpetual climb in its stock price and the ability that implied to fulfill contractual arrangements, thereby permitting continued access to new capital. Lower costs and increased control over transactions were also facilitated by the use of the EnronOnline trading technology. In sum, Enron was able to capitalize on unregulated gaps existing in the marketplace.

This strategy, even during its peak, was not without risks. Enron's choice of strategy and accompanying SEC disclosures highlights several financial risks for the firm and its investors. First, the lack of regulation in the industry allowed Enron to take advantage of a "knowledge gap" between gas buyers and gas sellers, but that very lack of regulation created the potential for volatility and high risk. Second, Enron made the strategic decision to move away from its highly successful core businesses into higher-risk dealer activities, as evidenced by contradictions with regard to the firm's industry classification and its formal change of Standard Industrial Classification code during the last quarter of 2000. Supporting this assertion is the mystical language used in the 1999 and 2000 annual reports to describe the firm's mission and the nature of its operations. Third, the pressure to secure future capital and maintain investor confidence led management to implement a self-declared intense focus on earnings per share, especially from 1999 onward. Finally, the performance of the firm's international high-risk, asset-heavy ventures and complex partnership structure sharply contradicted its asset-light philosophy and put strain on its capital budgeting and capital management systems. The inconsistencies between the need to maintain creditworthiness for operating purposes and the strategy of increasing financial or operating leverage and risk eventually led to the company's downfall, as Fusaro and Miller (2002) previously indicated.[3]

NOTES

1. In 1999, this publication won the prestigious American Accounting Association "Notable Contributions to Accounting Literature Award."

2. S. Bhatnagar and P. Tufano, *Enron Gas Services (Case #9-294-076)*, Boston: Harvard Business School Publishers, September 26, 1995.

3. The company's evaluation/incentive system that promoted extreme greed and fear (through heavy rewards for short-term performance and termination of the bottom 15%) certainly contributed to the excessive risk taking, which was detrimental to the firm and for which controls were inadequate (Cruver 2002).

REFERENCES

Altman, D. 2002. "Could Enron's Business Model Actually Work?" *New York Times* (January 28).

Babineck, M. 2002. "Analyst Fired for Urging 'Sell' Enron as Firm Touted Enron." *Associated Press State & Local Wire* (March 5).

Bellenir, K. 1998. "Natural Gas Distribution." In *Encyclopedia of American Industries*. 2d ed. Ed. S. Peck and T. W. Peck. Detroit: Gale Research.

———. 1994. "Natural Gas Distribution." In *Encyclopedia of American Industries*. Ed. K. Hillstrom and M. Ruby. Detroit: Gale Research.

Bhatnagar, S., and P. Tufano. 1995. "Enron Gas Services (Case #9-294-076)." Harvard
    Business School Publishers (September 26).
Collis, D., and C. Montgomery. 1998. "Creating Corporate Advantage." *Harvard Busi-
    ness Review*, 71–83.
Cruver, B. 2002. *Anatomy of Greed*. New York: Carroll and Graf.
David, F. 2001. *Strategic Management*. Upper Saddle River, N.J.: Prentice Hall.
Eisenman, T. R. 2002. "The Effects of CEO Equity Ownership and Firm Diversifica-
    tion on Risk Taking." *Strategic Management Journal* 23, No. 6: 513–534.
Enron Corporation Annual Report 2000. Houston: Enron Corporation.
Enron Corporation Annual Report 1999. Houston: Enron Corporation.
Enron Corporation Annual Report 1998. Houston: Enron Corporation.
Enron Corporation Annual Report 1997. Houston: Enron Corporation.
Enron Corporation Annual Report 1996. Houston: Enron Corporation.
Enron SEC 10-K Filings 2000 http://sec.gov.
Enron SEC 10-K Filings 1999 http://sec.gov.
Enron SEC 10-K Filings 1998 http://sec.gov.
Enron SEC 10-K Filings 1997 http://sec.gov.
Enron SEC 10-K Filings 1996 http://sec.gov.
Fink, R. 1999. "Balancing Act", *CFO Magazine* (June 1).
Fusario, D., and R. Miller. 2002. *What Went Wrong at Enron*. Hoboken, N.J.: John
    Wiley and Sons.
Hale, B. 2002. "Enron's Internet Monster." BBC News Online, http://news.bbc.co.uk/.
    (April 17).
Kaplan, R., and D. Norton. 2000. "Having Trouble with Your Strategy?" *Harvard
    Business Review* (September–October).
Lee, B. 2002. "Bill Would Close Trading Loophole Used by Enron." *Wall Street Jour-
    nal* (February 14), A8.
Lozano, J. A. 2002. "Analyst Says Fired for Urging Clients to Sell Enron Stock."
    Associated Press State & Local Wire (March 4).
Magretta, J. 2002. "Why Business Models Matter." *Harvard Business Review* (May).
McCann, J. C. 2001. "Industry Swept by Surging Gas Prices." *Standard and Poor's
    Industry Survey: Natural Gas Distribution Industry Survey* (January 25), 1–29.
McCann, J. C. 1997. "Convergence of Natual Gas and Electric Power Markets." *Stan-
    dard and Poor's Industry Survey: Natural Gas Distribution Industry Survey*
    (November 20), 1–25.
McLean, B. 2001. "Is Enron Overpriced?" *Fortune Magazine* (March 5).
Mergent Public Utility Manual. 2001. New York: Mergent, Inc. (pp. 1738–1755).
Moody's Public Utility Manual. 2000. New York: Moody's Investor's Service (pp.
    1763–1779).
————. 1998. New York: Moody's Investor's Service (pp. 2594–2063).
————. 1997. New York: Moody's Investor's Service (pp. 2665-2672).
Morgan, D. 2001. "Traders, Old Utilities Tangle over Wires." *Washington Post* (Au-
    gust 23), A1.
Palepu, K. G., P. M. Healy, and V. L. Bernard. 2000. *Business Analysis and Valuation
    Using Financial Statements*. 2d ed. Cincinnati: South-Western.
Porter, M. 1980. *Competitive Strategy*. New York: Free Press.
————. 1996. "What is Strategy?" *Harvard Business Review* 74, No. 6: 61–79.

Preston, R. 2001. "The Internet Didn't Kill Enron." *Internetweek.com*, http://www.internetweek.com (November 30).

Romaine, S. 2001. *Value Line Investment Survey Edition 3: Enron Corp.* New York: Value Line Publishing (September 21), 404–546.

Schonfeld, E. 2001. "Enron Is Dead. Long Live Enron." *Business 2.0*, http://www.business2.com (December 7).

Sridhar, V. 2002. "A Business Model of the Times." *Frontline* 19, No. 5 http://flonnet.com (March 15).

Smith, R. 2002. "The Analyst Who Warned about Enron." *Wall Street Journal* (January 29), C1, C17.

Schroeder, M., and G. Ip. 2001. "Out of Reach: The Debacle Spotlights Huge Void in Financial Regulation." *Wall Street Journal* (December 13), A1, A6.

Schwartzmann, T. 2000. *Value Line Investment Survey Edition 3: Enron Corp.* New York: Value Line Publishing (December 22), 408–542.

Swort, E. 1999a. *Value Line Investment Survey Edition 3: Enron Corp.* New York: Value Line Publishing (March 26).

———. 1999b. *Value Line Investment Survey Edition 3: Enron Corp.* New York: Value Line Publishing (June 25).

———. 1998. *Value Line Investment Survey Edition 3: Enron Corp.* New York: Value Line Publishing (December 25).

———. 1997. *Value Line Investment Survey Edition 3: Enron Corp.* New York: Value Line Publishing (December 26).

Thompson, A., and A. Strickland. 2001. *A Strategic Management.* Boston: McGraw-Hill Irwin.

U.S. Census Bureau. 2002. *North American Industry Classification System (NAICS).* http://www.census.gov/epcd/naics (May 18).

Yahoo Market Guide (Enron Business Description). 2002. http://www.yahoomarket guide.com/ (May 3).

5

Financial Analysts and Enron: Asleep at the Wheel?

Arline Savage and Cynthia Miree

EXECUTIVE SUMMARY

We attempt to replicate the duties of financial analysts by performing accounting and financial analyses for Enron, using information contained in the firm's Security and Exchange Commission filings and in annual and quarterly reports that were available to analysts prior to the firm's collapse. We focus on Enron accounting policies, estimates, and financial measures that reflect the key risk areas that we identified in our strategy analysis.

Given that the purpose of accounting analysis is to evaluate the degree to which a firm's accounting system captures its underlying economic reality, we attempt to assess the degree of distortion in Enron's reported numbers, based on our comfort level with management's choice of accounting policies and estimates. The purpose of our financial analysis is to assess the performance of the firm after its efforts to negate the effects of perceived distortions in the reported numbers. We ask, and attempt to answer, the question of whether financial analysts should have seen warning signs of Enron's collapse and should have warned investors of the firm's precarious financial situation long before the unfortunate event surprised stockholders and creditors alike.

Our detailed analyses show that from 1997 onward there was evidence of reporting and performance problems. We highlight areas of major concern about profitability and debt levels.

Although Enron management makes an abundance of information available to analysts, the language is not always clear; it is confusing even to accounting experts. The vast amount of information makes the analyst's job time consuming and tedious, yet essential information, such as separate disclosures of unrealized gains on trading activities, is not available. This does not, however, excuse analysts who overwhelmingly would not see the woods for the trees, and who continued recommending to clients that they buy or hold Enron stock.

Our investigation shows that the red flags were plentiful and that the situation was aggravated by the incidents of apparent disdain (reported in the news media) with which Enron's top management dealt with financial analysts. The results of our accounting and financial analyses raise issues about the competence, independence, and objectivity of analysts who continued to recommend this stock.

INTRODUCTION

The strategy analysis in the previous chapter allows us to focus on Enron's related key risk areas for accounting analysis purposes. The first was *the financial success of its dealer and trading activities*. This risk factor stems from Enron's move away from its successful low-risk core energy businesses into high-risk dealer and trading activities, including broadband and derivatives (the specifics of which cannot clearly be identified from strategy disclosures in public filings). The move put the firm at increased risk into new and ill-defined business operations. According to a group of analysts who questioned Enron's precollapse performance,

The sustainability of Enron's business model is based on its ability to create and exploit markets, whether they be in energy, bandwidth, freighter capacity, data storage or toilet paper. Its profit potential declines as a function of the rate at which the markets mature. . . . markets mature very quickly these days thanks to the increased sophistication and variety of risk management products and services and speed of information flows that enhance trading liquidity. (Wasden, Ayers, and Arias 2001, 6–7)

These analysts (whose opinion differed markedly from most of their peers) succinctly concluded that Enron's earnings could suffer from the very market efficiency that the firm had helped to unleash.

The second risk area concerned *the maintenance of investor confidence and access to financing resources*. This risk area became especially important from 1999 onward. Management's self-declared intense focus on earnings per share led to quality of earnings and income management concerns. In addition, management's emphasis on the continued access to financing resources provided strong motivation to manage ratios stipulated in debt covenants.

A third risk area is *the financial success of international high-risk, hard-asset ventures and complex partnership and equity ownership structures*. Investments in these ventures and entities contradicted management's apparent new asset-light philosophy. Examples included investments in the litigation-racked Dabhol power plant project in India and water plants in England. Enron also had complex ownership arrangements with many other companies and partnerships. These investments and ownership arrangements may have put a strain on the firm's capital budgeting and capital management systems.

We now use the conclusions reached in our strategy analysis to investigate Enron's accounting and financial information, in order to evaluate its financial performance and determine whether the firm's accounting and financial policies made sense. We believe that most financial analysts should have seen red flags and warned investors of the company's shaky financial situation. In this regard, we highlight actionable danger signals apparent in the financial statements and mandated Securities and Exchange Commission filings, signals that analysts should have recognized, identified, and warned stakeholders about.

ACCOUNTING ANALYSIS

Overview of Accounting Analysis

The purpose of accounting analysis is to evaluate the degree to which a firm's accounting system captures its underlying economic reality, given inherent management biases and the substantial accounting flexibility that management is empowered with (Palepu et al. 2000, 3-1). For this purpose we use Enron's precollapse publicly available and externally audited income statements, balance sheets, statements of cash flows, notes to the financial statements, management discussion and analysis (MD&A) reports, and independent auditor reports. We supplement this with other information that was readily available to analysts.

For each financial statement account category—assets, liabilities, shareholders' equity, revenues, and expenses—we use our knowledge of the firm's profit drivers and risk factors to identify key areas of accounting flexibility, bearing in mind that there are strong relations between the various categories (for example, revenue recognition policies directly impact assets). We evaluate the appropriateness of the accounting policies and estimates chosen by management, and we attempt to assess the degree of distortion in reported numbers. Where possible, we attempt to negate the effect of perceived distortions in reported numbers by using cash flow numbers, disclosures made in the notes to the financial statements, and qualified opinions given by the external auditors. This provides us a springboard from which to launch into financial analysis, using our own adjusted numbers (if deemed necessary) to improve the reliability of our financial analysis calculations (see Palepu et al. 2000, 3-1).

Another important part of accounting analysis is to demarcate the boundaries of the business by looking beyond the legal definitions that normally control financial reporting. As analysts, we should be far more concerned with economic substance than with legal form. We want to know what resources the firm controls, a much broader focus than the narrowly defined legal form of an entity. Generally, we would search for hidden commitments or losses from investments in other entities, the transfer of resources to other entities that the firm can somehow control (e.g., related entities owned or managed personally by Enron management), and possible investment in management pet projects that have high risk and a low return (see Palepu et al. 2000, 8-1). Therefore, we also perform entity accounting analysis.

When performing the accounting analysis, we take the following six steps, consistent with the Palepu et al. framework (2000, 3-7 to 3-13):

Step 1: Check the audit report. Is it "clean"? Identify and evaluate the key accounting policies that Enron uses to measure critical success factors and risk areas.

Step 2: Assess the flexibility that management has in choosing accounting policies and estimates, and try to discern management's most likely motivation (e.g., to improve earnings per share and debt covenant ratios).

Step 3: Evaluate accounting strategy. For example, was the strategy used to communicate business reality or to hide performance? Does management have strong motivation to manage earnings? Regarding earnings management, does the firm have debt covenants? Has management changed estimates and policies? Is there any evidence to suggest that Enron structures business transactions specifically to achieve certain accounting numbers?

Step 4: Evaluate the depth and quality of the disclosures. For example, do the notes to the financial statements adequately explain key accounting policies and assumptions? Does management adequately explain financial performance? What is the quality of segment disclosures? Does management aggregate many different businesses in a single segment? Does management disclose bad news in addition to good news? Does management adequately address performance problems? How good is Enron's investor relations program? How does management deal with analysts?

Step 5: Identify red flags that indicate potential accounting-quality problems and use these as starting points for further investigation. For example, are there unexplained changes in accounting? Are there unexplained or complex transactions? Is there an increasing gap between net income from operations and cash flow from operations? Is there an increasing gap between net income and taxable income? Is there evidence of unusual financing? Are there large and unexpected asset write-offs? Are there related-party transactions or transactions between related entities that may lack objectivity in the marketplace—especially in view of Enron's position of power due to vertical integration, which allowed it to control more than one stage of the industry's transactions, including that of market maker? Is there evidence that Enron exerts control over other entities that are not legally part of the group?

Step 6: Unravel possible accounting distortions by restating reported numbers. This is not always possible, because of lack of information. The notes to the financial statements and the cash flow statement may supply information useful for this purpose. By making these restatements as analysts, we do not accuse the firm of misstatement, but *we restate components of the financial statements based on our external perceptions of the underlying business reality of the firm*. In the event of an error in judgment, we would prefer to err on the side of caution.

Asset Analysis

Enron's audit reports from Arthur Andersen are clean. In both the 1999 and 2000 reports, however, Arthur Andersen specifically informs shareholders and the Board of Directors of the following (using identical wording for both years): "As discussed in Note 18 to the consolidated financial statements, Enron Corp. and subsidiaries changed . . . its method of accounting for certain contracts in energy trading and risk management activities in the first quarter of 1999" (1999 annual report, 40; 2000 annual report, 30). We will deal with the effects of this very significant accounting change—accounting for contracts (derivatives) in energy trading—under asset analysis.

Significant challenges face the financial analyst with regard to reported assets. Management often has considerable discretion over whether expenditures are capitalized or expensed. Decisions in this area can significantly affect profits and earnings per share, a ratio that stock market participants (including the financial news media) and Enron management (by its own admission) were particularly fixated on. We have already identified this self-declared fixation as a key risk area for Enron.

Instead of launching into an unstructured examination of Enron's financial statements, we will (to use the same term that Enron used with regard to earnings per share) "laser-focus" on the risk areas that we identified during strategy analysis and apply the six accounting analysis steps to each risk area.

The Financial Success of Dealer and Trading Activities

A major area of concern is the firm's move away from its successful core businesses into higher-risk dealer and trading activities, although this was not immediately evident to us from strategy disclosures in the firm's public filings but took some "digging" to discern. Accounting analysis may provide additional insight and either alleviate or strengthen our concerns. A related reported asset is called "assets from price risk management activities," and it was immediately apparent that a decided increase occurred in 2000, in both absolute and relative terms. The amount of this asset, with the percentage of total assets in parentheses, for each of the past five years was 1996, $2,473 million (15%); 1997, $2,384 million (11%); 1998, $3,845 million (13%); 1999, $5,134 million (15%); and 2000, $21,006 million (32%). This dramatic increase coincided with the introduction of Enron Online, which Web-enabled Enron's trading activities. A scrutiny of the quarterly Form 10-Q filings for 2000 reveals that at the end of the first quarter the amount was $6,567 million (18%), in the second quarter $10,924 million (24%), and in the third quarter $14,661 million (28%), a continual increase throughout the year.

Management explains Enron's accounting policy for this asset in footnote 1, "Summary of Significant Accounting Policies," of the 2000 annual report as follows (emphasis added by authors):

Accounting for Price Risk Management. *Enron engages in price risk management activities for both trading and non-trading purposes.* Instruments utilized in connection with trading activities are accounted for *using the mark-to-market method.* Under the mark-to-market method of accounting, forwards, swaps, options, energy transportation contracts utilized for trading activities and other instruments with third parties *are reflected at fair value and are shown as "Assets and Liabilities from Price Risk Management Activities" in the Consolidated Balance Sheet.* These activities *also include the commodity risk management component embedded in energy outsourcing contracts. Unrealized* gains and losses from newly originated contracts, contract restructurings and the impact of price movements are recognized as *"Other Revenues."* ... The market prices used to value these transactions *reflect management's best estimate* considering various factors including closing exchange and over-the-counter quotations, time value and volatility factors underlying the commitments. (p. 36)

The question that comes to mind is: What percentage of net income is attributable to these *unrealized* gains that are included in earned revenue? As the footnote mentions, revenues from price risk management activities are not shown separately on the income statement but are unobtrusively lumped in with "Other Revenue." Nevertheless, we attempt to quantify the revenue impact of these financial instrument trading activities by appealing to the statement of cash flows and the reconciliation between accrual-based net income (which is increased by these activities) and cash generated by operating activities (which excludes revenue from these activities because the revenue is unrealized and has not been collected). After taking into consideration Enron's disclosure of significant accounting policies—"Enron engages in price risk management activities for both trading and non-trading purposes,"—we decided on a wish list of what we would like to see in the statement of cash flows.

First, under "Cash Flows from Operating Activities," we would like to see the following line items for net price risk management assets: unrealized gains (losses) on trading price risk management assets and unrealized gains on non-trading price-risk-management assets.

Second, under "Cash Flows from Investing Activities," we would like to see the aggregate amount of expenditures on the portion of net price-risk-management assets reported as noncurrent (and hence nontrading net assets, in our view as outsiders without proprietary information or management disclosure to the contrary), as well as proceeds from the sale of such noncurrent net assets.

We are disappointed on both counts. An analysis and attempt at recalculation of the single line item of disclosure on "net assets from price risk management activities" under "Cash Flows from Operating Activities" reveals that current and noncurrent net assets have been lumped together; only the net asset increase has been disclosed (note that there is a $17 million unexplained discrepancy in 2000). Details of our calculations appear in table 5.1.

Table 5.1
Enron's Net Assets from Price-Risk-Management Activities (In Millions of U.S. Dollars)

	2000	1999	1998	1997
Current Assets	12,018	2,205	1,904	1,346
Current Liabilities	10,495	1,836	2,511	1,245
Net Current Assets	1,523	369	(607)	101
Non-Current Assets	8,988	2,929	1,941	1,038
Non-Current Liabilities	9,423	2,990	1,421	876
Net Non-Current Assets	(435)	(61)	520	162
Calculated Net Assets (Combined)	1,088	308	(87)	263
Calculated Net Change (Combined)	780	395	(350)	-
Net Change (Combined) per Cash Flow Statement*	763	395	(350)	(201)
Unexplained Difference	(17)	0	0	0

*Entire amount classified as resulting from "operating" activities as opposed to the long-term portion being classified as resulting from investing activities.

The effects of Enron's highly aggregated disclosure are first, that unrealized gains or losses in net income cannot be ascertained; and second, cash flow effects of *nontrading* risk-management activities have been excluded from "Cash Flows from Investing Activities" and diverted to the operating activities section of the cash flow statement. Enron does have nontrading activities in this regard, as evidenced by its disclosure that "Enron engages in price risk management activities for both trading and non-trading purposes." If we accept that the noncurrent net assets should be excluded from the operating section, the impact on operating cash flow would be positive, at $708 million instead of $350 million, for 1998; negative, at $976 million instead of $395 million for 1999; and negative at $1,154 million instead of $763 million, for 2000. Cash flows relating to investing activities would be affected by the same amounts but in the opposite direction.

The reported effects of the change in net assets from risk-management activities on operating cash flow from 1996 to 2000 are as follows (percentage impact on net income before tax is shown in parentheses): 1996, $15 million negative (*minus* 3%); 1997, $201 million negative (*minus* 191%); 1998, $350 million negative (*minus* 50%); 1999, $395 million positive (44%); and 2000, $763 million positive (78%). Scrutiny of the quarterly Form 10-Q filings for 2000 reveals that at the end of the third quarter the negative impact on cash flow amounted to $952 million, exceeding the net income amount of $919 million. This switch from a negative cash-flow impact situation (1996 to 1998) to a positive situation (1999 and 2000) may be related to the adoption at the beginning of 1999 of the Emerging Issues Task Force Issue No. 98-10, "Accounting for Contracts Involved in Energy Trading and Risk Management Activities," which requires energy trading contracts (including energy transportation contracts) to be recorded at fair value on the balance sheet (mark to market). This standard gave the rubber stamp to management to use its considerable discretion as buyer, seller, and market maker in determining the value of its price-risk-management assets and liabilities. The cumulative financial effect of this accounting change on net income was not separately quantified but was aggregated in the amount of $131 million, together with an amount relating to another accounting change made at the beginning of 1999. Taken at face value, the effect of the change does not appear to be material. The Accounting Pronouncements footnote states, "The first quarter 1999 charge was primarily related to the adoption of SOP 98-5," which requires the expensing of all startup and organization costs. However, once the new Emerging Issues standard on energy trading contracts was issued, the management of Enron was effectively given carte blanche on related net-asset valuations.

As discussed in the strategy analysis, Enron changed its SIC code during the last quarter of 2000, probably because of its focus on energy trading activities. This knowledge, coupled with our concerns about unrealized gains on risk-management nets assets, leads us directly into the second risk factor—management's self-declared sharp focus on earnings per share. Our concerns are heightened because management, by its own admission in the quoted accounting policy statement, largely determines the market value of these financial instruments, including energy transportation contracts, in an unregulated market. Coincidently, in late 2000 Congress passed legislation that exempted over-the-counter derivatives from regulation after some very aggressive lobbying by Enron (see Schroeder and Ip 2001; Schroeder 2002). This market was new and largely initiated by Enron, often without externally quoted prices upon which to base asset valuations. Enron, in its capacity as the market maker, was free to effectively manage its earnings. A major concern that comes to mind is whether management is using these unrealized gains to make up for possible poor performance in other high-risk ventures, such as the asset-intensive Dabhol power plant in India, water systems, and broadband.

Even if a firm chooses to blindly follow an accounting standard, without considering the underlying business reality, the resultant financial information can be misleading. The question is this: Does the selection of the policy or estimate result in the closest portrayal of business reality, fairly presenting the underlying economic conditions? If the analyst believes that business reality is not reflected, she or he should attempt to undo distortions caused by the selection of a particular accounting policy or estimate, regardless of its institutionalized general acceptance. This notion is not new (see Palepu et al. 2000), but it gained prominence with the spate of recent accounting failures. In an unprecedented and surprising move, a post-Enron SEC has taken this notion a step farther. In a warning by the chief accountant for the SEC's enforcement division (Liesman 2002), management and the auditors have been informed in no uncertain terms that it is possible to violate SEC laws while being in compliance with generally accepted accounting principles. Therefore, mere compliance with the rules without considering whether the results "fairly present" financial performance could lead to legal proceedings for securities fraud. It is in this light that we discuss briefly the FASB standards for derivatives, by which Enron justified its mark-to-market valuation approach.

Derivatives are initiated via legal contracts, without any immediate significant expenditure. These contracts represent legal rights and obligations, from which assets and liabilities arise. Enron to some degree highlighted this problem when during the first half of the 1990s it took the lead and incorporated mark-to-market accounting for energy-related derivative contracts and thereafter used it on an unprecedented scale. Under mark-to-market rules, assets and liabilities resulting from the legal rights and obligations of the contracts are recorded at fair market value. The determination of a fair value at which to record these rights and obligations as assets and liabilities is a major problem in accounting for markets that are largely unregulated and not well established, with no quoted prices. Enron began trading in a variety of these markets as a first-mover (for example, trading in energy-related derivatives, bandwidth, data storage, paper, and weather derivatives) and essentially caught accounting standard setters off guard. Firms like Enron were free to develop and use discretionary valuation models to value their assets and liabilities, allowing considerable management discretion. The resultant unrealized gains or losses were used to determine net income. Existing financial instruments standards had not been prepared with unregulated markets (such as those that Enron created) in mind. The latitude that Enron had, by which it acted as buyer, seller, and market maker, exacerbated this situation, regardless of whether or not it followed FASB standards. Consequently, we do not feel at all comfortable with the quality of these earnings.

From a financial analysis perspective, because of Enron's multiple roles (buyer, seller, market maker) and resultant quality of earnings concerns, we argue for the reversal of unrealized gains until such time as realization warrants recognition as revenue. In the event of a net unrealized loss, we support a transfer to the income statement, invoking the conservatism concept in accounting as justification for the disparate treatment. As we cannot determine the amount of the unrealized gains because of insufficient disclosure in the cash flow statements, we will use the cash flow numbers as reported by Enron (although we strongly suspect that these are also flawed, because noncurrent price risk net assets are treated as current and operating). However, we will adjust net income to the best of our ability to negate the effect of increases resulting from these activities. The cash flow does provide an alternative benchmark for reporting (Palepu et al. 2000, 3-13). This is the route we will take for

Enron in undoing distortions before performing our financial analysis. As a result, net income will change materially for 1999 and 2000, with a resultant decrease in earnings per share, and net assets from price risk management activities will be reduced. We acknowledge that our adjustment has limitations, in that the full amount of the increase in net assets (included in our adjustment because these amounts have not been disclosed separately on the cash flow statements) does not have an effect on net income. The effect is limited to unrealized gains, which cannot be determined because of lack of information in Enron's disclosures.

We will now proceed with an examination of the company's ventures into broadband. We analyze the MD&A and the Broadband Services business segment, which makes its debut in the 2000 annual report, although Enron had dabbled in broadband since 1998 at the very latest but had been incorporating it in other business segment disclosures. The MD&A disclosure includes the following statement: "Broadband Services is constructing . . . a nationwide fiber-optic network that consists of both fiber deployed by Enron and acquired capacity on other non-Enron networks and is managed by Enron's Broadband Operating System software. Enron is extending its market-making and risk management skills from its energy business to develop the bandwidth intermediation business" (2000 annual report, 25). The segment disclosure shows identifiable assets ($1,313 million) and capital expenditures ($436 million) for the 2000 fiscal year. This is a new industry, and the risk is high. In theory, this could be a very successful venture for Enron, but if a glut of fiber-optic capacity develops, Enron may have to take a hit against its asset values. This would, in turn, reduce net income. We cannot predict an outcome, but the risk is high, especially since, after three years of experimentation, broadband generated a net loss of $60 million for the 2000 fiscal year (2000 annual report, 51).

The Maintenance of Investor Confidence and Access to Financing Resources, and Resultant Focus on Earnings per Share and Components of Other Key Financial Ratios

Assets are often components of key ratios, either as an absolute amount, or because of the key role that asset valuation plays in income determination, stemming from the relationship between assets and revenues and assets and expenses. A major concern regarding this risk area is covered in the preceding discussion on Enron's change in operating activities. However, we want to determine whether there are any other asset amounts that we need to examine more closely, after we consider the degree of risk with regard to possible asset misstatement.

To get a feel for this risk, we ask the following questions: How good is Enron's investor relations program? How does management deal with analysts? Here, we resort to external sources for answers.

We could find only a few voices of dissent in the analyst community prior to November 2001. For example, as far back as March 2001, the Reed Wasden Research team wrote: "At the risk of offending Enron's *mighty investor relations army* [emphasis added], we will attempt to paint a simplistic portrait of what we believe Enron really is" (Wasden, Ayers, and Arias 2001, 4). This firm appears to have emerged unscathed after questioning Enron's future prospects, but other dissenting analysts were not as fortunate. One of these was Chung Wu of UBS PaineWebber (Lozano 2002; Babineck 2002). Another was Daniel Scotto, a bond analyst in New York for BNP Paribas, a French securities firm (Smith 2002).

Wu sent an e-mail message to his clients on August 21, 2001, expressing concern about Enron's financial future and advising them to sell their Enron stock. He was fired the same day. This happened a week after Jeffrey Skilling resigned as Enron's chief executive officer. At the time, Enron stock was in the range of $36, less than half of its peak earlier in the year. In a regulatory filing dated August 31, 2001, to the National Association of Securities Dealers, Wu made the following statement: "Enron management was not pleased and due to the employee stock option relationship UBS PaineWebber has with them, the pressure came from my corporate office to the branch level (Houston) to dismiss me." (For detailed newswire reports, see Lozano 2002; Babineck 2002.) UBS PaineWebber did not deny that it had sacked Chung, nor did the firm deny that the dismissal came after complaints about the e-mail from the Enron executive in charge of its stock option program (*Washington Post* March 28, 2002, A47).

Another example is that of Scotto, a thirty-year Wall Street veteran, who issued a research report to his clients on August 23, 2001, in which he lowered his recommendation on Enron from "buy" to "neutral" and suggested that Enron be used as a "source of funds" (i.e., in analyst language, "consider selling the stock to raise funds for other investments"). He followed up his written report with a conference call, recorded from the firm's trading floor, wherein he advised his clients to dump Enron securities. Shortly afterward, he was demoted, put on leave, and then terminated. BNP Paribas declined to give reporters reasons for Scotto's termination but made the statement that it "was completely unrelated to any research he wrote on any company, including Enron." Scotto, however, claims that BNP Paribus had an investment-banking relationship with Enron. (For the detailed business news report, see Smith 2002.)

Management's seemingly aggressive and intimidating manner of handling adverse analyst reports should have incensed the financial analyst community, as it impairs its independence. The Reed Wasden quote shows that analysts were well aware of the "mighty investor relations army." This behavior toward analysts does not inspire confidence in reported numbers. One has to ask the question: What is Enron trying to hide? It is in this light that we scrutinize asset balances and the related accounting policies.

The following asset balances catch our eye: first, "Investments in and advances to unconsolidated equity affiliates," which increased by 211% between 1996 and 2000, from $1,701 million to $5,294 million; second, "Other investments," which increased by 236%, over the same period, from $1,626 million to $5,459 million. A related accounting policy intensified our interest: "Investments in unconsolidated affiliates are accounted for by the equity method, except for certain investments resulting from Enron's merchant investment activities which are included at market value in 'Other Investments' in the Consolidated Balance Sheet. See Notes 4 and 9. Where acquired assets are accounted for under the equity method based on temporary control, earnings and losses are recognized only for the portion of the investment to be retained" (2000 annual report, 37). On reading footnotes 4 and 9, we decide that this is a major area of concern and that these assets will best be discussed under the Equity Accounting Analysis subsection.

Second, we would like to see more transparency on "Other" assets, classified under "Investments and Other Assets." The amounts are material—for example, $5,459 million for 2000 and $4,681 for 1999. Without knowing the nature of these assets, it is difficult to determine whether we would prefer to expense part or all of these assets.

The Financial Success of International High-Risk, Hard-Asset Ventures and Complex Partnership and Equity Ownership Structures

Footnote 4 (2000 annual report, 40), "Merchant Activities," shows a split between "Merchant Investments" in the amount of $601 million (included in "Other Assets" on the balance sheet) and "Merchant Assets" of $89 million (included in "Investments in and Advances to Unconsolidated Equity Affiliates").

The cash flow statements show that both merchant investments and merchant assets are generators of net income from operating activities, despite the fact that a large portion is included under noncurrent assets on the balance sheet. This suggests the possibility that cash flow from operations may be overstated (as was possible with net assets from price-management activities). In this regard, disclosures in the cash flow statements show how accrual-based net income is converted to cash flow from operations. In 2000, the line item "Additions and Unrealized Gains" on merchant assets and investments is deducted from net income to arrive at cash flow from operating activities, to the tune of $1,295 million. Comparative amounts for this line item were 1999, $827 million; 1998, $721 million; 1997, $308 million; and 1996, $192 million. We have already decided to adjust net income from operations downward for unrealized gains on price-risk-management activities; a similar adjustment for "Additions and Unrealized Gains" on merchant assets and investments has a profound negative affect on net income, especially for 2000. "Other Assets" will also be decreased, for duality purposes. Although the cash flow statement better fulfills our information requirements for merchant assets and investments than it did for net assets from risk-management activities, we are concerned about the additions and unrealized gains being aggregated and shown on a single line item. This severely hampered our ability to make accurate adjustments for unrealized gains, which may have much less of an impact on net income than we are surmising. There is a lack of disaggregated information disclosure for this line item, but due to the potential for management manipulation of these numbers, we decided to treat this line item as an unrealized gain in its entirety, as we did for net assets from risk-management activities. The potential impact is too great for us to ignore such an adjustment, and we would rather err on the side of caution. We do, however, realize that our adjustment has limitations, in that the "additions" component of the line item "Additions and Unrealized Gains" does not have an effect on net income. Our adjustment is therefore misstated by the amount of the unknown cost of these additions.

Hard-asset, high-risk ventures, such as Dabhol Power and Wessex Water, are included in unconsolidated affiliates, and as such the assets are kept off Enron's balance sheet. This issue is dealt with under Entity Accounting Analysis.

Liability Analysis and Shareholders' Equity Analysis

There are two types of claims against a firm's assets: liabilities and shareholders' equity. Equity is, by definition, a residual value. Therefore, fair valuations of assets, liabilities, revenues, and expenses automatically result in a fair residual value. Accounting questions concerning equity generally revolve around hybrid securities, interest rates used to value long-term debt, and the allocation of equity amounts between reserves, retained earnings, and capital. Some important questions concerning Enron's liabilities are: Does the firm have a business strategy that appears to favor off–balance sheet financing to improve debt ratios? Are these significant? (see Palepu et al. 2000, 5-1 to 5-2, 5-14). We now examine liabilities and equity under each of the key risk areas.

The Financial Success of Dealer and Trading Activities

Enron's "Accounting for Price Risk Management" is described under Asset Analysis. Just as these contracts have asset implications to capture rights, they also capture Enron's contractual obligations. The difference between the assets and liabilities for each contract results in unrealized gains or losses, using the mark-to-market method of valuation, which has already been discussed under Asset Analysis. The resultant liabilities are shown as *"Liabilities from Price Risk Management Activities"* on the Consolidated Balance Sheet. We have already discussed the reasoning behind our decision to reverse such unrealized gains, even though the exact amount could not be determined due to incomplete information.

The Maintenance of Investor Confidence and Access to Financing Resources, and Resultant Focus on Earnings per Share and Components of Other Key Financial Ratios

Footnote 7 of the1998 annual report (p. 55) delineates an important timeframe with regard to debt: "Enron has credit facilities with domestic and foreign banks which provide for an aggregate of $1.67 billion in long-term committed credit and $1.37 billion in short-term committed credit. Expiration dates of the committed facilities range from April 1999 to June 2002. . . . Certain credit facilities contain covenants which must be met to borrow funds." From this quote, it is clear that continued financial success during this window period is essential to the company's ability to maintain external financing. It provides a very strong incentive for management to maintain the ratios stipulated in the debt covenants.

In the 2000 annual report, in the MD&A (p. 27), management confirms this risk factor: "Enron is party to certain financial contracts which contain provisions for early settlement in the event of a significant market price decline . . . or if the credit ratings for Enron's secured, senior long-term debt obligations fall below investment grade. . . . Enron's continued investment grade status is critical to the success of its wholesale businesses as well as its ability to maintain adequate liquidity." According to the 1998–2000 annual reports, Enron consistently maintained its credit ratings. But the possibility of an understatement of liabilities is a key consideration, especially when favorable credit ratings are so critical to the firm's success.

To get a feel for long-term debt obligations, we summarize the disclosures on annual maturities of long-term debt outstanding for 1998 to 2000 (see table 5.2).

In the 2000 annual report (p. 41), long-term debt due during 2001 rocketed to $2.1 billion, from $569 the year before. The sudden escalation in the amount of this debt is a major cause for concern, especially when compared to prior year long-term debt levels. We will place particular emphasis on this risk area when we do ratio analysis in the financial analysis section.

The Financial Success of International High-Risk, Hard-Asset Ventures and Complex Partnership and Equity Ownership Structures

Unconsolidated affiliates provide management with the opportunity to understate liabilities. This topic is fully investigated in the subsection dealing with entity accounting analysis, and it is a major area of concern.

In addition, Enron entered into complex equity arrangements and commitments, and the related disclosures are confusing, to say the very least. The disclosure in the 2000 annual report illustrates the difficulties confronting an analyst:

Table 5.2
Enron's Reported Long-Term Debt Maturity Values (In Millions of U.S. Dollars)

Matures ►►	1999	2000	2001	2002	2003	2004	2005
1998 Report	541	413	666	182	656	N/A	N/A
1999 Report	N/A	670	569	432	494	493	N/A
2000 Report	N/A	N/A	2,112	750	852	646	1,592

In 1999, Enron entered into a Share Settlement Agreement under which Enron could be obligated, under certain conditions, to deliver additional shares of common stock or Series B Preferred Stock to Whitewing for the amount that the market price of the converted Enron common shares is less than $28 per share. In 2000, Enron increased the strike price in the Share Settlement Agreement to $48.55 per share in exchange for an additional capital contribution in Whitewing by third-party investors. . . . Absent certain defaults or other specified events, Enron has the option to acquire the third-party investors' interests. If Enron does not acquire the third-party investors' interests before January 2003, or earlier upon certain specified events, Whitewing may liquidate its assets and dissolve. (p. 43)

Whitewing is one of Enron's 50 percent unconsolidated equity affiliates. This is but the tip of the iceberg. A separate disclosure note reveals (2000 annual report, 42), "In 2000 and 1999, Enron sold approximately $632 million and $192 million, respectively, of merchant investments and other assets to Whitewing. Enron recognized no gains or losses in connection with these transactions." This is but one of many very troubling and confusing disclosures of intermingled "unconsolidated affiliate" disclosures.

Revenue Analysis

Revenue should only be recognized if Enron has provided all, or substantially all, of the goods or services to the customer and if the customer with reasonable confidence is expected to pay cash.

The Financial Success of Dealer and Trading Activities

The 2000 quarterly results show increasing and unprecedented levels of revenue for each quarter. For example, revenues for the third quarter skyrocketed from $16.9 billion for the preceding quarter to $30 billion, a 77 percent increase. The fourth quarter shows revenues of $40.8 billion. A partial explanation is that unrealized gains resulting from "Assets from Price-Risk-Management

Activities" were included in "Other Revenues" on the income statements, an issue addressed as part of asset analysis. The cash-flow statements also show that merchant assets and investments generated unrealized gains. From a revenue-recognition perspective, the issue revolves around the ability to eventually collect the cash related to unrealized gains, which management recorded as revenue. We choose to exclude these gains from revenues for purposes of financial analysis.

The Maintenance of Investor Confidence and Access to Financing Resources, and Resultant Focus on Earnings per Share and Components of Other Key Financial Ratios

Management included revenues from unconsolidated equity affiliates (related parties) of $150 million in 2000, $674 million in 1999, $563 million in 1998, and $219 million in 1997. We believe that these transactions should be eliminated on consolidation, and we will deal with this issue under entity accounting analysis. However, we find an obvious contradiction and a very strong warning signal in wording that Enron uses in an explanatory small-print footnote to its reporting on "Unaffiliated Revenues" amounts: "Unaffiliated revenues include sales to unconsolidated equity affiliates" (2000 annual report, 51). Enron's so-called unaffiliated revenues, which have shown a rampant increase, include non–arm's length sales to affiliates. Examples of percentage holdings in these affiliates are Azurix Corp., Citrus Corp., Dabhol Power, and JEDI—all 50 percent; Jacare Electrical—51 percent; Enron Teesside—100 percent (disclosed in the 2000 annual report, 56).

The Financial Success of International High-Risk, Hard-Asset Ventures and Complex Partnership and Equity Ownership Structures

By consolidating unconsolidated equity affiliates (see Entity Accounting Analysis), we may be able to partially undo revenue distortions with regard to this risk area.

Expense Analysis

Reporting challenges related to expenses arise when resources provide benefits over multiple accounting periods (e.g., goodwill), the timing and amount of future payments are uncertain (e.g., pension benefits); it is difficult to determine a value for resources consumed (e.g., stock option compensation) and the decline in value of unused resources (e.g., asset impairments and changes in the value of financial instruments). Typically, we appeal to the matching and conservatism principles to arrive at a fair value (Palepu et al. 2000, 7-1 to 7-16).

The Financial Success of Dealer and Trading Activities

If the broadband business segment proves to be unsuccessful, it could result in a write-off of a portion, or all, of the broadband assets of $1,313 million. The future profitability of this new business area, far removed from Enron's core area of expertise, is uncertain and risky, but we do not know enough to make any adjustments to the numbers. This possibility was discussed under the asset analysis. We also discussed unrealized losses resulting from trading in derivatives under asset analysis.

The Maintenance of Investor Confidence and Access to Financing Resources, and Resultant Focus on Earnings per Share and Components of Other Key Financial Ratios

Enron's focus on earnings per share leads us to consider the possible under-statement of expenses, rather than overstatement. Specifically, we consider whether any reported assets should be expensed (e.g., goodwill and other in-tangibles) and whether there are expenses that have been completely omitted (e.g., stock-option remuneration). We also look for large and unexpected asset write-offs, which may indicate management reluctance to incorporate chang-ing business conditions into accounting estimates, especially if unfavorable to earnings per share (Palepu et al. 2000, 3-12).

First, we consider "Goodwill" and "Other" assets (which are disclosed just below the goodwill line item). These are reported as follows. For Goodwill: 1996, $0.87 billion; 1997 and 1998, $1.9 billion; 1999, $2.8 billion; 2000, $3.6 billion. For Other: 1996, $1.6 billion; 1997, $3.7 billion; 1998, $4.4 bil-lion; 1999, $4.7 billion; 2000, $5.5 billion. These assets have increased pro-gressively and form a substantial portion of total assets, but we have no way of estimating possible overstatements or impairments. It is unusual to see assets in the billions classified as "Other." We would like to see more disclosure on the nature of these assets.

Next, we consider employee stock option expenses. Companies are not re-quired to include employee stock-option expenses in net-income calculations, even though the expense can be material. This expense should appear on the income statement, but the Financial Accounting Standards Board bent to in-tense corporate lobbying and political pressure and in 1995 released FASB Statement 123, which compromised by requesting that the expense be recorded but allowing it to be disclosed in the footnotes if the company wished, effec-tively allowing for overstatement of net income and earnings per share. We are not surprised that Enron chose the footnote-disclosure route. Fortunately, FASB Statement 128 requires disclosure of diluted earnings per share, which includes the effects of unexercised options. Therefore, the reported impact of unexercised stock options (an unrecorded expense) can be estimated by examining the mandatory reconciliation between basic and diluted earnings per share. The impact of including this stock option expense is a decrease in after-tax net income as follows: 2000, $93 million; 1999, $66 million; 1998, $29 million; 1997, $39 million; and 1996, $22 million.

The Financial Success of International High-Risk, Hard-Asset Ventures and Complex Partnership and Equity Ownership Structures

The MD&A (2000 annual report, 21) mentions a $326 million impairment charge for Azurix, a water and wastewater "unconsolidated equity affiliate" and one of Enron's new ventures. This impairment is not separately disclosed on the face of the income statement. We cannot determine whether further impairments are likely.

By consolidating unconsolidated equity affiliates (see Entity-Accounting Analysis), we may be able to partially undo distortions with regard to this expense risk area.

Another problem we experienced is the lack of disclosure on foreign assets. We were unable to determine whether the reported value of foreign assets could be impaired.

Entity-Accounting Analysis

Entity-accounting analysis is crucial in determining reporting boundaries for financial analysis purposes. The focus is on resources that an entity controls in evaluating performance rather than on legal definitions of control. The accounting challenge is whether to aggregate the financial performance of two or more reporting entities (see Palepu et al. 2000, 8-1). Enron has a complex and confusing myriad of related unconsolidated affiliates and related parties. A convolution of financing and other arrangements, combined with bewildering disclosures, make this a difficult and troubling area to examine.

The Financial Success of International High-Risk, Hard-Asset Ventures and Complex Partnership and Equity Ownership Structures

Footnote 9 (2000 annual report, 42–43) makes warning bells go off. Enron's unconsolidated equity affiliates are mostly 50 percent holdings. Are we to believe that a company of Enron's size, stature, and aggressiveness does not exercise control over these affiliates? This is especially pertinent when we consider the power that Enron management appears to exert over financial analysts. In addition, Enron guarantees the performance, liabilities, and lease obligations of some these affiliates to the tune of over $2.5 billion. Is this the action of a third party without control over these entities? Is it possible that

Enron purposely structured its holdings to be exactly at 50 percent mainly to avoid consolidation? Some of the unconsolidated affiliates even exceed the rule-of-thumb limit of 50 percent. For example, on December 31, 1998, Enron's ownership interest in one unconsolidated affiliate, Enron Teesside Operations, was 100 percent. Enron's position is that it intended to ultimately hold a voting interest of no more than 50 percent and therefore chooses not to consolidate. We beg to differ.

Asset-heavy Dabhol Power Company and Wessex Water are included in these unconsolidated affiliates, along with the JEDI and JEDI II and other partnerships. Enron states in the footnote that it has also entered into various arms-length administrative service, management, construction, supply, and operating agreements with these affiliates, but based on the percentage holdings, we discount this assertion. The footnotes include a summary balance sheet of all the affiliates combined. In our adjustments, we will use the information obtained from the financial statements and shown in table 5.3 to consolidate these affiliates. This affects not only asset balances but also liabilities, shareholders' equity, and net income for 1996 to 2000.

Table 5.3
Financial Information for Unconsolidated Equity Affiliates (In Millions of U.S. Dollars)

	2000	1999	1998	1997	1996
Investment in Affiliates	5,294	5,036	4,433	2,656	1,701
Equity in Earnings (Losses)	87	309	97	216	215
Balance Sheet					
Current Assets	5,884[a]	3,168[a]	2,309[a]	3,611	2,587
Property, Plant & Equipment (net)	14,786	14,356	12,640	8,851	8,064
Other Non-Current Assets	13,485	9,459	7,176	1,089	902
Current Liabilities	4,739[b]	4,401[b]	3,501[b]	1,861[b]	2,381
Long-Term Debt	9,717[b]	8,486[b]	7,621[b]	5,694[b]	5,230
Other Non-Current Liabilities	6,148	2,402	2,016	1,295	1,139
Owners' Equity	13,551	11,694	8,987	4,701	2,803
Income Statement[c]					
Operating Revenues	15,903	11,568	8,508	11,183	8,258
Operating Expenses	14,710	9,449	7,244	10,246	7,335
Net Income	586	1,857	142	336	226
Distributions Paid to Enron	137	482	87	118	68

Source: Notes to the Financial Statements in 1998, 1999, and 2000 annual reports; 1997 Form 10-K.

[a]Includes Receivables from Enron: 2000, $410 million; 1999, $327 million; 1998, $196 million.

[b]Includes Payables to Enron: 2000, $302 million; 1999, $84 million; 1998, $296 million; 1997, $569 million.

[c]Enron recognized revenues from transactions with unconsolidated equity affiliates: 2000, $510 million; 1999, $674 million; 1998, $563 million; 1997, $219 million.

Another footnote of interest, "Related Party Transactions," appears for the first time in the 1999 annual report (p. 59). A major concern is that these transactions may lack the objectivity of the free market and consequently have the potential to materially distort financial information. Extracts from Enron's footnote include: "In June 1999, Enron entered into a series of transactions involving a third party and LJM Cayman. . . . A senior officer of Enron is the managing member of LJM's general partner"; "An officer of Enron has invested in the limited partner of JEDI and from time to time acts as agent on behalf of the limited partner's management." The thirty-seven lines of related party disclosure in 1999 increase to ninety lines in 2000, indicating increased activity in this area. The proxy statement for the 2001 shareholders' meeting (available around the time of the release of the 2000 annual report) identifies the senior official as Andrew Fastow, Enron's chief financial officer. The limited partner is unknown. The footnote goes on to describe some of the related party transactions and discloses pretax gains for Enron of approximately $16 million, which is not material. However, in 2000, the related party footnote more than doubles in length (2000 annual report, 48–49). It starts as follows: "In 2000 and 1999, Enron entered into transactions with limited partnerships (the Related Party) whose general partner's managing partner is a senior official of Enron." The pretax effects on net income from transactions with these partnerships appear to be in excess of $550 million. This is a substantial portion of Enron's pretax earnings of $1,413. This raises serious questions about the quality of earnings. Ideally, our consolidation adjustments for unconsolidated affiliates will adjust for these transactions, but we are not given enough information to be completely confident.

Consolidation of these unconsolidated affiliates increases Enron's reported debt equity ratio at December 31, 2000, by almost 40 percent, which could result in violation of debt covenants. This ratio will be discussed in more detail when we perform the detailed financial analysis.

Additional Red flags

In addition to the concerns already raised, we review the relationships between Enron's reported net income and cash flow from operating activities and its reported net income before taxes and taxable income.

Table 5.4 clearly shows large and inconsistent fluctuations between net income and operating cash flow (especially in 2000), as well as enormous differences in reported net income (before taxes) and taxable income. This is an indication that quality of earnings may not be high. In particular, the large gap between 2000 net income of $979 million and cash generated by operations of $4,779 requires more explanation. Is it possible that cash flow from investing activities was diverted to cash flow from operating activities? We have already put forth an argument for this in regard to noncurrent price-risk-management activities.

Table 5.4
Enron's Relationships between Income, Cash Flows, and Taxes (U.S. Dollar Amounts in Millions)

	1996	1997	1998	1999	2000
1. Net Income	$584	$105*	$703	$893	$979
Cash Flow from Operations	$884	$211	$1,640	$1,228	$4,779
% Net Income to Cash Flow	69%	50%	43%	73%	15%
2. Income before Income Taxes	$855	$15*	$878	$1,128	$1,413
Tax Payable on Income	64	84	88	83	227
% Tax Payable	7.5%	560%	10.1%	7.4%	16.1%
% Deferred Tax	24.2%	(1160%)	9.9%	1.8%	14.6%
% Effective Tax	31.7%	(600%)	20%	9.2%	30.7%

*Includes unusual nonrecurring contract restructuring charge of $675 million.

We also scrutinize the 1998 to 2000 annual reports for evidence of large fourth quarter fluctuations, as annual reports are audited, whereas quarterly reports are (normally) merely reviewed (Palepu et al. 2000, 3-12). Management could make adjustments in the fourth quarter to satisfy the external auditors; this would heighten our concern about the credibility of the numbers. We do notice an anomaly during the fourth quarter of 2000. Revenues increased by 36 percent over the third quarter, and yet net income decreased by 79 percent. We now feel even more comfortable with our decision to make adjustments to revenues.

Undoing Perceived Accounting Distortions

Before proceeding to financial analysis, we will undo accounting distortions as we believe warranted, based on our accounting analysis interpretations. We had additional concerns, but we do not have enough information to quantify and adjust for them. The adjustments we decided on for financial analysis purposes are as follows:

Possible unrealized gains from price risk management activities (included in "Other Revenues" on the income statement): Restate revenues (and net income before tax) for 1999 and 2000, and reduce Retained Earnings. Income before tax decreases materially as follows: 2000, $763 million; and 1999, $395 million. "Assets from price risk management activities" decreases as well, to complete the double entry. We also adjust for deferred taxation at the statutory federal income tax rate.

Possible unrealized gains on merchant assets and investments: Reduce revenues (and net income before tax) and "Other Assets" as follows: 2000, $1,295 million; 1999, $827 million; 1998, $721 million; 1997, $308 million; and 1996, $192 million. We also adjust for deferred taxation at the statutory federal income tax rate.

Adjustment for impact of stock option expense as a decrease in after-tax net income as follows: 2000, $93 million; 1999, $66 million; 1998, $29 million; 1997, $39 million; and 1996, $22 million.

Consolidate unconsolidated affiliates as best we can with the incomplete information available to us (see table 5.3). Our consolidated financial information is subject to the following limitations: we have only aggregated amounts for all affiliates; we do not have individual affiliate ownership interest percentages, acquisition dates, amounts, and preacquisition equity information; and we do not have the breakdown of revenues and expenses that are not operating revenues/expenses and cannot split these expenses between interest, income tax, and other expenses or revenues. Because of the above limitations, assets may be understated, because we could not determine at-acquisition goodwill. We achieve duality by adjusting the reported amount for Minority Interests.

FINANCIAL ANALYSIS

Overview of Financial Analysis

The purpose of financial analysis is to assess the performance of the firm. We use two tools for this purpose: ratio analysis and cash flow analysis. In ratio analysis, we determine how selected financial statement line items relate to each other, and we assess the firm's profitability. In cash flow analysis, we analyze liquidity and evaluate cash flows from operating, investing, and financing activities (Palepu et al. 2000, 9-1).

Our financial analysis is somewhat limited by a lack of information on the unconsolidated affiliates. For example, we do not have the details of interest expense, income tax expense, and cash flow for these affiliates. Therefore, we could not calculate the ratios that require this information (e.g., Earnings before Income Tax margins), and consequently we could not use the Palepu et al. (2000, 9-1 to 9-29) financial analysis model in its entirety. Although our financial analysis may not be as comprehensive as we would like it to be, we believe that the key ratios that we could calculate provide us with enough information to make an informed decision about Enron's financial results and condition.

Ratio Analysis

The ratios that we use for our personal decision-making purposes are summarized in table 5.5. These calculations are based the adjusted amounts that we calculated, not on Enron's reported amounts. Where relevant, we use the average of the beginning and ending balances for assets, liabilities, and shareholders' equity in our ratio calculations. The only exception to this is for 1996, because we do not have adjusted amounts for 1995.

The starting point for analyzing a firm's profitability is return on equity. ROE indicates how well management has used shareholders' funding to generate returns. On average, over long periods, large public U.S. firms have tradi-

Table 5.5
Enron Ratio Analysis after Adjustments to Reported Amounts

	1996	1997	1998	1999	2000
Return on Equity	12.2%	-3%	3.5%	0.4%	-4.9%
Return on Assets	1.7%	-0.5%	0.5%	0.1%	-0.6%
Financial Leverage	7.2	6.5	6.6	6.6	7.9
Net Profit Margin	2%	-0.4%	0.5%	0.1%	-0.4%
Asset Turnover	0.8	1.1	1.0	1.0	1.6
Gross Profit Margin	6.5%	4.1%	4.9%	4.1%	0.8%
Basic EPS	0.86	-0.28	0.29	-0.05	-0.73
Net PP&E Turnover	1.4	1.9	1.9	2.1	4.4
Current Ratio	1.1	1.4	0.9	0.9	1.1
Debt Equity Ratio	5.7	4.5	5.0	4.2	7.2

tionally generated ROEs of 11 to 13 percent (Palepu et al. 2000, 9-3). Enron's ROEs are: 2000, *minus* 4.6 percent; 1999, 0.4 percent; 1998, 3.2 percent; 1997, *minus* 2.5 percent; and 1996, 12.2 percent. The return for 1996 is the only one that is within the normal range. The subsequent years (1997 to 2000) are well below this range, with 2000 being the worst year by far. Problems with overall profitability appear to surface as early as 1997. A review of a Reed Wasden Research publication (Wasden et al. 2001, 2-8) shows that Enron's ROEs (even the preadjustment ROE) fall far short of those of its comparable peers—AES, Calpine, Constellation, Duke, Dynegy, TXU, and Williams Companies. For example, peer 2000 ROEs were 17.21 percent, 20.21 percent, 10.6 percent, 13.5 percent, 19.29 percent, 11.3 percent, and 9.14 percent, respectively. Even Enron's preadjustment ROE of 7 percent is the lowest for this group. Yet, as the report indicates (Wasden et al. 2001, 2), Enron was trading at a substantial valuation premium over its peers.

A further decomposition of ROE can be done, into return on assets or ROA (*Net Income/Average Assets*) to determine how profitably assets have been employed and financial leverage (*Average Assets/Average Shareholders' Equity*), which shows how big the firm's asset base is relative to shareholder investment. Enron's ROAs are 2000, *minus* 0.5 percent; 1999, 0.06 percent; 1998, 0.4 percent; 1997, minus 0.4 percent; and 1996, 1.7 percent. An already low ROA declined sharply from 1996 to 1997 and has remained at extremely low or negative levels. Ratios for the peer group ranged between 2.45 and 5.37 for the 2000 fiscal year.

Financial leverage ratios, which show how many dollars of assets the firm deploys for each dollar of shareholder investment, were fairly constant, except for the increase shown during the 2000 fiscal year: 2000, 9.3; 1999, 6.2; 1998, 7.1; 1997, 6.1; 1996, 7.2. The main problem appears to be with the ROA factor of ROE.

ROA can be further decomposed into *Net Income/Sales* multiplied by *Sales/ Average Assets*, the net profit margin and asset turnover ratios, respectively (see table 5.5). Enron's profit margins are dismal, dropping from 2 percent in 1996 to –0.4 percent in 1997 and 2000. The two positive returns of 0.5 percent and 0.1 percent in 1998 and 1999 are well below those of six of Enron's seven peers. Comparative peer ratios for 2000 were: 9.58 percent, 16.32 percent, 8.9 percent, 3.6 percent, 1.70 percent, 4.78 percent, and 5.19 percent (Wasden et al. 2001, 8). The asset turnover ratio appears to be reasonable, given the heavy asset investment requirements that are characteristic of energy companies. Once again, profitability appears to be problematic. Gross profit margins (calculated with limited information as follow: [*Operating Revenues – Operating Costs and Expenses*]/*Operating Revenues*) indicate a problem in 2000. The ratios remained fairly constant from 1997 to 1999 but then dropped from 4.1 percent in 1999 to 0.8 percent in 2000, despite an increase of 129 percent in the amount of operating revenue from 1999 to 2000. In summary, we are concerned about Enron's operating management. Restated earnings per share strongly reinforce our concerns (1997, from 0.16 to *negative* 0.28; 1998, from 1.07 to 0.29; 1999, from 1.17 to *negative* 0.05; and 2000, from 1.22 to *negative* 0.73). How do these deteriorating profit ratios justify the increase in stock price of nearly 90 percent in 2000?

With regard to long-term asset management, the only ratio that we could calculate was the property, plant & equipment (PP&E) turnover ratio (*Sales/ Average Net PP&E*), which shows the efficiency with which PP&E was used. The only major fluctuation that we noted was the increase in this ratio from 2.1 in 1999 to 4.4 in 2000, a result of the dramatic increase in operating revenues in 2000, without a comparable increase in PP&E. As previously discussed, we opine that the 2000 revenues are of questionable quality.

Finally, we evaluate financial management. Enron' current ratio (*current assets/current liabilities*) appears to be consistently low, ranging between 0.9 and 1.4 for 1996 to 2000. From a debt and long-term solvency perspective, our concerns center round the vastly deteriorating debt equity ratio in 2000. Our restated consolidated amounts indicate an increase in the debt equity ratio from 4.2 in 1999 to 7.2 in 2000. Also, reported debt/equity and restated debt/ equity showed a deterioration of close to 40 percent. This, along with earnings management concerns, does not inspire investment confidence.

However, we will analyze Enron's cash flow numbers before reaching to a final conclusion.

Cash Flow Analysis

We do not have the required unconsolidated equity information to adjust Enron's reported cash-flow information. Therefore, we will perform certain aspects of cash-flow analysis based on reported amounts. We are particularly interested in the large gap between Enron's reported net income ($979 million) and cash flow from operating activities ($4,779 million) for the 2000 fiscal year, a difference of $3.8 billion. In contrast, the difference for 1999 was a mere $335 million. Also, net cash from operating activities increased by $3,551, or 289 percent, in 2000. Enron's management explains this enormous difference as "primarily reflecting decreases in working capital, positive operating results and a receipt of cash associated with the assumption of a contractual obligation" (2000 annual report, 26). Our concern is that cash flow from investing activities (e.g., sale of investment assets) may have been diverted to cash flow from operating activities. Proceeds from the sale of merchant assets and investments are recorded at $1,838 million. We also notice an amount of $1,113 million cash inflow, described as "Other operating activities." The comparative amount for 1999 was a mere $174 million. Is this the contractual obligation of which management briefly makes mention? What is the nature of this obligation? Should this obligation possibly be better classified as a financing activity? We do not have the answers to these questions, but we do not feel comfortable with the cash flow disclosures. We would like to see more of an explanation from management, because of the materiality of the difference between net income and cash flow from operating activities. If this business generated this much in cash from operations, why is the current ratio so low and the debt equity ratio so high at the end of 2000?

CONCLUSION

Based on the foregoing analyses, we would not recommend this stock. From 1997 onwards, our analyses indicate reporting and performance problems. We have major concerns about profitability and debt levels.

Enron throws an abundance of information at financial analysts in its Form 10-K filings (which are generally in excess of 200 pages). The language is not always clear; it can be downright confusing, even to accounting experts—a major red flag in and of itself. The quantity of information makes the analyst's job time consuming and tedious, effectively drowning the analyst in paper, and yet essential information (e.g., separate disclosures of unrealized gains on trading activities) is not available. Nonetheless, this does not excuse those analysts who overwhelmingly would not see the woods for the trees and who continued recommending clients that they buy or hold Enron stock.

Our investigation shows that the red flags were plentiful, and the situation was aggravated by the apparent disdain (judging by incidents reported in the news media) with which Enron's top management dealt with financial analysts. Coupled with the results of our accounting and financial analyses, we should be very concerned about the competence, independence, and objectivity of financial analysts who continued to recommend this stock. This raises the question of whether these analysts were remiss in the discharge of their fiduciary duties.

We posit that financial analysts may have been buying into the mindset of financial management, if one believes that the pre-Enron CFO literature reflects what was happening within financial management circles. When reviewing this literature, bear in mind that the purpose of financial reporting is to reflect underlying business reality so that external users can make informed economic decisions. We conclude this chapter with examples from this literature, which was freely available to financial analysts.

Ronald Fink, a senior editor of *CFO Magazine*, wrote about Enron's substantial need for capital in June 1999: "But conventional financing techniques to exploit the industry's current and potential size would jeopardize the BBB+ credit rating Enron earns. . . . The financial balancing act that this situation requires has turned Enron into a master of creative financing. . . . Enron does not consolidate a number of highly leveraged subsidiaries in which it owns—or plans to own—no more than 50 percent of the voting stock. Under current practice, Enron can use the equity method of treating these subsidiaries' results, which keeps their debt and assets off Enron's own books." The article goes on to describe the "creative financing" that Fastow used to keep some $10 billion in long-term debt and other liabilities off Enron's balance sheet. The writer concludes: "No wonder Fastow goes to great lengths to convince financial analysts that such nonrecourse debt shouldn't be consolidated, regardless of FASB's position." A second article appears in the same publication in October 1999 (Banham 1999), singing Fastow's praises for "walking the tightrope" of creative financing: "Fastow's expert balancing act, in fact, has earned him this year's CFO Excellence Award for Capital Structure Management." The very acts that resulted in this Excellence Award are contrary to the purpose of financial accounting, which is to help external decision makers make informed decisions about the economic activities of the firm.[1]

NOTE

1. Enron's employee evaluation/incentive system that provided high rewards for good short-term performance reports and termination for the bottom 15 percent "performers" certainly created a fertile environment for accounting manipulation and distorted reports (Cruver 2002). This fact must be taken into consideration for any firm having or considering such a system.

REFERENCES

Babineck, M. 2002. "Analyst Fired for Urging 'Sell' Enron as Firm Touted Enron." *Associated Press State & Local Wire* (March 5).

Banham, R. 1999. "How Enron Financed Its Amazing Transformation from Pipelines to Piping Hot." *CFO Magazine* (October 1).

Cruver, B. 2002. *Anatomy of Greed*. New York: Carroll and Graf.

Fink, R. 1999. "Balancing Act: Will a New Accounting Rule Aimed at Off-Balance-Sheet Financing Trip Up Enron?" *CFO Magazine* (June 1).

Liesman, S. 2002. "SEC Accounting Cop's Warning: Playing by Rules May Not Ward Off Fraud Issues." *Wall Street Journal* (February 12), C1, C8.

Lozano, J. A. 2002. "Analyst Says Fired for Urging Clients to Sell Enron Stock." *Associated Press State & Local Wire* (March 4).

Palepu, K. G., P. M. Healy, and V. L. Bernard. 2000. *Business Analysis and Valuation Using Financial Statements.* 2d ed. Cincinnati: South-Western.

Schroeder, M. 2002. "As Enron's Derivatives Trading Comes into Focus, Gap in Oversight Is Spotlighted." *Wall Street Journal* (January 28), C1, C15.

Schroeder, M., and G. Ip. 2001. "Out of Reach: The Debacle Spotlights Huge Void in Financial Regulation." *Wall Street Journal* (December 13), A1, A6.

Smith, R. 2002. "The Analyst Who Warned about Enron." *Wall Street Journal* (January 29), C1, C17.

Wasden, C. D., S. Ayers, and P. Arias. 2001. "Enron Mystique Exacts Premium." *Prometheus File: Global Energy Technology Weekly* (March 31).

6

Prepaid Forward and Leasing Contracts: A Critical Analysis of a Potentially Useful Form of Financing Employed by Enron

Usamah A. Uthman

EXECUTIVE SUMMARY

Prepaid forward contracts, or salams, have existed for hundreds of years and in many places around the world, yet they have probably never been traded in organized markets. An interesting example of the use of salams is provided by Enron. Enron's utilization of the contracts was unfortunately abusive in a way that got the company and others into trouble. We explain what Enron and its bankers should have done as a better use of these prepaid forward contracts.

The primary purpose of this chapter is to discuss the securitization of the salam and leasing contracts in a way that alleviates their abuse and to provide a reasonable alternative to financial debt to raise capital. Furthermore, the chapter discusses the possibility of using the resulting instruments for conducting fiscal and monetary policies. The essential feature of salam certificates (SCs) and leasing certificates (LCs) is the issuer's obligation toward the investor, not different from what the market in the real sector pays on the due date of payment. Because the investor's income is not guaranteed and is geared to a specific commodity or project, SCs and LCs seem to be self-financing; there is no need for further debt to finance their payment. The instrument holder has an uncertain, confined claim against the issuer. Hedging in the case of SCs and the near annuity-bond feature in the case of LCs, on the one hand, and liquidity via the securitization of both, on the other, should make these instruments attractive for both real and financial investors.

INTRODUCTION

Both governments and businesses frequently need external financing to continue in operation and expand. The typical means of financing is the issuance of securities that promise, or provide the potential to make, future cash payments in return, either in the form of promised interest and principal, or in the form of dividends from the residual income of the organization. A somewhat unusual alternative is the *salam*, an ancient form of financing that is essentially a forward contract, with the cash payment for the spot commodity or asset underlying the contract made up front instead of at the time of delivery. Enron provides and example of a company that has used a form of the salam in recent history. Essentially, the company used forward contracts to obtain financing from J. P. Morgan & Company (Sapsford and Raghavan 2002). In particular, Morgan, having set up an offshore company called Mahonia Ltd. to deal in energy forward contracts, would pay Enron $150–250 million up front for the periodic future delivery of natural gas or crude oil. Although the transaction had similarities to a collateralized loan, with the repayment being in kind instead of in cash, the transaction was treated as a trade instead of as a loan. As a result, Enron was able to keep the liability for delivery of the commodity from being treated as a loan on its balance sheet; instead, the liability to delivery the energy commodities apparently was listed as a deposit in the liability section of the balance sheet.

Once delivery of the commodities occurred, the gain or loss had to be booked into the income statement. If Enron hedged its obligation to deliver the commodity through some forward contract with a third party or through the futures market, it would automatically suffer a loss every time it delivered on its forward contract liability with Morgan (as the cash paid up front by Morgan would have to be at a discount to the forward market price to give Morgan a profit margin that would reflect the effective interest rate on the up-front financing). However, Enron was able to postpone delivery, and thus any gains and losses, into the future any time it wished by simply entering into a new forward contract to deliver the energy the next year. This scheme created the apparently legal possibility of smoothing or inflating income as Enron chose, as well as a way of deferring taxes on any gains indefinitely. Doug Carmichael, a professor of accounting at New York's Baruch College stated, "It certainly makes sense as a tax strategy" (Sapsford and Raghavan 2002).

J. P. Morgan was willing to maintain the scheme with Enron for about a decade, because it earned between 7 percent and 8 percent from the difference between the cash paid up front and the actual forward price prevailing at the time. As time went, and as Enron's situation worsened, J. P. Morgan asked for guarantees of delivery on the contracts; Enron offered "surety bonds" through some insurance companies and a line of credit from a German bank (Sapsford and Raghavan 2002). When Enron filed for bankruptcy, the insurers refused to honor their commitments, "alleging that Mahonia was a fabrication meant to disguise loans in the form of Commodity trade" (Sapsford and Raghavan 2002). J. P. Morgan's bad debts from these deals mounted to $2.6 billion.

While the overall financing concept was a good one, Morgan did make some mistakes in its implementation. In particular, Morgan should not have rolled over the forward contracts at Enron's wishes. In addition, Morgan could have securitized the forward contracts in the market to reduce its exposure to Enron's debt.

The purpose of this chapter is to evaluate two financial instruments that may satisfy some of the financing needs of governments and corporations. Salam and leasing certificates are the suggested alternatives. Although the forward and leasing contracts have existed for hundreds of years, and in many places around the world, they are still not traded in organized financial markets. Consequently, textbook treatments of salam and leasing certificates are rare. Our purpose is to discuss first the economics of the securitization of salams and leasing contracts and second their use not only by the private sector but also by governments.[1] The essential feature of salam and leasing certificates (SCs and LCs) is the fact that the issuer's obligation toward the investor is not different from what the market in the real sector pays on the due date of payment. Because the investor's income is not guaranteed and because it is geared to a specific commodity or project, SCs and LCs are self-financing. There would be no need for further debt to finance their repayment. The instrument holder has an uncertain, confined claim against the treasury.

SALAM CERTIFICATES

Salam certificates can be issued against the future delivery of a commodity, product, or service. The certificates represent a sort of forward contract. A government that controls a major natural resource, such as cotton, copper, iron, petroleum, or the like, issues certificates for the future delivery of such products, which are fully paid for on the spot by investors, who receive certificates of purchase in return. For example, a country that produces oil may want to expand its refining facilities. Instead of borrowing on the basis of interest, it may sell salam (forward) contracts of refined oil products to an American company based in Houston. Each contract is five thousand barrels, for $18 per barrel, to be delivered in Houston, one year after the date of payment of the full value of the contract (5,000 × $18). The buying company may choose to hold onto the SC and receive the shipment on the designated date, or it may elect to sell its contract before the date of delivery at whatever possible market price, to another investor. An SC may change hands between the beginning of the contract and its date of maturity. Actual delivery and receipt, and not just paper settlement, are binding on the salam issuer and the final holder of the certificate. Net realized income to the buyer of the salam would be the difference between the current spot price paid now and the spot price in the future. The difference may be positive, zero, or negative. Salam contracts can be nonstandardized, but in order to securitize them, they should be standardized. The certificates can be of different denominations and of different maturity periods. (See appendix 6.1 for some jurisprudence elements of salam.)

The basic attraction of salam certificates to a government (or to any issuer) is the fact that they do not represent a financial debt burden on the government, and no interest has to be paid on their nominal principal. Since salam certificates tie finance, production, and sale into one contract, the risk of changing prices of the commodities, products, or services represented by SCs is transferred to those who invest in them. The basic attraction of salam to an investor (buyer) is the provision of the required hedge against price increases, in addition to liquidity via securitization. A mathematical evaluation of the pricing of salams is provided in appendix 6.2.

Salam Certificates Compared to Swaps

Myers (1992) explains that a *swap* is an agreement whereby one party replaces one cash flow (or commitment) by another that is indexed to some price or interest rate. A country that obtained a conventional loan from a bank, for instance, exchanges its fixed debt obligation with another firm that undertakes to assume these obligations toward the bank in exchange for payments based on the price of some commodity. The country benefits from a price fall, while the firm hedges against a price rise. Thus both parties are better off.

In spite of the expected benefits of swap agreements, they may not be among the best instruments, for the overall transaction costs associated with them may be very high. First of all, there are the costs of searching for, negotiating, and drafting a loan contract. Second, there are also costs when it comes to selling (swapping) a loan contract. Third, the time lag between the two contracts may not be short, especially if domestic or international economic conditions are not favorable. Fourth, the swap does not eliminate debt; it only transfers it from one party to another, and there is a limit to how much debt a firm or country can absorb.

A salam contract can bring about the benefits of the swap at a lesser cost. As a forward contract, it gives the buyer the required hedge against possible future price increases in addition to liquidity via securitization. The salam contract gives the seller the required "downside price protection." Salam reduces the need for a banker, since the seller can get financing directly from buyers. Needless to say, a bank can participate as a buyer of salam. However, salam does not eliminate the need for a commodity exchange if it is to be securitized. However, for a simple salam, a commodity exchange may not be needed. Also, salam eliminates fixed interest payments. Needless to say, the transaction costs associated with a salam contract are likely to be much lower than those of a swap. The salam contract also avoids any predetermined cash debt on either party.

Salam Certificates Compared to Commodity-Indexed Bonds

Myers also explains that in the case of commodity indexed bonds (CIB), both the principal and coupon payments are indexed to the price of some commodity. Payments rise and fall according to a predetermined schedule as the price of the commodity fluctuates. This is less risky to the producer than a conventional loan at a variable interest rate, because payments in the latter case are unrelated to the profitability of the borrowing business. Interest-indexed payments may be sticky or even rising when commodity prices and profits are falling. A supply shock (such as a crop failure) may cause prices to go up but lower overall revenues and hence weaken the borrower's ability to meet his obligations. Linking the debt service to the commodity's revenue may reduce the risk for the producer. There is, however, a moral hazard problem here— the borrowing country has a disincentive to increase (and an incentive to underreport) production levels (Myers 1992).

Obviously, while revenue-indexed bonds may reduce the risk for the borrower, they may increase it to the lender both because of a greater variation in payments and because of the increased default risk. The salam contract converts a cash debt into an in-kind debt, not some fixed or variable amount of cash. This provides the required price hedge for the buyer, while at the same time it protects both the buyer and seller from the respective risks of revenue and price-indexed debts. There is less incentive on the part of the seller to transfer more risk to the buyer by manipulating his reported revenues. Part of the variation in revenue has been already transferred to (and accepted by) the buyer in the form of a predetermined price, and the other (quantity) part is contractually fixed. The manipulation of actual or reported production by the seller only delays and increases the fulfillment of his obligations but does not bring him any reduction in these obligations.

Salam Certificates Compared to Options

Myers describes an option bond as another commodity-linked instrument, except for the fact that it has the usual principal and interest payments. At maturity, the holder has an option to buy (a call option) or sell (a put option) a predetermined quantity of a specific commodity at a predetermined price (the strike price). This added feature makes option bonds either sell at a premium to conventional bonds or have lower coupon rates, thereby lowering the cost of servicing the debt to the issuer. The "payment [of debts] occurs, however, at a time when commodity prices are high and the producer can best afford to pay. The producer has forgone the opportunity to reap the gains above the strike price in exchange for lower interest payments" (Myers 1992).

The attraction of the option feature should not blind us to the fact that an option bond is essentially a debt instrument and thus has the ramifications of any debt. As is shown in appendix 6.2, it should be very easy to design a salam certificate coupled with an option with no cash debt element involved. The ramifications and policy implications of salam and the other suggested instrument, leasing certificates, is discussed toward the end of the chapter.

LEASING CERTIFICATES

Leasing certificates may be issued as original financial instruments for projects to be started afresh, or they could be issued against already-existing projects.

Suppose a government would like to build an airport but it is short of the necessary funds. The government will sign a contract with a contractor to build the airport, but at the same time, it will lease the airport to the public. The value of the lease (equal to or greater than the cost of construction) will be divided over a large number of "shares" of different denominations and maturities, and called "leasing certificates." In other words, different investors may participate in the lease contract for different periods. The government will pay the contractor from the proceeds of the lease. Holders of LCs will sublease the airport, through some government agency, to whatever companies and industries are using the airport. LC holders will accept whatever variable income is received on a monthly, quarterly, or annual basis. The government is not obliged to pay investors anything different from actual income from the facility.

Leasing certificates are in a way similar to revenue bonds in the United States in the sense that they are backed by expected revenues from the project to be financed.[2] However, the return from LCs is absolutely variable, with no guarantee on the part of the government of any interest income or principal. Like salam certificates, LCs have the important feature of avoiding any predetermined financial debt in government finances. Certificates of different maturities can be issued to satisfy different investors' preferences. The longer the maturity of a certificate, the more coupons it carries and hence the higher its price (other things being equal). At the time of distributing revenues, all certificate holders, regardless of the length of time to maturity, share equally in the project's revenues. Naturally, the government prices a certificate below the nominal sum of all expected future coupon payments, in order to generate a positive rate of return to the investors. At the end of the lease the government has the right to collect whatever salvage value the physical asset may retain.

Income from LCs can be either out of the project's net income or out of total revenue. The first scheme implies that investors are indirectly responsible for the profitability of the physical assets and hence is more risky.

If the issuing agency finances its operations partially by stocks and partially by LCs side by side, equilibrium requires that a stock and a perpetual LC should have the same price and also that the rate of return on any LC (of any maturity period) be equal to the rate of return on a stock that is held for the same period. Otherwise there would be an opportunity for arbitrage.[3] Whether this is the case or not remains an empirical matter.[4] The absence of data precludes any empirical testing. A theoretical analysis of leasing certificates is provided in appendix 6.3.

Types of Risk Associated with LCs

Because of the direct relationship between revenue (or dividends) of an LC and its price, the price risk and the revenue reinvestment risk tend to reinforce each other (as in stocks).[5] This is contrary to the case of bonds, where the price risk and the coupon reinvestment risk tend to offset each other. The absence of any data on LCs makes it difficult to judge how risky LCs are relative to bonds and stocks. Empirical research on stocks and bonds in the United States tells us that stocks have a much higher average rate of return but a higher standard deviation than those of bonds (Ibbotson and Sinquefield 1982). While returns from both common stocks and LCs are variable and not guaranteed, common stocks have an added advantage in that they represent a claim against real physical assets. Since this is not the case with LCs, it may be reasonable to conclude that, generally speaking, LCs are more risky than either stocks or bonds.[6] But because of different maturity periods of LCs, one wonders if there is a term-structure problem similar to that in the case of bonds.

The Term Structure of Returns on LCs

The term structure of interest rates on bonds describes the relationship between the yield and maturity of securities, holding other things (including prices) constant. The case of LCs in this regard is somewhat more complicated, for more than one reason. First, a LC does not carry a fixed coupon payment. Second, realized revenues are shared equally between holders of different maturity certificates. This implies that while the "coupon payments" may be variable over time, they are equal at any point in time for different outstanding denominations. Third, and because of the previous point, longer maturities (which carry more coupons) should command higher prices. Consequently, it can be inferred that the term-structure problem of LCs (if any) involves three variables at the same time—yield, maturity, and price.

As the problem in question is more complicated than it first appears, we may ask the following question: What is it that the theory of the term structure of interest rates tries to explain? It tries to explain the behavior of what is essentially intended to be a contractually fixed rate of return—the coupon rate. Market forces, however, influence the interest rates on subsequent issues of debt and thus change the prices of outstanding debt and hence the actual rate of return—the yield—on these instruments. The function of a debt contract of a longer maturity is thus to reflect expectations about, and guard against, future changes in contractually fixed rates of return. The theory of the term structure implicitly discusses the structure of contractual incomes over time. Since there is no contractually fixed income in the case of LCs, an LC yield reflects no such attempt to deal with uncertainty of coupon payments. It can be concluded that there is a term structure problem with LCs only to the extent that there is such a problem with stocks where average holding periods serve as proxies for maturity periods.[7]

Duration

It may be argued that since a LC has a specific maturity date, a measure of the duration for the LCs ought to be possible to calculate. This is not accurate, however. In order to calculate a duration measure, the value of the "coupon payment" must be known in advance. Since this is not the case with LCs, no duration measure can be calculated. One could argue that the average of expected "coupon payments" could be used as a proxy for the fixed interest payments. But this implies that there will be as many duration measures for an LC as there are expectations about its "coupon payments." The best that can be done, then, is to estimate the probability distribution and parameter values for an LC's duration.

SOME POLICY IMPLICATIONS OF SALAM
AND LEASING CERTIFICATES

John Hicks (1939) explains that uncertainty about changes in wants and resources represents the "limiting factor" against the spread of futures contracts (p. 136). But we may also note that it is uncertainty itself that motivates forward trading. In many cases a country's (or firm's) delinquency on payment does not necessarily stem from inability to produce but more often from inability to sell. Hicks explains that there are objective reasons why the market for forward trading tends to be one of net hedging. This is because "technical conditions give the entrepreneur a much freer hand about the acquisition of inputs than about the completion of outputs. Thus while there is likely to be some desire to hedge planned purchases, it tends to be less insistent than the desire to hedge planned sales" (p. 137). In spite of the importance of technical conditions, one may argue that we can imagine their removal in the long run through invention and innovation. The psychological factor may loom large and highly unpredictable. The relative weakness on the demand side of commodities, products, and services may create a shortage of liquidity that is aggravated by the very nature of conventional financial debt—the fixity of debt may not respond to changing economic conditions.

At the microeconomic level, a firm that finances some physical assets with a loan will record the value of the asset on the assets side of the balance sheet, and the value of the loan on the liability side. From an accounting point of view the two entries tend to balance each other. From an economic point of view, however, the firm actually winds up with two fixities—a sticky asset and an unforgiving debt. The implied risk of investment is definitely higher, if not doubled. From an economic point of view, then, there is an underaccounting of actual costs. Compare this to another method of finance, such as equity. It makes tremendous difference whether the owners of the asset owe its financing to themselves or to outsiders. There is only one fixity here—the value of the asset itself. It is the increased degree of risk associated with debt that forces firms to ask for a higher minimum attractive rate of return in order to embark on investment.

The more advanced an economy is, the more specialized is labor [and capital], and hence the more specific would become the firm's assets. In an advanced economy, asset specificity is the rule and not the exception. In such an economy, and in accordance with Williamson's [1988] rule (of using more equity the more specific the assets are), equity financing, contrary to Williamson's conclusion, should be the rule and not the last resort. . . . Because there is more discretion in profit sharing arrangements, there is necessarily more provision (safeguarding) for unforeseen contingencies. . . . What we see, then, in debt finance (of leveraged buy-outs) is a market mechanism that may facilitate opportunistic tendencies. (Uthman 1994, 3–4, 6)

Leijonhufvud (1981) discusses a theory of "Effective Demand Failures" and observes that "Realized sales appear (i) as a proxy for expected income, (ii) as a constraint on current purchases, and (iii) as a constraint on the demand signals" (p. 115). He asks the following question: "when would we then expect to observe effective demand failures, sizable multiplier coefficients and the rest? In brief, when liquid buffer stocks have been squeezed out of the system" (pp. 122–123). Salam and leasing certificates provide liquidity not only in terms of finance but also in terms of sales. This is especially true once they are securitized.

The irony is that while conventional futures contracts provide a means of generating sales if actual delivery ever takes place, they are neither genuine investment nor finance. Since margin requirements are usually a fraction of a price to be paid in the future, a conventional futures contract is more risky to the producer than a salam contract. It is no wonder that a buyer of salam commands a higher "coordination return" in the sense of a lower price paid to the issuer of salam relative to both a spot-payment/spot-delivery price and a conventional futures price.

There are, however, several ramifications with salam certificates. First, the number of certificates that can be issued is governed by the extent of the reserves of those natural resources (or crops) available for sale and the state of the market for these particular commodities. In contrast, government bonds are not constrained by any natural limit and are dependent on no particular market. Second, since most commodities markets are usually (but not always) short-term markets, the maturities of the SCs can be mostly short ones. This weakens the case for use of SCs to finance long-term government projects.

Government bonds, on the other hand, can be issued for a wide variety of maturity periods, including in perpetuity. But one should hasten to say that different products may facilitate the issuance of different maturities, including long-term ones.[8] Third, SCs pay earnings (and the principal) only once—at the maturity date. Expected earnings are the difference between the spot price paid and the expected future price. Accordingly, SCs are in a way like discount (zero coupons) bonds, but since the earnings are absolutely variable, they are in another way like common stock. Fourth, due to their nature as described above, SCs may be useful mostly as short-term tools for the conduct of monetary policy. In general, however, the fiscal and monetary uses of SCs depend on the elasticity of demand and market structure of the commodity in question. Needless to say, that the use of SCs in monetary policy is contingent upon the development of a reasonably effective domestic market of financial instruments.

Leasing certificates can be used not only to finance governments' and companies' expenditures but also by central banks to influence the money supply via open-market operations. One may ask what the impact is of the issuance of SCs and LCs on the market interest rate and the price level. It may be argued that if the private sector is not buying bonds or paying taxes, it will be buying future contracts. Thus the budget constraint is equally affected. In other words, whatever the instruments issued by the government, they represent a demand for loanable funds in the face of a constant supply of funds in the short run. Nevertheless we can explain why the proposed instruments could have a different effect on the interest rate and the price level. Interest, whether it is explicit (as in bonds) or implicit (as in SCs and LCs) increases the cost of production and the minimum required rate of return (the hurdle rate). The major difference between conventional debt and our proposed instruments is that under the former, the risk of change in price is transferred to the producer–borrower, while under the latter the risk of change in prices is transferred to the buyer–lender. Furthermore, the economic process under conventional debt can be represented by the following flow diagram.

Finance (cash received by the borrower) → production → sale → fixed and guaranteed cash repayment

The financier may be, and mostly is, a different entity from the buyer, and cash has to be generated to complete the cycle. Under our instruments—this is especially clear under SCs—the buyer and the financier are one and the same entity. Sales are generated at the same point in time of finance. Under LCs the economic responsibility of investors for sales is generated at the same point in time of finance. We have to remember that LCs are akin to common stocks. The economic process under salam and LCs (and any other instruments like them) can be stated as follows:

Finance and sales (or responsibility for sales) → production →
fixed in-kind repayment in case of Salam
(or variable nonguaranteed cash payment in case of LCs)

The coupling of finance and selling in one entity and at one point in time in our instruments reduces transaction costs in terms of search for information and negotiation and thus improves welfare.

There may be a moral hazard problem associated with leasing certificates—those in charge of the leasing assets may not do their best to maximize the present value of future lease payments. One way to go about it is for some of the major investors to sit on the board of directors, involved in day-to-day management. We should remember that the securitization of LCs provides a way for people to get in and out of an investment. Should the rate of return go well below the expected rate, and as people sell their certificates, there will be reputational pressures on the management to improve its performance. One can always relate the payment and raises of management to some minimum standard of performance. Still another method is to stipulate that managers should have the last access to lease payments should the return go below some minimum level. The bonding mechanisms that can be designed are a function of what the law allows and what it does not.

It should be remembered that under conventional finance, the fixity of financial debt and the risk of foreclosure make the hurdle rate required by producers even higher. (Sovereign states risk the foreclosure of their foreign assets and deprivation from further borrowing should they borrow abroad [Myers 1992]). Hedging to the producers and the removal of financial fixity should reduce the hurdle rate. If we believe in the neoclassical theory of the interest rate (Ricardo, *The Principles of Political Economy*, 1817), it is the profit rate that determines the interest rate in the long run, not the rate of growth of money supply. Since salam implies the acceptance of a lower rate of return by producers, it should be expected that pervasive salam-like contracts that are used for a long period of time should lead to a lower discount (interest) rate. The reduction in hurdle and interest rates should lead to a lower price level.

Reverting to Hicks, a salam contract may lead to a lower general price level not only because hedging via salam results in a lower price (relative to a spot price), but also because salam provides a coordination mechanism of finance, purchase of inputs, production, and sales that is absent in the interest-based finance. Moreover, the conversion of a cash commitment into an in-kind obligation softens the pressure on the producer's cash flow. These factors together provide for greater stability in economic activity and contribute to a lower general price level.

The effect of salam and salam-like contracts will be felt even more when the budget deficit tends to grow. Under conventional debt, the growth of deficit calls for more debt, more taxes, or both. Salam and salam-like contracts reduce the urgency for further borrowing or taxes in subsequent periods, in that previous obligations have been, or will be, paid for in kind; no more cash from taxes or borrowing will be needed to pay for them. This is how the pressure on the cash flow of government and the private sector is reduced. This should place less pressure on interest rates to go up. Furthermore, the reduction in the government's financial obligations improves the credit rating of the country and thus should lower the interest rate it would be charged should it borrow internationally. Imagine what would have happened to interest rates and investment in a country like the United States had the American Government not had to pay the equivalent of 3.1 percent of U.S. GDP in interest on government borrowing in 1990, or the projected 3.2 percent of GDP in 1997. When we consider the cost of rolling over a debt, salam could be a cheaper way of finance. The same argument is applicable for leasing certificates; non-revenue-generating projects are helped indirectly by the proposed instruments, since the government's revenue from the sale of these certificates releases funds for other projects.

Of course, one could argue that the U.S. Government spends far more than salam and leasing certificates could raise. The point is that salam-like contracts may help to reduce financial debt. The elimination of the deficit requires far more economic reform than just these two instruments, especially the tax system and the Social Security system. Such instruments are more helpful if politicians are willing to reduce or hold constant government spending. The state of Texas owns petroleum resources on state-owned lands; thus Texas might even be a more natural user of salam-like contracts than the federal government.

LCs can be used in any country, rich or poor, by government or business. Only governments that control the major part of production can use SCs of goods and commodities. The private sector can definitely use them too. However, SCs can be issued by any government, developed or developing, to finance public projects, such as public utilities, unless the production in such areas is delegated to the private sector. People receive a service, such as some number of kilowatt-hours of electricity, instead of cash payments.

The expected government income stabilization using the Salam contract may be compared to some historical experience. We may ask, how does a combination of traditional debt financing plus a price-stabilization fund compare to a forward contract? Since governments of industrial countries are not in direct control of major economic assets, they are not expected to issue forward contracts, so industrial countries are not covered by the question. When it comes to developing countries, Dunn and Ingram (1996, 222–224) explain that international commodity-price-stabilization programs assume that the industrial importing countries are willing to provide initial finance and that "a normal" target price can be agreed upon. They explain however, that "such programs have a very poor track record. . . . Target prices have been . . . always too high. The fund . . . soon runs out of money. . . . If quotas are agreed upon, countries frequently cheat. . . . A recent World Bank study concluded that only five major programs have been set up in recent decades and that four of these had ceased operating, leaving only the rubber program as of 1993. The four that failed covered the markets for coffee, cocoa, tin and sugar." In other words, since price-stabilization programs have been deemed a failure, they have not helped governments' budget deficits. Our proposed forward contracts stabilize prices, generate sales, provide finance, and convert a financial debt into an in-kind debt, and thus soften the pressure on the government cash flows.

It may be worth reemphasizing the significance of SCs and LCs. A bondholder is always assured (at least by the intent of the contract, but not in the case of bankruptcy and liquidation) of a total nominal sum that is higher than the par value. The government has a specific, predetermined obligation toward the bondholder, who has a claim against the government's treasury at large.[9] The payment of debt will have to come either from tax proceeds or from further issuance of debt (assuming no moneytization of the outstanding debt). What the government cannot generate from one sector must be supported by other sectors or ways and means.

When it comes to salam and leasing certificates, the holder accepts the possibility that he may wind up getting a total nominal sum that is less than the par value of the instrument. There is no specific, predetermined income from the government. There is more risk acceptance on the part of the investor and hence more relief for the treasury. The essential feature of SCs and LCs is that the government's obligation toward the investor is not different from what the market in the real sector pays on the due date of payment. Because the investor's income is not guaranteed and because it is geared to a specific commodity or project, salam and leasing instruments are self-financing, and there is no need for further taxes or debt to finance their payment. The instrument holder has an uncertain, confined claim against the treasury.

SUMMARY

Budget deficits of many governments and the wave of the latest corporate scandals that started with Enron's bankruptcy highlight the difficulties associated with the existing ways and means of financing public and private expenditures, and call for the search for new instruments. Salam certificates are instruments issued against the future delivery of a particular commodity or product.

A major factor that may contribute to the superiority of Salam as a financial instrument to the conventional debt and futures contracts is that salam combines genuine financing of production along with marketing and sales. Because salam is riskier to investors than conventional futures, goods sold on a salam basis command a lower price and a higher rate of return. The only case where the two contracts are of equal value is when the risk-free rate of return in the market is zero (see appendix 6.2).

Leasing certificates represent another financing tool. The issuer guarantees no interest or principal whatsoever. At one extreme, a single-payment LC is in a way similar to a pure discount bond. At the other extreme, a perpetual LC is in a way like common stock. An LC price converges to the expected value of the last coupon payment, while that of a regular bond converges to the par value of the bond. The time path of an annuity bond is a mirror image of that of an LC, converging to the annuity value (see appendixes). The price risk and the revenue reinvestment risk in LCs (as in stocks) tend to reinforce each other. Since the return from LCs is absolutely variable while not entitling the investor any claims against physical assets, LCs may be more risky than both stocks and bonds.

The price of an LC increases with the length of time to maturity and hence cannot be assumed to be constant. Consequently, the term-structures problem of LCs, if any, involves three variables: yield, maturity, and price. The term structure problem in bonds involves only the first two (holding other things, including price, constant). The calculation of duration of a LC is another difficulty with LCs, for the coupon payments are variable.

Why should these instruments be desirable by investors? Stated very briefly, hedging and the near annuity-bond feature, on the one hand, and liquidity via securitization, on the other, should make these instruments attractive for both real and financial investors. Also, the new instruments expand the choice set to investors in terms of risk and return preferences.

SCs and LCs will help to lower the interest rate through two channels. First, they reduce the need to borrow in the future to pay back previous debts. Second, a lower rate of return to producers because of hedging should lead to a lower interest rate. Ricardo (1817) argued that the interest rate in the long run is regulated by the profit rate. A lower interest rate should lower hurdle rates and thus the price level.

Once again, salam and leasing certificates are financing instruments that replace financial debt with an "in kind" debt, one that is more geared to the productivity of the real sector. The essential feature of a SC and a LC is that the government's obligation toward the investor is not different from what the market in the real sector pays on the due date of payment. Because the investor's income is not guaranteed and because it is geared to a specific commodity or project, salam and leasing instruments appear to be self-financing and not to require further taxes or debt to finance their payment. The instrument holder has an uncertain, confined claim against the treasury.

One may ask why these instruments have not existed before. Salam (forward) and leasing contracts existed in many places around the world, but only in the private sector. They have never been securitized, however, anywhere either for the use of the private sector or for the government. In Western economies, the fact that governments have much less direct control over real assets of the economy may explain the resort of governments to debt finance. In third world economies, where government's control over economic assets is much larger, weak financial systems may have prevented the evolution of new instruments. Myers (1992) explains that sovereign risk is the most important problem in the securitization of any form of government-issued instruments. This may lead to high-risk premiums, which adds another barrier. Myers then asks a very important question: "Would commodity-linked securities help developing countries overcome the restrictions on lending arising from sovereign risk?" He answers that the default problem will always exist: "What changes however, is the probability of default. Because commodity-linked securities provide a hedge against movements of commodity prices, debt service is positively correlated with the ability to pay." We have to remember, however, that Myers's proposed instruments are financial debt instruments. It has already been discussed in this chapter how the proposed instruments may provide the same benefits of those of Myers's while at the same time avoiding the problems of financial debt.

Salam in commodities can be issued mainly in countries where governments control major natural resources, commodities, or products. Leasing certificates can be issued in almost any country to finance public services. But both instruments may be used for the purpose of conducting monetary policy anywhere in the world. It should not be difficult, however, to design salam certificates to finance public utilities. The economics of salam in utilities, however, is not exactly the same as that in commodities and products. It deserves treatment in a separate paper.

APPENDIX 6.1: SOME ELEMENTS OF THE JURISPRUDENCE OF THE SALAM CONTRACT

1. Definition: Salam is the exchange of a price (capital of salam) paid on the spot for a good to be delivered in the future.
2. Salam is a sale and the general conditions of selling are applicable to it. The object (good) of a sale is a debt.
3. Collateral and guarantees are permissible.
4. The general conditions of salam are
   a. The object of exchange (the good) must be clearly describable in terms of weight, size, volume, color, quality, grade, and the like in a way that avoids disputes in the future.
   b. The object has to be delivered in a specific date in the future (see m, below).
   c. The place of delivery must be known.
   d. The price must be specified and paid in full in advance.
   e. Foods cannot be exchanged for each other in salam or money.
   f. The capital (price) of salam is money, but it could be a service.
   g. Capital cannot be paid in installments.
   h. Debt of the buyer against the seller cannot be used as a capital of salam.
   i. Debt of the buyer against a third party cannot be used as a capital of salam.

j. After capital is received by the seller, it can be redeposited by the buyer.

k. The price of salam cannot be made conditional upon a market price in the future.

l. The time to maturity should be long enough that prices may change.

m. Installments in delivery of a good are permissible.

n. Salam cannot be in a particular existing unit of a good or asset.

o. The object of salam can be an agricultural, industrial, or natural good or a service.

p. Salam has to be in goods that customarily exist in markets.

q. The seller of salam does not have to be an owner or a producer of the good.

r. The salam contract is conclusive and final. It cannot be optional.

s. Salam can be abrogated with the consent of both parties.

t. The seller of salam can rebuy his contract before maturity for the same price he received or less, but never for more.

u. Salam can be delivered before the date of maturity if it does not cause the buyer inconvenience (Omar 1992).

APPENDIX 6.2: THEORETICAL ANALYSIS OF SALAMS

The Rate of Return on a Salam Contract

Bodie and Rosansky (1980) analyzed the performance of conventional commodity futures over the period from 1950 through 1976. They found that commodity futures are quite similar to common stocks in terms of risk and return. While it seemed that the two types of investment were equally attractive, a combination of the two would perform better. The lack of data about salam contracts precludes empirical comparison. A theoretical comparison may be possible, however. It may be argued that on the demand side, commodity-linked instruments such as salam are relatively illiquid in comparison to financial securities. As a result, there could be a cost premium that could drive up the required rate of return. However, the above-mentioned research of Bodie and Rosansky shows that such illiquidity problems may not actually arise, especially in well-organized markets.

For a conventional futures contract, we usually assume that a speculator in a long position in futures invests the price of the futures, P^f, in a riskless security first, until the investment in the futures is closed at time T, when settlement of futures is due. Income from the riskless asset is $(1 + r_f) P^f$. The actual holding period rate of return is

$$1 + r_a = 1 + r_f + \frac{[P^T_s - P_f]}{P^f} \qquad (A6.2\text{-}1)$$

where P^T_s is the commodity's spot price at time T, r_f is the riskless rate of return, and r_a is the actual rate of return.

The actual rate of return can be split into two components, simply because investment is composed of two steps.

By contrast, such a breakdown in the case of salam is not possible, simply because salam is a one-step investment—a full payment today for delivery in the future. Investment by the buyer in a riskless asset prior to the delivery date is not possible. The relationship between the salam spot price paid today, P^0_s, and the spot price at time T is

$$P^T_s = P^0_s (1 + r_a), \qquad (A6.2\text{-}2)$$

where $P^T_s \gtreqless P^0_s$.

The distinguishing case of salam is when $P^T_s = P^0_s$. We are tempted to conclude that $r_a = 0$—that is, when the investor breaks even (in an accounting sense), his rate of return is zero. But in an economic sense his *loss* is equal to r_f. By contrast, in the conventional futures contract, if the expected spot price equals the futures price, the investor will expect to earn only the riskless rate (in an accounting sense). Furthermore, the attainment of $r_a = r_f$ under a salam contract may take place only by mere coincidence. We may conclude that the opportunity cost of investing in a salam contract is higher and thus should command a higher rate of return than a conventional futures contract. The attainment of a higher rate is contingent upon a lower equilibrium price.

One may note here that on the demand side there are two risks associated with salam. First, there is the risk of default on the part of the seller. But such risk exists with any commodity-linked instrument; it is not specific to salam. (See earlier parts of the chapter for more detail on this point.) Second, there is the risk that the price at period T is less than the prepaid salam price at period zero. But we have to remember that the buyer hedges against the up side of the market (See earlier parts of the chapter for more detail on this point.)

A Digression: The Inclusion of Carrying Costs

The analysis to this point assumes zero carrying costs for both futures and salam contracts. Herbst, Kare, and Marshall (1993) have shown that for a direct hedger, the relationship between the future and spot prices is affected by the carrying costs and the time to maturity of the futures contract. This in turn affects the minimum risk-hedge ratio (the ratio of futures to spot position).

Carrying costs can be included in the rate of return of futures and salam contracts. We want to keep the assumption of an investor in a long position. The following observations can be made.

First, salam involves no cash settlement. Actual physical delivery is a must. This has the important consequence that if the buyer is a mere speculator, the contract in his hand becomes like a hot potato that he must get rid of before maturity. Time is less crucial in this respect for active (actual) users of the product. For a mere speculator the saving in inventory-carrying cost is zero.

Second, salam has to be in things that usually exist in markets but are not in the possession of the seller at the time of contracting. The buyer either cannot find the product in the market at the time of contracting or it is inconvenient for him to buy it at that time. This implies that in one case the buyer's saving in inventory-carrying cost is zero; in another it is positive. Third, for both speculators and active users of goods, the contract carrying cost may include the opportunity of forgone profits from other ventures. But for the active buyer, if the forward price is less than the spot price at the maturity of the contract, he may be compensated for that loss. However, if at the time of maturity the spot price turns out to be less than the forward price paid, he loses that much.

A futures contract for the buyer implies a saving in inventory carrying cost if the buyer is an actual user of the commodity; otherwise his inventory carrying cost is zero. The term r_a in both of equations (A6.2-1) and (A6.2-2) above can be thought of as the net rate of return.[10] The carrying cost in salam for an active user is

$$P^0_s(r_f - n),$$

where n is the storage cost rate as a fraction of the spot price paid in salam. The net actual rate of return is

$$\frac{p^T_s - P^0_s}{P^0_s} + n - r_f = r^s_a.$$

If $P^T_s = P^0_s$ in equation (A6.2-2) above, the salam holder may be profiting or losing depending on whether n > or < rf. In case of the futures contract, the actual net rate of return to the actual user is

$$\frac{p^T_s - P^f}{P^f} + n - r_f = r^s_a.$$

The general formula for a minimum risk hedge ratio is not different from that developed by Herbst et al. (1993).

What Price Should a Buyer of Salam Be Willing to Pay?

If an investor is offered the choice of paying for and receiving an asset immediately, on the one hand, or paying on the spot but receiving the asset in the future (i.e., buying a salam contract), he will take the latter only if he expects to make a rate of return equal at the minimum to the riskless rate, such that

$$P^0_s = \frac{P_0}{(1 + r_f)^T}, \tag{A6.2-3}$$

where P_o is the current price paid in a spot-payment/spot-delivery transaction, assuming zero carrying and storage costs, and $P^o{}_s$ is the salam price. Relation (A6.2-3) can be called the current salam spot prices parity relationship. Also, if the spot transactor holds his asset until period T and requires (expects) a rate of return K, he should not pay a price more than

$$P_o = \frac{E(P_T)}{(1 + K)^T} \qquad (A6.2\text{-}4)$$

where $E(P_T)$ is the expected spot price at period T, and $K \geq r_f$, is the required rate of return.

But if he is going to buy on salam basis and requires a rate of return L, the price he pays should not be more than

$$P^o{}_s = \frac{E(P_T)}{(1 + L)^T} \qquad (A6.2\text{-}5)$$

Since the opportunity cost of buying salam is higher than buying on spot, L must be greater than K. From (A6.2-3) and (A6.2-4), we get

$$P_o = P^o{}_s \ (1 + r_f)^T = \frac{E(P_T)}{(1 + K)^T}$$

$$\qquad (A6.2\text{-}6)$$

$$P^o{}_s = P^o{}_s \ = \frac{E(P_T)}{(1 + r_f)^T \ (1 + K)^T}$$

Equation (A6.2-6) gives us an expression of the price the buyer of a salam contract should be willing to pay. It implies that when the spot required rate of return is K, the expected spot price in the future, E (PT), in the salam contract, should be discounted by a factor greater than $(1 + K)$. By contrast, assuming the required rate of return in a conventional futures contract is also K, the futures price is

$$F_O = E(P_T)\left[\frac{1 + r_F}{1 + K}\right]^T \quad \text{(Bodie et al. 1989, p.650)} (A6.2\text{-}7)$$

In equation (A6.2-7), $E(P_T)$ is discounted by a factor smaller than $(1 + K)$. Obviously, this says that F_O (equation [A6.2-7]) should always be greater than $P^o{}_s$ (equation [A6.2-6])—the price of a conventional futures contract is always greater than the price of a Salam contract. The differences between the two prices (and rates of return) are natural results of differences in opportunity cost. If we substitute for $P^o{}_s$ from equation (A6.2-5) into equation (A6.2-6), we get

$$(1 + L) = (1 + r_f) (1 + K) \qquad\qquad (A6.2\text{-}8)$$

Equation (A6.2-8) implies that the buyer should require a rate of return on salam, L, that is equal to the required rate of return on the conventional futures, compounded by the riskless rate of return. In order for the two prices to be equal,

$$F_O = E(P_T) \; = \frac{(1 + r_f)}{(1 + K)} = \frac{E(P_T)}{(1 + r_f)(1 + K)}$$

Rearranging, we get $(1 + r_f)^2 = 1$, which implies that $r_f = 0$. In other words, for the prices of the futures and salam contracts to be equal, the riskless rate of return must be zero, and the two contracts must be of equal opportunity cost. The example below may help to explain further the contrasts and comparisons between the two contracts.

A Comparison of a Futures and a Salam Contracts for a Seller

The following examples should give us an idea about the rate of return to the sellers of futures and salam contracts. The two examples are not related. They merely show the mechanism of return from two contracts.

Basic Information

Spot price of oil/barrel (for immediate delivery) is $18.00.

Spot price of oil/barrel (for immediate payment but delivery in one year) is $17.00.

Futures price (for delivery in one year and payment in one year) is $18.50. Seller sells oil he owns at t = 0 and simultaneously buys a futures contract.

Interest rate is 10%.

Transaction cost is 3%.[11]

Futures	Salam
At t = 0, sell 5,000 barrels paying 3%. Transaction cost @ $18.00	At t = 0, sell 5,000 barrels for future delivery @ $17.00 and receive proceeds on spot
Receive (5000 × $18 × .97) = $87,300	5000 × $17.00 = $85,000
Invest proceeds @ 10%	Use proceeds to expand refinery
Buy 5,000 barrels for delivery in one year (futures contract) @ $18.50	Saving in interest payments @ 10% per year = $8,500
At t = 1 collect invested proceeds 5,000 × $18X.97 × 1.1 = $96,030	At t = 1, deliver 5,000 barrels (no proceeds from buyer)
Accept delivery of oil and pay 5,000 × $18.50 = $92,500	Actual revenue from salam sale = 5,000 × $17.00 × 1.1 = $93,500

Net proceeds = $96,030 - $92,500
    = $3,530.

or $85,000 + $8,500 = $93,500

Value of contract on t = 1 @ $18.50
(spot price in 1 year) = 5,000 × $18.50
= 92,500

Net gain = $93,500 − $92,500 = $1000
to seller.

The difference in net gain between the two contracts should not give the impression that a futures contract is a better strategy. Numbers can be manipulated quite easily to make salam more profitable. More important, the futures contract does not by itself finance real production, and gains in futures can be driven down to zero in efficient financial markets. When it comes to salam, even though the seller in this particular example may have sacrificed ($18.50 − $17.00 = $1.50, or 8.1%), he has guaranteed sales, reduced his risk against the down side of the market, increased his net worth, and reduced his debt/ asset ratio, which should reduce his risk further, as well as the cost of financing in the future.

For the buyer, as long as his opportunity cost is less than his explicit expected rate of return from salam ($1.50/$17.00 = 8.82% in the above example), he should be willing to go for it. But even if his explicit rate of return is less than the market interest rate (8.82% < 10%), the implicit benefit to the buyer is to hedge against the upper side of the market, guaranteeing supplies and making the task of planning his production and marketing easier if he is to keep the contract to maturity.

It may seem from the salam example that there is a positive relationship between the seller's net gain, today's spot price, and the interest rate, but a negative relationship between his net gain and the spot price in the future. The opposite is true for the buyer of salam.

But the seemingly positive impact of a higher interest rate on the seller's net gain should not mean that the seller would welcome a rise in interest rates. On the contrary, a higher interest rate may force the seller to accept a lower spot price, in order for salam to offer a better substitute to investors. At the same time, higher interest rates increase the opportunity cost to the buyer of salam and thus may entice him to offer a lower spot price and/or build a strategy around a higher expected spot price in the future. Whenever that is not possible, the process of exchange between buyers and sellers becomes more difficult.

Imagine a situation under which interest-based financing is not available, for whatever reason. The immediate result of such a situation is the removal of the urgency for the seller (buyer) of salam to accept (offer) a lower spot price. The spread between the expected sacrificed return by the seller and expected rate of return by the buyer is reduced. In addition, the pure forces of supply and demand in the real sector are much in line with the rate determining the rate of return to both parties.

Salam Certificates with Options

Myers (1992) argues that high-risk premiums and weak awareness about the usefulness of commodity-based instruments are major reasons behind the limited trade in such instruments. An important forward step would be to explain to governments and businesses the attractive features of such instruments relative to the ramifications of conventional debt. A second step is the issuance of small denominations of instruments that make them accessible to laymen. A variety of instrument designs should make them attractive for both the issuers and the investors. In case of delinquency in delivering (and in contrast to financial debt), the value of the in-kind salam debt is not compounded over time. Consequently, if SCs are to be sold at some discount rate to attract investors, the issuing agency may still want to do that even if the discount rate is higher than the interest rate on a conventional loan. The equilibrium point between the two methods of finance will be where the discount rate on a SC is equal to interest rate plus the expected cost of rolling over the financial debt. Needless to say, the cost of rolling over a debt, rod in equation (A2.2-9), in terms of increasing the number or amount of payments, will raise the effective interest rate. The issuing agency can afford a discount rate L such that

$$(1 + L)^T \le (1 + r_f)^T (1 + rod)^T \qquad\qquad (A2.2\text{-}9)$$

To put it differently, considering the cost of delinquency and assuming the two debts are of equal maturities, salam is expected to be cheaper to the issuer than conventional debt. To see this, we have from equation (A2.2-6):

$$(1 + L)^T = (1 + r_f)^T (1 + k)^T \le (1 + r_f)^T (1 + rod)^T$$
$$(1 + k)^T \le (1 + rod)^T$$

This implies that $K \le rod$, which means that the cost of rolling over a debt could also exceed the required rate of return by the investor in a conventional futures contract.

Another feature of SCs that should increase their marketability is to include the option of inflicting a penalty on the issuer in case of delinquency—either the stated price is reduced or the quantity to be delivered increased. Both would imply a reduction in the effective per-unit price. Such a penalty should increase the value of an SC, which at the same time implies a reduction in the risk premium required by investors and makes an SC more liquid. Needless to say, it is up to the instrument holder to exercise the penalty option.

It may be argued that the penalty option is in the nature of rolling over the in-kind debt in-kind terms. This is true despite the benefits explained above of such a penalty. But it is also true that in many cases a country's (or a firm's) delinquency on payment does not necessarily stem from the inability to produce; more often it stems from the inability to sell. Furthermore, even if an in-kind penalty has to be inflicted, there is a reduction in transaction costs by eliminating the need to search for a buyer of the commodity first, securing cash receipts from sales, and then paying for the debt. Moreover, creditors are paid in kind at whatever price the market may fetch.

It may be useful to analyze the value of a salam contract. Rubinstein (1987) explains that the present value (pay-off function) of a forward contract is

$$V(C^*) = V(S^* - F) = V(S^*) - V(F), \qquad (A2.2-10)$$

where S^* is the price of the underlying asset (a stock for example) on the delivery date, and F is the previously agreed-upon forward price to be paid, for certain, on the same delivery date.

Assuming that r is one plus a riskless discount rate and t is the period to maturity,

$$V(C^*) = V(S^*) - Fr^{-t} \qquad (A2.2-11)$$

When it comes to the salam contract, since the price of the underlying asset (commodity) is paid on the spot, the present value of the Salam forward contract is

$$V(Csc) = S^*_{sc} r^{-t} - P^o_s \qquad (A2.2-12)$$

where P^o_s is the salam spot price, and S^*_{sc} is the expected price of the commodity on the delivery date.

A salam contract can be designed so that it carries a "call option" by allowing the buyer to buy on the maturity date an additional amount at the same unit price of the underlying contract. It should be emphasized that the exercise of the option is contingent upon the commitment to honor the original contract. In other words, the option is not to be bought and sold separately in the market. The present value of the SC becomes

$$V(C^{CO}_{SC}) = S^*_{sc} r^{-t} - (P^o_s + m) + V \{max[O, S^*_{sc} - K_{sc}]\} \quad (A2.2-13)$$

where $V(C^{CO}_{SC})$ is the value of a salam contract with a call option, m is the premium paid for the option, and K_{sc} is the striking price and $K_{sc} \leq P^o_s$.

Since a salam with a call option is more valuable than a salam without one, it commands a price, $P^o_s + m$, higher than the price of a simple Salam, P^o_s. The last term on the right hand side represents the value of the option. Alternatively, equation (A2.2-13) can be rewritten as

$$V(C^{CO}_{SC}) - S^*_{sc} r^{-t} - (P^o_s + m) + V \{max[O, S^*_{sc} - \delta P^o_s]\} \quad (A2.2-14)$$

where $\delta \leq 1$, $K_{sc} = \delta P^o_s$.

Equation (A2.2-14) implies that the smaller the d, the larger the difference between the spot and strike prices; the larger the difference between the expiration price, S^*_{sc}, and the strike price, K_{sc}, the larger the value of the option, and thus the larger the value of the SC. This is a composite contract, which combines forward and option contracts. Rubinstein (1987) explains that in order for an underlying asset to replicate the payoff function of a derivative asset, the required strategy for a forward contract is one of buy-and-hold, while for an option the strategy is a dynamic one that requires investors to change their portfolio at each moment in time. But in our case when we consider the composite contract as a package deal, a buy-and-hold strategy will be the dominating one. Otherwise a dynamic strategy may turn the spot price itself into a stochastic parameter. This implies that while an option may increase the average rate of return from buying an SC, it may also increase its variance too.

Figure 6.1 shows the profits and losses from holding (selling) a pure salam contract (represented by the solid lines) and from holding (selling) a salam-plus-call (put) option contracts (represented by the broken lines). It is assumed that the salam price, P^o_s, equals the strike price, K^s_c. When the contract price, P^o_s (which is fixed) is less than the price of commodity on the delivery date (which may be variable), a buyer of salam makes a gain and the value of the buyer's position becomes positive. The opposite is true if the ranking of prices is reversed; the position of the seller is a mirror image of the buyer's. An option on salam provides a chance for greater gains and greater losses.

Since a salam certificate actually represents a form of a commodity-linked instrument, it is useful to analytically compare and contrast SCs with other commodity-linked instruments (CLI). Three instruments are analyzed in appendix 6.3.

Figure 6.1
Profits and Losses from Holding (Selling) Salam a

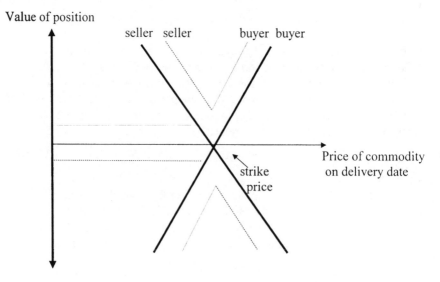

APPENDIX 6.3: THEORETICAL ANALYSIS
OF LEASE CERTIFICATES

The Economics of Leasing Certificates

At one extreme, a single-payment LC is in a way similar to a pure discount bond, with the difference that the par value of a pure discount bond is contractually guaranteed, while in the case of a LC no guarantee whatsoever is made. At the other extreme, a perpetual LC is in a way like a common stock; there is no maturity date, stated rate of return, or guarantee of a par value. The difference between stocks and LCs in general is that a common stock entitles the holder to a permanent right of ownership in the real assets of the firm and any capital gains therefrom, in addition to rights in realized income. A nonperpetual LC holder has the last type of rights, and only for a fixed period of time to maturity, plus any possible capital gains from holding the certificate.

Because holders of certificates share equally in whatever variable revenues are realized in any period, the longer the maturity of a certificate, the larger the number of its coupons, and the higher the price it should command (assuming the same expected rate of return and degree of risk). The closest proxy in this case is the amortized (constant annuity) bond that can be represented by the following formula:

$$P = C\left[\frac{1 - (1 + i)^{-n}}{i}\right]$$

where   P = the price of the amortized bond
C = the constant coupon annuity
i = the discount rate
n = the number of periods.
Differentiating[12] P with respect to n (holding C and i constant), we get

$$\frac{\partial P}{\partial n} = \frac{-C}{i}\left[\frac{-\log(1 + i)}{(1 + i)^n}\right]^2 > 0$$

This should make sense, because if an investor has a choice between two annuity bonds of the same coupon payments and rates of return and risk, he should be willing to pay a higher price for the longer-maturity bond, which entitles him to more coupon payments, assuming rates are not expected to rise. The difference, between leasing certificates and annuity bonds is that in the case of LCs the "coupon payments" are variable and not contractually guaranteed, while in the case of bonds they are constant and guaranteed.

The time path of a LC price can be compared to that of a regular bond (i.e., one that pays interest over a number of periods with the principal paid at maturity). Figure 6.2 illustrates the case of bonds. Assume that the par value of a

Figure 6.2
**Time Path of the Value of a 10 Percent Coupon, $1,000 Par Value Bond When
Interest Rates Are 5 Percent, 10 Percent, and 15 Percent**

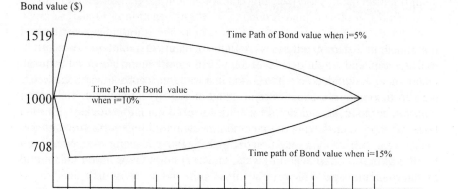

bond is $1,000 and the interest rate is 10 percent. If the interest rate does not
change, the price of the bond shall remain at par until the date of maturity. If
the interest rate falls (or rises) to 5 percent (or 15%) and remains constant at
that level, the bond's price will rise (fall) initially and then decline (rise) over
time. Whatever happens to interest rates, the bond's price will converge with
its par value as it comes closer to the maturity date.

Compare the above to the time path of a LC price. If the initial price of a LC
is P_o, and if the actual and expected rates of return are equal to each other
throughout the lifetime of the certificate, its price will decline steadily until it
reaches the expected revenue in the last period. If, however, the actual rate of
return, i_a, overshoots (undershoots) the expected rate, i_e, the certificate's value
will overshoot (undershoot) the constant-rate price line. Whatever happens to
the actual rate of return, the value of the certificate will converge with the
expected value of revenue in the last period as it nears the maturity date. Figure 6.3 illustrates this case.

The time path of a LC price can be represented by the following equation:

$$P_t = \alpha - \beta t \pm \gamma \ [E\ (Ct) - \beta],$$

where α is the IPO (initial public offering) price, which is assumed to represent the PV of all expected future payments; t is the number of expired periods
and already-paid coupons; β is the equivalent of a risk-free coupon payment
per period; $E(C_t)$ is the expected coupon payment in period t; and γ (>0) is the
adjustment coefficient.

Figure 6.3
Time Path of the Value of an LC (When $i_a \gtreqless i_e$)

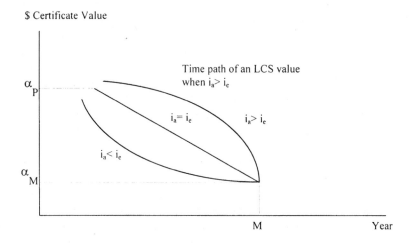

$ Certificate Value

Time path of an LCS value
when $i_a > i_e$

$i_a = i_e$

$i_a > i_e$

$i_a < i_e$

α_P

α_M

M   Year

In case E (Ct) = β, the time path is represented by a downward-sloping straight line. Otherwise, the time path of the LC prices either overshoots (in case of excess demand) or undershoots (in case of excess supply). In a more complicated situation, β does not have to be a constant—it could be itself a function.

Since the coupon payments from an LC are variable, we can assume that the intrinsic value, V_o, (or the IPO value), of an LC has the same general form as a common stock, such that

$$VO = \frac{E(C_1)}{1+i} + \frac{E(C)}{(1+i)^2} + \frac{E(C_3)}{(1+i)^3} + \dots$$

$$= \sum_{t=1}^{n} \frac{E(C_t)}{(1+i)^t}$$

where *i* is the market capitalization rate.

An LC resembles a common stock in the sense of a direct relationship between price and earnings. The picture in the case of an amortized (annuity) bond will be a mirror image of that in figure 6.3, simply because of the inverse relationship between the interest rate and the bond's price. The case is illustrated in figure 6.4. No matter what happens to the interest rate, the value of an annuity bond will converge with the value of the annuity as it nears the maturity date.[13]

Figure 6.4
Time Path of the Value of an Annuity Bond (When $i_a \gtreqless i_e$)

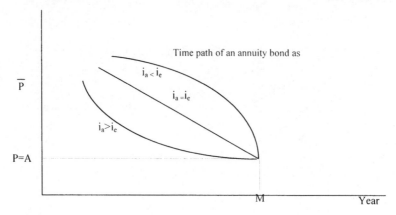

$ Annuity Bond Value

NOTES

The author is thankful to Anthony Herbst, Said Elfakhani, Stephen Figlewski, Jawad Fazal Seyyed, and anonymous referees for useful comments and suggestions. They are absolved from any mistakes that may be found in the paper. Financial support from KFUPM is gratefully appreciated.

1. Less resource-rich countries may have less chance in using these instruments. Other instruments may have to be developed to meet their needs.

2. LCs may be compared and contrasted with *primes* and *scores*. Jarrow and O'Hara (1989) explain that these are financial derivatives of some underlying common stocks, brought about via the creation of a trust by a private firm. They explain that "the prime component receives all dividend payments and any increase in the stock price up to a termination value. The score receives any appreciation above the termination value. The termination price is set at the beginning of the trust and has generally been at a 20–25 percent premium to the current stock price. A trust may not accept further shares once the stock price exceeds the termination value." In contrast to primes and scores, the issuing agency of LCs relinquishes some (or all) of its proceeds from its own equity for some period of time. In other words, proceeds are *stripped* from the physical productive assets. Accordingly, an LC holder is not entitled to any capital gains in the value of the projects' assets, but he is entitled to any capital gains in his own certificate. There is no termination price for any LC, and its rate of return is absolutely variable. Because of the way in which primes and scores are designed (in terms of the existence of termination price on primes), there are two constraints on the number of primes and scores that can be issued: the termination price itself and the number of shares of the underlying stock. The issuance of LCs is more flexible, however, since the termination-price constraint is absent.

3. A lucid discussion of the arbitrage principle is found in Varian (1987).

4. The same argument is applicable in the case of salam certificates.

5. The same argument may be applicable in the case of salam certificates.

6. Jarrow and Ohara (1989) observed that the sum of primes and scores prices exceeds the price of the underlying stock. They reasoned empirically that a score, which is a five-year option, might be economizing on the transaction costs of dynamic hedging and thus may be the source of overpricing.

7. A similar argument may be made about salam certificates.

8. This is, of course, an empirical matter, for it is known that there is an active market for zero coupon bonds. The difficulty with a long-term SC is that the price risk may be larger for longer maturities.

9. A number of authors (for example, Brayant and Wallace 1979) have argued that under the assumption of perfect substitutability between money and (consumption, for example), the payment of interest on bonds but not on money is a distortion, since money and bonds are both costless to produce. Is the same argument applicable in the case of LCs? While LCs may be costless to produce, yet income from LCs may not be distortionary, simply because the government does not guarantee neither the income from an LC nor its principle value. In other words, while interest from bonds is a purely financial income (from the mere act of finance), income from an LC is related to the actual performance of the real sector.

10. Herbst (1986) explains, however, that in a normal, carrying-charge market for a physical commodity, the futures price is higher than the spot, or cash, price today, because it reflects the costs of storage. The difference between spot price and futures price is the "basis" for the futures contract. Because of either delivery of the commodity, or cash settlement, the basis must vanish as maturity of the contract approaches. A short hedger is short the futures contract, long the cash commodity. The short hedger gains the basis, while the long hedger loses it. (Thus there is no "free lunch" to be gained by trying to use futures contracts as a substitute for inventory in order to save storage costs.)

11. This assumed commission is far higher than one would pay in practice with futures contracts. Typically it is fixed $50 per futures contract. However, if one includes all advisory or consulting fees and administrative costs, this hypothetical amount is not unreasonable. Use of a lower assumed commission would only make the net difference even larger than indicated in this example.

12. This is like $P = \dfrac{b}{a^x}$ where $b = \dfrac{-C}{I}$, $a = (1 + i)$,

and $X = n$.

13. Unlike annuity bonds and leasing certificates, the time path of salam certificates does not converge to a particular value toward maturity.

REFERENCES

Bodie, Zvi, and Rosansky. 1980. "Risk and Return in Commodity Futures." *Financial Analysts Journal* (May/June).

Bodie, Zvi, Alex Kane, and Alen J. Marcus. 1989. *Investments*. Homewood, Ill.: Irwin.

Brayant, John, and Neil Wallace. 1979. "The Inefficiency of Interest-Bearing National Debt." *Journal of Political Economy* 87 (April): 365–382.

Dunn, Robert M., Jr., and James C. Ingram. 1996. *International Economics*. 4th ed. New York: John Wiley and Sons.

Herbst, Anthony. 1986. *Commodity Futures: Markets, Methods of Analysis, and Management of Risk*. New York: John Wiley & Sons.

Herbst, Anthony, Dilip Kare, and John Marshall. 1993. "A Time Varying Convergence Adjusted Hedge Ratio Model." *Advances in Futures and Options Research* 6: 137–155.

Hicks, John R. 1939/1946. *Value and Capital*. 2nd ed. Oxford: The Clarendon Press.

Ibottson, Roger G., and Rex A. Sinquefield. 1982. *Stocks, Bonds, Bills and Inflation: The Past and the Future*. Charlottesville, Va.: Financial Analysts Research Foundation.

Jarrow, Robert A., and Maureen O'Hara. 1989. "Primes and Scores: An Essay on Market Imperfections." *Journal of Finance* 44, no. 5 (December): 1263–1287.

Leijonhufvud, Axel. 1981. "Effective Demand Failures." In *Information and Coordination*. New York: Oxford University Press, 103–129.

Myers, Robert. 1992. "Incomplete Markets and Commodity-Linked Finance in Developing Countries." *World Bank Research Observer* 7, no. 1 (January): 79–94.

Omar, Mohammed Abdulhaleem. 1992. *The Jurisprudence, Economics and Accounting Framework of the Sale of Salam*. Jeddah, Saudi Arabia: The Islamic Institute for Research Training, The Islamic Development Bank.

Ricardo, David. 1817/1960. *The Principles of Political Economy and Taxation*. London: Dent and Son.

Rubinstein, Mark. 1987. " Derivative Assets Analysis." Journal of Economic Perspectives no. 2 (Fall): 73–93.

Samuelson, Paul, and William Nordhaus. 1995. *Economics*. 15th ed. New York: McGraw-Hill.

Sapsford, Jathon, and Anita Raghavan. 2002. "Trading Charges: Lawsuit Spotlights J. P. Morgan's Ties to the Enron Debacle." *Wall Street Journal*, January 25, A1, A4.

Sharpe, William F. 1985. Investments. 3rd ed. Upper Saddle River, N.J.: Prentice Hall International.

A Special Issue on Euroland. 1999. *Newsweek* (November 1998–February 1999).

Uthman, Usamah A. 1994. "Debt and Equity Contracts in the Theory of Social Economy." *Review of Islamic Economics* 3, no. 1: 1–18.

Varian, Hal R. 1987. "The Arbitrage Principle in Financial Economics." *Journal of Economic Perspectives* 1, no. 2 (Fall): 55–72.

Williamson, Oliver. 1988. "Corporate Finance and Corporate Governance." *Journal of Finance* 43, no. 3.

7

A Modern Financial Analysis of the Titanic *Disaster: A Timeless Case Study of Excessive Risk-Taking*

Austin Murphy and Don Bloomquist

EXECUTIVE SUMMARY

This chapter applies option-pricing theory to the financial situation of the company that owned the *Titanic* at the time of its infamous sinking nearly a century ago. The investigation illustrates the potential losses to creditors, consumers, and others that can result from the incentive that firms have to attempt to enhance the value of the equity call by taking excessive risk.

The case also provides some evidence that markets nearly a century ago were fairly efficient in reflecting the implications of modern option-pricing models. In particular, this case illustrates that option-pricing theory can actually represent a practical method of valuing stocks, bonds, and other securities. For instance, equity can be valued as a call option on the value of the firm, with the strike price of the call being equal to principal value of the liabilities (and with the exercise price of the common equity being equal to the principal value of all the liabilities plus the prior liquidation claim of the preferred stock). In addition, debts themselves have embedded call options in the form of prepayment rights that can be valued and analyzed using complex option-pricing models (for which inexpensive and easy-to-use software exists).

INTRODUCTION

It has been asserted that Enron and other recent corporate disasters may have been motivated by company leaders being pressured by a short-sighted and inefficient market of investors to take actions that are excessively risky and detrimental to the long-term value of companies (Fuller and Jensen 2002).

However, to some extent at least, the behavior of corporate managers in taking risks that seem excessive from the point of view of a company's entire set of stakeholders (and of society as a whole) can be explained even in efficient markets by the basic financial theory that the owners of company essentially hold on the value of a firm a call option that is maximized by increasing risk. This fact can be illustrated by a case that predates that of Enron by nearly a century—the financial situation surrounding the infamous sinking of the *Titanic*.

The financial effects of the sinking of the *Titanic* have previously been the subject of one brief research study by Khanna (1998), who computed the loss incurred by the equity stakeholders in the company that owned the ship to be approximately $2.6 million within two days of the maritime disaster on April 15, 1912. In particular, trading on the New York Stock Exchange (NYSE) indicated that the shareholders of the International Mercantile Marine (IMM) trust that owned the *Titanic* suffered a 14.8 percent market-adjusted drop in the value of the preferred share certificates and a 25.3 percent market-adjusted fall in the price of the common within two days of the sinking. Since the *Titanic* had been built for $7.5 million but was insured for only $5.0 million, the stock market value decline was very close to the $2.5 million in direct and immediate losses suffered by IMM. Khanna (1998) concluded that the market was semistrong efficient in reflecting this loss.[1]

Unfortunately, Khanna's (1998) research ignored several important facts related to the case. In particular, he did not consider the many indirect costs associated with the sinking of the *Titanic*, which, due to reputation issues alone, would seem to indicate losses significantly in excess of the $2.5 million in out-of-pocket costs. A market that neglected such significant indirect costs would actually be inefficient. However, in this case, the market may have very well been very efficient, insofar as Khanna's (1998) failure to consider some indirect losses associated with the maritime disaster may have been offset by his neglect of other factors involved. For instance, besides ignoring some important indirect costs incurred as a result of the calamity, Khanna (1998) also ignored the change in the market value of IMM's liabilities that occurred as a result of the ship's sinking.

Using modern financial theory, this research expands the investigation of IMM to examine all the costs associated with the sinking of the *Titanic* and to evaluate their effect on the company's liabilities, as well as on the equity. It is found that the total market value decline to the company was over double the $2.6 million estimated for the equity holders alone. Using the general implications of option-pricing models, this finding is discovered to be supportive of the hypothesis that both the bond and stock markets were semi-strong efficient nearly a century ago. In addition, and most importantly, examining IMM's overall financial situation around the time of the sinking of the *Titanic*, it is deduced that the corporate risk-taking that led to the sinking of the *Titanic* can be rationally explained by option-pricing theory within the context of an efficient market.

INFORMATION AND BACKGROUND ON THE CASE

To apply modern financial analysis to the case study of IMM around the sinking of the *Titanic*, information on IMM's financial situation was obtained from *Poor's Manual of Industrials*. Stock market prices were obtained from the *Wall Street Journal*, with the midpoint between the reported closing bid and ask prices utilized to avoid the effects of changing spreads and varying closing transactions at the bid or ask. Before the sinking of the *Titanic*, IMM common stock sold at under 1/15 of its $100 par value, and IMM's cumulative preferred equity, upon which dividends had not been paid for almost a decade (since December 1, 1902), was selling at under 1/4 of its own $100 par value. This low stock market valuation reflected the operating problems of the company, which had allocated virtually all of its cash flow over the previous ten years to a subjective "depreciation fund" reserve that substituted for an actual fixed depreciation expense in those days, implying virtually no true economic profits.

Originally incorporated in the United States in 1893 as the International Navigation Company, the firm changed its name to IMM in 1902 as the famous American financier J. P. Morgan sought to consolidate much of the ocean transportation business into a U.S. holding company that could crush the remaining international competition with low prices and then proceed to fix rates at a much higher level that would permit a rise in profitability from the very competitive situation in existence at the time (Wade 1986). Morgan's plan failed, however, and IMM entered into financial trouble due to the continued robust competition from other ocean carriers, such as the British Cunard Line and "opulent German liners," which had faster ships (Wade 1986).

IMM may have also overextended itself financially with its 1902 acquisition of the Oceanic Steam Navigation Company for a price equal to ten times its earnings in a peak year related to the Boer War (Wade 1986). This latter acquired company owned the British White Star Line, the fleet of which eventually included the *Titanic*. In 1907, IMM leaders concocted a plan to have the *Titanic* (and similar ships) built for the White Star Line in an attempt to develop and profit from a reputation for extremely large, safe, and luxurious ships that rapidly crossed the Atlantic Ocean (Wade 1986). Despite the distressed financial state of IMM early in 1912, the outlook appeared to be improving prior to the initial sailing and sinking of the *Titanic*, as indicated by the company's stock prices reaching levels in early April 1912 that had not been seen since 1910.[2]

APPLYING OPTION-PRICING THEORY TO THE CASE OF THE SINKING OF THE *TITANIC*

Given the overall depressed financial situation of IMM, it is likely that a significant portion of the losses associated with the sinking of the *Titanic* was incurred by IMM's bondholders. In particular, modern financial theory indicates that equity merely represents a call option on the firm's assets (Merton 1974). The less such a call is in the money, the more any company losses are inflicted on its bondholders (Leland and Toft 1996). As a result, the fact that an equity call is less in the money provides more incentives to the equity owners to increase risks, as those risks provide large upside potential to the holders of the equity call, while the potential downside losses are largely absorbed by creditors (who have a long position on the value of the firm but are effectively short the equity call).[3]

Although the complex financial situations typically existing at most companies today may require simulations/iterations to accurately incorporate the effect of the many different options existing on the many different securities outstanding (Parrino and Weisbach 1999), the simplicity of IMM's capital structure in 1912 enables an illustrative estimation of the value of the company's securities before and after the sinking through a straightforward application of the simple option-pricing theory (Black and Scholes 1973). In particular, on April 13, 1912, IMM had $77.7 million in book value of bonds outstanding, of which most ($52.7 million of 4½22 bonds) was due on October 1, 1922. It also had additional liabilities of $14.0 million. It is reasonable to assume that the company would either need to have a value on October 1, 1922, in excess of its liabilities (in order to be able to obtain financing to pay off the bonds), or it would have to allow the creditors to seize the firm's assets. As a result, the company's equity can be valued as an option with an exercise price of $77.7 + $14.0 = $91.7 million. Employing the typical option-pricing model assumption of absolutely no transaction costs (including those associated with bankruptcy), the appraised value of the existing liabilities would equal the estimated value of the entire company less the option value of the equity calls.

Because IMM's cumulative preferred stock mandated a dividend of 6 percent per year, which it had merely accumulated since 1902, the total preferred claim in 1922 would be $61.5 million above its par value of $51.7 million, or $51.7 + $61.5 = $113.2 million. As a result, the exercise price for the residual common stock would be $91.7 + $113.2 = $204.9 million, while the preferred stock would be valued as a package consisting of a long call option with an exercise price of $91.7 million (sold by the creditors) and a short call option (sold to the common stockholders) with an exercise price of $204.9 million. On April 13, 1912, the last trading day before the catastrophic collision of the *Titanic* with an iceberg, there were 3,821 days to the assumed October 1, 1922, expiration of these options.

At the same time, the long-term interest rate on high-grade debt was then 3.89 percent, which was the yield to maturity on New York State bonds maturing in 1961. Except for some U.S. government bonds that had abnormally low yields (possibly for bank liquidity and regulatory reasons), the 3.89 percent was the lowest yield for the long-term bonds listed in the Wall Street Journal around the time of the sinking. That yield can therefore serve as the risk-free rate in the option-pricing model.

Given the lack of dividend payments on IMM's equities, the payout on the company's assets may be assumed to be equal to the interest payments on its debt, which totaled $3.9 million in 1911. The pricing model requires the latter estimate in order to value options on assets that make cash payments not available to the option holders prior the expiration date (Rubinstein 1976).

With these data, it is possible to solve jointly for the market value of the assets and the volatility that sets IMM's common and preferred equities equal to their market values of $3.1 million and $12.5 million, respectively, just prior to the sinking of the *Titanic*. Iterations using Rubinstein's (1976) dividend-adjusted option-pricing model indicates that the assets were worth $93.8 million and that the volatility of the assets was 20.5 percent. The company's preferred stock was therefore just barely in the money, while the company's common was far out of the money. Subtracting the equity market values from the estimated asset values implies that the appraised value of the company's liabilities was $93.8 − 12.5 − $3.1 = $78.2 million prior to the sinking, as summarized in table 7.1.

After the April 15, 1912, maritime disaster, it is once again possible to iterate to solve jointly for the market value of IMM's assets and volatility. Using the fact that the market value of the common and preferred equity fell to $2.4 million and $10.6 million, respectively, two days after the sinking of the *Titanic*, the option-pricing model indicates that the value of the assets declined to $88.6 million, while the volatility rose only slightly to 20.7 percent. Thus, the value of the company's assets is computed to have dropped by $93.8 − $88.6 = $5.2 million. As also shown in table 7.1, use of other parameter estimates for the risk-free rate and for the time to expiration did not materially affect this estimate.[4] The option-pricing model therefore implies that the value of IMM's liabilities fell by $5.2 − $2.6 = $2.6 million as a result of the tragedy.

A MORE DETAILED ANALYSIS OF THE LOSSES TO IMM'S LIABILITY HOLDERS

Although market values for all of IMM's liabilities were not available, it is possible to observe the initial price reaction on the company's publicly traded 4½22 bonds. These bonds were secured by a first lien on various properties, including IMM's White Star Line subsidiary that owned the *Titanic*, and by a second lien on most of IMM's other assets. The bonds fell in price from 69.125 percent of par to 64.25 in the two trading days after the sinking of the *Titanic,* for a total percentage return of −7.1 percent.[5]

IMM also had outstanding $18.1 million of 5s29 bonds (under the company's original name of International Navigation), the prices of which could be observed in some April 1912 *Wall Street Journals*. In particular, these bonds traded at a price of 82 on April 10 (when the 4½22 bonds were selling at 69.75), at 81.75 on April 15, and at 81 on April 16. The April 10 and April 16 prices indicate a market value loss of only 1.2 percent related to the sinking of the *Titanic*. The 5s29 bonds were secured by a first lien on IMM's principal subsidiaries not related to the White Star Line, which owned the *Titanic*, and so it seems rational for their percentage market value loss to be lower than for the 4½22 bonds (since the value of the collateral for these bonds was largely unaffected by the sinking).

Market prices for IMM's $20.9 million in other liabilities (consisting of $6.9 million of bonds that had a prior claim on some of the subsidiaries' ships, $8.6 million in loans and bills that were partially secured by mortgages, $1.0 million in accrued interest that was also secured like the principal, $4.1 million in accounts payable, and $0.3 million in miscellaneous accounts) were not observable. However, they may also have fallen only a slight amount in value as a result of the sinking of the *Titanic*, as some were secured by ships that had not sunk, and many others were short-term liabilities. If they fell by the same amount as the 5s29 bonds, the total market value loss for IMM liabilities would be

> IMM Liability Value Decline
> = (.04875x\$52.7) + (.012x\$18.1) + (.012 × \$20.9)
> = \$3.0 million,

which is very close to the $2.6 million drop predicted by the option-pricing model.

The fact that the total $5.6 million estimated loss to IMM security holders ($2.6 million in losses to stockholders, along with the $3.0 million in losses to liability holders) is $0.4 million greater than predicted by the option-pricing model ($2.6 + $2.6 = $5.2 million) may stem from the effect of bankruptcy costs. In particular, a higher probability of bankruptcy for IMM (caused by the sinking of the *Titanic*) would increase the expected value of bankruptcy costs, which are not incorporated into the Black–Scholes option-pricing model, which essentially assumes frictionless markets. The increase in the expected value of future cash flows related to bankruptcy would lead to a drop in the company's value greater than the $5.2 million estimated by the frictionless model. The extra decline in value (here estimated to be $0.4 million) would fully be absorbed by the creditors, since the claim of the equity holders, who would be entitled to nothing in bankruptcy, would be unaffected by bankruptcy costs (Murphy 2000).

To further evaluate the price declines of IMM's publicly traded bonds, a model can be employed that incorporates transaction costs and other factors, such as call features and sinking funds, that affect bond values. In particular, Murphy's (1988) dynamic option-pricing model of fixed income securities is selected because of its theoretical and empirical robustness.[6] Information from the previous option-pricing analysis of the IMM company is utilized to estimate default risk parameters in the model.

The prior analysis indicated that IMM can be rationally assumed to have an annual probability of default equal to the annualized chance of the equity call on the firm at $91.7 million being out of the money over the ten-plus years to 1922. This assumption indicates the probability of bankruptcy for IMM to have been

Table 7.1
Option Model Values of IMM Securities

Security	Days to Exp.	Risk-Free Rate	Strike Price	Implied Assets' Value	Implied Assets' Volatility	Option Model Security Value	Securi. Market Value
April 13, 1912 (expiration date=10/1/22; Risk-free asset=NY 4s61)							
All Equity	3821	3.89%	$91.7	$93.8	20.5%	$15.6	$15.6
Common (Long @ 204.9)			$204.9			$3.1	$3.1
Preferred (Long @91.7; Short @204.9)						$15.6-3.1= $12.5	$12.5
Liabilities (Long @0; Short@91.7)						$93.8-15.6=$78.2	?
April 16, 1912							
All Equity	3818	3.89%	$91.7	$88.6	20.7%	$13.0	$13.0
Common			$204.9			$2.4	$2.4
Preferred						$13.0-2.4=$10.6	$10.6
Liabilities						$88.6-13.0=$75.6	?
EFFECT OF ALTERNATIVE PARAMETER ESTIMATES							
April 13, 1912 (expiration date=2/1/29; Risk-free asset=US 2s30)							
All Equity	6133	1.93%	$91.7	$109.3	18.30%	$15.6	$15.6
Common (Long @224.5)						$3.1	$3.1
Preferred (Long @91.7; Short @224.5)						$15.6-3.1=$12.5	$12.5
Liabilities (Long @0; Short @91.7)						$109.3-15.6=$93.7	?
April 16, 1912							
All Equity	6133	1.93%	$91.7	$104.0	18.40%	$13.0	$13.0
Common						$2.4	$2.4
Preferred						$13.0-2.4=$10.6	$10.6
Liabilities						$104.0-13.0=$91.0	?

Note: All option model values were estimated with the Rubinstein option-pricing model, assuming that the annual payout on the underlying assets equaled the interest payments on the company debt of $3.9 million (all dollar amounts in the table are in millions of U.S. dollars), as there were no dividend payments on the firm's equity (the preferred stock dividends, which had not been paid since 1902, were assumed to cumulate as per the contractual 6% terms of the issue, to $113.2 million by 1922 and, in the alternative parameter estimate case, to $132.8 million by 1929). The alternative parameter estimation case is provided for illustration purposes, setting the expiration date of the equity call equal to the maturity of IMM's longer-term bond issue (5s29), and setting the risk-free rate equal to the yield to maturity on U.S. government bonds with especially low yields.

$1 - .3641134^{365/3821} = 8.20$ percent before the sinking and $1 - .3178^{365/3818} = 10.38$ percent after the sinking. Given these values (and given the fact that the 4½22 bond was callable at 105, while the 5s29 bond had a $250,000–$500,000 annual sinking fund), it is possible to use the Murphy (1988) model to solve for the expected payoffs on the bonds in default that would set the model value equal to the prices. The expected value of the 4½22 bonds in default is thereby estimated to be 73 percent of par before the sinking and 64 percent afterwards, compared to 86 percent and 85 percent for the 5s29 bond, respectively. The (.73 – .64) × $52.7 = $4.7 million drop in the value of the collateral underlying the 4½22 bonds implied by the bond pricing model is consistent with the fact that almost all the losses related to the sinking of the *Titanic* were concentrated in that ship's White Star Line, which represented collateral for those bonds.

Because of the transaction costs of bankruptcy, the liability values in default estimated by the Murphy (1988) model naturally indicate larger overall losses to liability holders than implied in table 7.1 by the simple option-pricing model payoff on the company's $91.7 million in liabilities. In particular, if bankruptcy costs are 5 percent of assets (Murphy 2000), the overall payoffs would have to be reduced to .95 × $78.2/$91.7 = 81 percent (from the $78.2/$91.7 = 85% listed in table 7.1) before the sinking, and to .95 × $75.6/$91.7 = 78 percent (from $75.6/$91.7 = 82%) afterward. In addition, it should be mentioned that the Murphy (1988) model payoffs in default represent the present value (at the time of default) of the actual expected payoffs after the typical multiyear bankruptcy proceedings. Those values therefore underestimate the true payoffs, which may occur years after default, given little or no interest compensation in the meantime (Murphy 2000).

While the bond market seemed to react rather rationally to the sinking, one IMM official stated at the time, referring to the 4½22 bond price decline of 7.1 percent, that he knew "no material reason why the bonds sell off," making the argument that the loss of the ship would be fully covered by external insurance and transfers from reserve accounts so that reported earnings and book value would not be directly affected (*Wall Street Journal* 1912c). However, investors in the market at the same time apparently analyzed the effects of the sinking of the *Titanic* in a manner that was more consistent with modern financial theory. Although today's most advanced theories had not yet been developed by 1912, dynamic option-pricing models (assuming a normal distribution) did exist at that time (Bachelier 1900), and it seems that investors were able to make valuation appraisals that may have applied such models, at least intuitively.

INITIAL SECURITY PRICE REACTIONS
TO THE SINKING

Despite the apparent efficiency of the market in determining security prices, it should be noted that on the first trading day after the sinking the market may have reflected some initial confusion as to the value of IMM, especially since some newspapers, including the *Wall Street Journal* (1912a), were still, even in their April 16 morning editions, disputing the report that the ship had sunk. Possibly as a result of the mixed information on April 15, early on the day of the sinking, IMM's preferred equity price fell over 15 percent and its common stock price over 10 percent (*Wall Street Journal* 1912b), but they both recovered later in the same day to post only a slight loss of 2.4 percent and 3.0 percent on volumes of 3,740 and 2,300 shares, respectively (both of which were more than triple the average daily volume earlier in April 1912). At the same time, the 4½22 bond price opened at 67.25 and fell to a low of 67 before closing at its high for the day of 67.875 (for a net loss of 1.8 percent on volume of $114,000 in bond par value).

The initial investor confusion can perhaps be explained by a delay in public communication of the disaster, as wireless messages from the rescue ship, the *Carpathia*, were initially confined to official ones to the ship's owners (the White Star Line subsidiary of IMM) and personal ones from survivors (*Boston Globe* 1912f). In particular, there is some evidence that reporting about the sinking may have been restricted by wireless operators in order to permit an exclusive interview with a newspaper to be compensated in four figures later (Spignesi 1998). The initial trading action on April 15 may therefore have been caused by an excess of sell orders at the beginning of the day from knowledgeable traders who had access to some of the private wireless messages that the rescue ship sent. On the other hand, investors who were ignorant of that information or skeptical of the rumors and conflicting reports in the absence of any official announcements may have seen the resulting decline in IMM's security prices as an opportunity to buy them for what they perceived to be bargain prices. Those purchases may have driven the market price back up near the presinking appraised value later in the day.

Once investors were fully aware of the sinking, IMM's security prices fell sharply on April 16 and subsequently did not change radically from their much lower April 16 level. For instance, the equity values fell only a further $0.2 million by the end of the month and declined another $0.8 million by the end of the year, while the market value of the 4½22 bonds rose $0.3 million from April 16 to the end of April and increased a further $0.9 million by the end of the year.

CAUSES OF LOSSES EXCEEDING THE VALUE OF THE UNINSURED PORTION OF THE *TITANIC*

The fact that the total losses to IMM security holders far exceeded the cost of the ship less the insurance proceeds appears very rational. In particular, it would seem logical for investors to have believed that the maritime disaster would result in lawsuits and harm to the company's reputation that would lead to a significant loss of future business.

There had been many very rich people on the *Titanic* (*Boston Globe* 1912a), and while there had been actually very little valuable property on board other than personal jewelry (Eaton and Haas 1996), rumors floated around soon after the sinking that property such as diamonds and bearer bonds valued in the millions of dollars had been lost with the ship (Spignesi 1998). Over $16 million in liability claims related to the sinking of the *Titanic* were eventually filed against the company owning the ship, although the actual total payout on the total claims was only $663,000 (Eaton and Haas 1996).[7]

Besides the cost of lawsuits, the sinking of the *Titanic* probably resulted in a loss of net present value (NPV) from the ship, as well as from possible similar ocean liners that in the future might have been built and promoted as "unsinkable" if the *Titanic* had not sunk. Some evidence of investors' having perceived IMM's investment in the *Titanic* to have a significantly positive NPV is provided by a run-up in IMM's stock prices prior to its sailing, which had increased shareholder value by $2 to $3 million.[8] It is important to point out that the NPV expected from such ships represents the amount by which the present value of the expected net cash flows from such ships exceeded their building cost (which was $7.5 million for the *Titanic*). A recovery of IMM's loss of NPV here would not be possible by merely building new "unsinkable" ships, because of the adverse publicity created by the loss of the "unsinkable" *Titanic*.

In addition, given that the sinking of the *Titanic* probably had a very negative effect on IMM's overall image, especially with respect to safety and reliability, it would have been rational for investors to forecast that the company's other operations would suffer a serious loss of future revenues. Wade (1986) has indicated that IMM's business situation did worsen after the sinking of the *Titanic* in early 1912. As reported in *Moody's Manual of Railroad and Corporate Securities*, the company's earnings were $132,334 in 1912 and $315,602 in 1913, compared to profits of $772,477 in 1911 before the maritime catastrophe. IMM defaulted on its bond obligations in 1914 and went into receivership in 1915.[9]

With the value of actual payouts to *Titanic* customers for damages equaling about a half-million dollars, with the loss in NPV potentially being more than $2 million as a result of the sinking, and with losses related to a damaged image being nontrivial, it would seem rational for the market to assume at least $2.5 million in value declines to IMM over and above the out-of-pocket losses (which alone equaled a loss of $2.5 million from the sinking of the $7.5 million ship's net of $5.0 million in casualty insurance proceeds). Thus, the market price drop of over $5.0 million appears to have been very rational.[10]

THE RELATIONSHIP BETWEEN IMM'S FINANCIAL SITUATION AND THE *TITANIC*'S SINKING

The option-pricing analysis and IMM's financial distress may help explain some of the risk-taking actions that led to the sinking of the *Titanic*. In particular, the high speed at which the *Titanic* was traveling at the time of the collision could be considered reckless in light of the iceberg warnings and sightings that had previously been made in the area (Behe 1997). However, IMM's directors saw an ocean crossing in record-breaking time as an opportunity to gain publicity to help attract new business by meeting the competitive advantage of the faster ships of other companies (Wade 1986). Thus, despite the risks, a rapid sailing represented one method for IMM to gamble itself out of virtual insolvency. The gamble offered high upside potential for the equity holders, who were protected from much downside risk of a sinking, since their effective call option on the firm was only barely in the money. Because the upside potential for the stockholders (and the downside risk of bondholders) is maximized when company debt maturities (and the expiration date of the equity call) are more long-term (Parrino and Weisbach 1999), the motivation to take such a gamble was very large in the case of IMM as principal payments on its major bond issues were not due for over ten years.

There is indeed some anecdotal evidence supporting the hypothesis that IMM was deliberately taking calculated business risks with respect to having the *Titanic* steam at high speed in the midst of icebergs. In particular, witnesses reported having overheard IMM President Bruce Ismay (a passenger who survived the sinking) making suggestions to the *Titanic*'s captain to try to set a speed record (Eaton and Haas 1996). In addition, other testimony of witnesses at investigative hearings was also consistent with the IMM chairman's demanding high speed (Behe 1997).

This situation prompted the famous American Admiral George Dewey to remark in reaction to news of the sinking, "The greed for money making is so great that it is with the sincerest regret that I observe that human lives are never taken into consideration" (*Boston Globe* 1912e). It is important to observe that even though the IMM president's own life might have been endangered by the monetary gamble, the true extent of his personal risk might be indicated by the fact that he managed to find a safe place in one of the lifeboats. In any event, Myers's (1977) model of firms in financial distress overinvesting in high-risk projects and underinvesting in low-risk projects may help explain the expensive investment in the high-risk operation of the *Titanic* at the same time that there was an underinvestment in low-risk safety equipment like lifeboats.

It should also be mentioned that although brochures put out by IMM prior to the completion of the *Titanic* stated that it was "designed to be unsinkable" (Lynch 1993), her designer (Alexander Carlisle) had never considered the *Titanic* to be unsinkable but had merely designed the ship "to minimize the risk of ordinary accident" (*Boston Globe* 1912d). Eaton and Haas (1996) indicate that despite the visible employment of high-quality construction materials, the *Titanic* could have been more maneuverable (and thus able to steer effectively away from sighted icebergs), could have had better iceberg watch facilities (such as with respect to searchlight and binocular availability), and (most important) could have been able to withstand greater and more extensive water entry (such as with more watertight compartments, especially higher up, which would have saved the ship). As it was, the British-registered ship was not even outfited to meet minimum U.S. safety codes with respect to the number of lifeboats or life rafts (*Boston Globe* 1912c); as IMM had rejected Carlisle's original plan to have sufficient lifeboats for all passengers and crew (Eaton and Haas 1996). Although IMM reported shortly after the sinking that the cost of the ship had been no greater than $8 million, there were outside estimates as high as $10 million (Spignesi 1998). The higher cost estimates might have reflected the value of the ship as perceived by investors who were swayed by IMM's deliberate creation of an image of having spared no expense to build a magnificent and unsinkable ship (Eaton and Haas 1996).

While IMM's business leaders were certainly well aware of the actual vulnerability of the ship, her captain (who went down with the ship) may have been deceived in this matter, as indicated by his stated personal belief in the unsinkability of the ship prior to sailing (*Washington Post* 1912). Alternatively, it is also possible that the *Titanic*'s captain may have been motivated to talk and act imprudently by monetary rewards, such as a nice retirement package that was often offered by IMM's White Star subsidiary to cooperative employees. Behe (1997) has provided evidence of a cover-up of the entire affair by the White Star Line, which had previously engaged in similar actions, demanding high speed in ocean crossings and promising lifetime employment and pensions to those who remained silent when mishaps occurred.

CONCLUSION

This research applies option-pricing theory to the valuation of corporate assets, liabilities, and equities in the case of the *Titanic*'s infamous sinking. The analysis is important not only for educational and historical purposes but also to illustrate the semi-strong efficiency of security markets in immediately reflecting all public information.

In particular, even at the beginning of the last century, when today's communication systems and financial models did not exist, investors were able to react fairly rationally to confusing and ambiguous reports and to set stock and bond market prices that were fairly consistent with complex financial analysis. For instance, given the stock price changes surrounding the sinking of the *Titanic*, it can be concluded from the option-pricing model that bond prices reacted rationally. Similarly, it can also be concluded that given the bond price changes surrounding the sinking, stock prices also reacted rationally. In addition, the size of the overall security market value changes appear to be consistent with the underlying real fundamental losses that were incurred.

Perhaps even more important, this research, based on the option-pricing model, illustrates the risk imposed on existing and potential liability holders as a result of the equity holders' call option on a firm's assets, providing them with the incentive to use their managerial power to increase the variance of the firm's value. While these risks may exist for all firms, the incentives to maximize such risks are greater for diversified owners of firms in greater financial distress, as their call option values become nearly worthless if they do not try to gamble their way out of that distress. Although some of these risks to creditors can be mitigated, such as through short-term maturities and restrictive indenture clauses for bondholders (Parrino and Weisbach 1999), the risks of excessive company gambling can remain large for many existing and potential future liability holders, such as customer and worker victims of excessive risk-taking and recklessness by companies in desperate financial straits.

Researchers have long been aware of the fact that lax and delinquent government deposit insurance programs create incentives for financial institutions in distress to take excessive risks (Guttentag 1983). However, the motivation created for distressed companies by nongovernment debt obligations to engage in activities that are far too risky for (and not in the best interests of) creditors, customers, and other stakeholders has not been thoroughly investigated or illustrated. Note that the ability of companies to engage in excessively risky ventures is inhibited in a situation of debt immediately due (Parrino and Weisbach 1999), just as it is in the case of a government deposit insurer that immediately closes insolvent depository institutions.

However, it should be mentioned that whether companies are in financial distress or not, financial inhibitions in practice have historically been too weak to prevent major disasters, as many recent examples have shown. For instance, in the recent tobacco scandals, it was revealed that the allure of enormous profits was sufficient to make tobacco companies addict their customers with unhealthy products (Enrich 2001), which in turn eventually threatened the financial health of the tobacco firms once the facts were uncovered, lawsuits settled, and alternatives developed by competitors (Pascual 2001).

NOTES

We would like to thank Aman Awan, Matej Blasko, and Rong Yang for their very useful assistance in gathering data for this study, as well as Pat Behe, James Galbraith, and Karack Osborn for the information they provided on the *Titanic*. A portion of this research was funded by a grant from Oakland University.

1. Because the overall stock market return was negligible over that time period, the two-day total drop in the market-adjusted value of IMM's equity was $2.6 million, which was identical to both the rounded raw figure, as well as to the Brown and Warner (1985) market model residual estimated using the prior fifty-two weeks of pricing data on the Dow Jones Industrials as the market index. In particular, over the two trading days after the sinking of the *Titanic*, the *Wall Street Journal* indicates that an index of twelve industrial stocks appreciated by 0.1 percent, while an index of twenty railroad equities increased 0.2 percent. The two indexes rose by 0.7 percent and 0.8 percent on the first day, respectively, but both fell by 0.6 percent on the second day. The *Boston Globe* (1912b) actually declared one of the reasons for the overall market decline on the second day after the sinking to be related to the fact that "the shocking *Titanic* disaster was keenly felt throughout the financial district." The latter statement may not be surprising given that the passengers on the *Titanic* itself had wealth in excess of a half-billion dollars (*Boston Globe* 1912a), which was an incredibly large sum of money at the time. Thus, instead of the overall equity market conditions significantly affecting IMM's security prices, the impact may very well have run in the reverse direction, if anything.

2. The peak prices in 1910 had been surpassed in prior years. Between 1905 and 1912, the preferred stock price had ranged between a low of $12.625 in 1910 and a high of $49.75 in 1905, while the common equity price had ranged between $2 and $17 (both of the latter extremes were experienced in 1905). For many of these years, IMM had been milking its White Star Line subsidiary in order to have sufficient cash flow to pay creditors, with that subsidiary's dividend to IMM being doubled to 60 percent of par value in 1911 (for an annual dividend of close to $2 million).

3. The shareholder–bondholder conflict of interest can also result in companies being motivated to make excessive payouts to shareholders (Smith and Warner 1979), but it does not appear that that particular strategy was employed by IMM, which was not making any payouts to shareholders at all at the time.

4. As explained in table 7.1, these other estimates employed 1929 as the equity option expiration date because of the existence of another IMM obligation coming due at that time and utilized the U.S. 2s30 bond as the risk-free asset. Although the change in the value of the company's assets was not materially affected by these changed parameter estimates, the overall asset values were much higher than the liability book values, which would be inconsistent with the empirical fact of IMM bond prices selling at a discount discussed in the next section. Given that the size of the 1929 bond issue was only a small fraction of that of the 1922 bond ($18.1 million versus $52.7 million) and given that the U.S. 2s30 bond may have had special liquidity and regulatory advantages that caused its yield to be abnormally low, the results using these parameter estimates are probably not very meaningful except to illustrate the robustness and sensitivity of the results. Parrino and Weisbach (1999) provide an example of utilizing Monte Carlo simulations to evaluate the effects of incorporating more complex capital structures into such analysis, which may be even more relevant today, when most companies have a much more diverse set of liabilities and debt maturities.

5. In contrast, the prices of other bonds, including similar distressed bonds selling at a substantial discount from par value, were little changed over the two days. For instance, the Allis Chalmers 1st 5s bond fell from 66 on April 13, 1912, to 65.625 on April 16. The Missouri Pacific 4s bond remained unchanged at 74.5. In addition, short-term interest rates on commercial paper were constant at 3.5 percent by 3.75 percent over the two-day period, as were the prices of the U.S. government 4s25 and 2s30 bonds.

6. The model employs parameters for default risk premiums that are consistent with those found empirically by Elton, Gruber, Agrawal, and Mann (2001). It values call features by integrating across a truncated normal distribution of possible future bond prices (assuming a 13% standard deviation for long-term risk-free T-bond prices in lieu of the existence of implied volatility estimates from T-bond futures options at the time) and iterating to determine the optimal trigger points that maximize those values in a world of transaction costs (assumed to be 1.2% for refundings). The model has been shown to be empirically consistent not only with the valuation of corporate debt subject to regular and sinking fund calls (Murphy 1988, 1989, 2001a), but also with the pricing of many other callable securities, including municipal bonds (1998), mortgages (2001b), and convertible preferred stock (Murphy, Kleiman, and Nathan 1997). An updated test of the model was conducted on all newly issued callable fixed-rate bonds listed in the *Mergent Bond Survey* between 1999 and 2001 for which offer yield and credit rating data were available. A simple regression of the model yields on the offer yields indicated a statistically significant regression coefficient of .97 with a

standard error of .22 (while the intercept was statistically insignificant at .06 with a standard error of 2.14). The latter research was funded by Oakland University (which owns the copyright to the data and results).

7. The payout on the claims, which included a maximum individual claim of $1 million for loss of life and a maximum personal property claim of $177,352.74, was finally made on July 28, 1916, after several years of legal battles that culminated in an out-of-court settlement (Eaton and Haas 1996). The actual decision of the plaintiffs in the *Titanic*-related litigation to settle for less than 5 percent of their claims, tentatively agreed to in December 1915 (Eaton and Haas 1996), was made while the company was in receivership and may have at least partially reflected the subordinate creditor status of the claimants in comparison to most of the other liability holders, who were largely secured creditors. The priority of claims in this legal setting is relevant today in many cases, such as with respect to the widespread asbestos liabilities that may rank junior to secured or senior debt (and which may therefore end up with a much lower payoff than senior debt).

8. In particular, the *Wall Street Journal* (1912b) reported that IMM's preferred stock price had risen from its February 1912 range of $19.625–$21.75 to $24.75 on April 9 before falling back slightly to $24.125 on April 13, the last trading day before the *Titanic*'s collision with an iceberg. At the same time, the common equity price had risen from a February 1912 range of $4.25–$4.75 to $6.625 on April 9 before declining to $6.25 on April 13, 1912.

9. IMM's preferred, common, and bond prices suffered large declines in the several years after the sinking, falling by the end of 1913 to $14, $3.75, and 60, respectively, and to $3, $0.75, and 30.125 by the end of 1914.

10. Given IMM's bankruptcy in 1914, it could be argued that investors underestimated the drop in the total firm value of IMM. However, it should be mentioned that while there was little reported trading in IMM stock for much of 1915, the bond prices bounced back sharply that year, as IMM's operations recovered due to a World War I shipping boom. The company emerged from receivership in 1916 and exchanged its bonds for higher coupon debt, allowing it to pay a large amount of the previously accumulated preferred dividends between 1917 and 1922. However, losses for the company resumed in 1922 and continued through 1927 until after it sold its Oceanic Steam Navigation Company subsidiary, which had owned the *Titanic*. As a result of the losses, the preferred dividends were suspended again after 1922, and the preferred shareholders accepted an offer to have their stock converted into common in return for a $20 cash payment per share in 1929. At the same time, the common stock price rose to a high of $39.125 in 1929, before it fell in the Great Depression to a low of $0.875 in 1932. Wade (1986) has referred to IMM as J. P. Morgan's "one conspicuous failure."

REFERENCES

Bachelier, Louis. 1900/1964. "Theory of Speculation." In *The Random Character of Stock Market Prices*. Translated by James Boness, edited by P. Cootner. Cambridge: MIT Press, 17–78.

Behe, George. 1997. *Titanic: Safety, Speed and Sacrifice*. Polo, Ill.: Transportation Trails.

Black, Fischer, and Myron Scholes. 1973. "The Pricing of Options and Corporate Liabilities." *Journal of Political Economy* 81: 637–659.

Boston Globe. 1912a. "Passengers of Great Wealth." April 16, 4.

———. 1912b. "Prices Weak Most of the Time Today—*Titanic* Disaster an Influence." April 16, 9.

———. 1912c. "*Titanic* Had 20 Lifeboats." April 17,1.

———. 1912d. "*Titanic*'s Side Torn Out, Belief." April 17, 6.

———. 1912e. "Life Boats Too Few, Says Dewey." April 18, 6.

———. 1912f. "Knew Bergs Near—Ismay." April 20, 3.

Brown, Stephen, and Jerold Warner. 1985. "Using Daily Stock Returns: The Case of Event Studies." *Journal of Financial Economics* 14: 3–31.

Eaton, John, and Charles Haas. 1996. *Titanic: Destination Disaster.* New York: Norton.

Elton, Elton, Martin Gruber, Deepak Agrawal, and Christopher Mann. 2001. "Explaining the Rate Spread on Corporate Bonds." *Journal of Finance* 56: 247–277.

Enrich, David. 2001. "Jeffrey Wigand." *U.S. News & World Report*, August 20–27, 70.

Fuller, Joseph, and Michael Jensen. 2002. "Just Say No to Wall Street: Putting a Stop to the Earnings Game." *Journal of Applied Corporate Finance* (Winter): 41–46.

Guttentag, Jack. 1983. "A Note on Hedging and Solvency: The Case of a Phoenix." *Journal of Futures Markets* 3: 137–141.

Khanna, Arun. 1998. "The *Titanic*: The Untold Story." *Financial Analysts Journal* 54 (September/October):16–17.

Leland, Hayne, and Klaus Toft. 1996. "Optimal Capital Structure, Endogenous Bankruptcy, and the Term Structure of Credit Spreads." *Journal of Finance* 51: 987–1019.

Lynch, Don. 1993. "The 'Unsinkable' *Titanic*, as Advertised." *Titanic Commutator* 16 (February-April):4–6.

Merton, Robert. 1974. "On the Pricing of Corporate Debt: the Risk Structure of Interest Rates." *Journal of Finance* 29: 449–470.

Murphy, Austin. 1988. "A Discounted Cash-Flow Model of Fixed-Income Securities Subject to Multiple Calls." *Southern Economic Journal* 55: 21–36.

———. 1989. "A Discounted Cash-Flow Model of Convertibles Subject to Multiple Calls in a World of Refunding Costs and Stochastic Interest Rates." *Southern Economic Journal* 56: 87–104.

———. 1998. "An Empirical Investigation into the Components of Long-Term Municipal Bond Yields." *Journal of Private Portfolio Management* 1 (Spring): 27–36.

———. 2000. *Scientific Investment Analysis.* Westport, Conn.: Quorum Books.

———. 2001a. "A Comparison of Taxable and Tax-Deductible Preferred Yields." *Research in Finance* 18: 169–193.

———. 2001b. "A Comparative Analysis of the Price-Process Model of Mortgage Valuation." *Review of Financial Economics* 9: 65–82.

Murphy, Austin, Robert Kleiman, and Kevin Nathan. 1997. "The Value of Convertible Preferred Stock in Transactions with 'Relationship Investors' like Warren Buffett." *International Review of Financial Analysis* 6: 241–256.

Myers, Stewart. 1977. "Determinants of Corporate Borrowing." *Journal of Financial Economics* 5: 147–175.

Parrino, Robert, and Michael Weisbach. 1999. "Measuring Investment Distortions Arising from Stockholder–Bondholder Conflicts." *Journal of Financial Economics* 53: 3–42.

Pascual, Aixa. 2001. "LeBow Turns Over a New Leaf." *Business Week*, May 7, 71–72.

Rubinstein, Mark. 1976. "The Valuation of Uncertain Income Streams and the Pricing of Options." *Bell Journal of Economics* 7: 407–425.

Smith, Clifford, and Jerold Warner. 1979. "On Financial Contracting: An Analysis of Bond Covenants." *Journal of Financial Economics* 7: 117–161.

Spignesi, Stephen. 1998. *The Complete Titanic*. Secaucus, N.J.: Birch Lane Press.

Wade, Wyn. 1986. *The Titanic: End of a Dream.* New York: Penguin.

Wall Street Journal. 1912a. "Liner *Titanic* Struck by Berg but Passengers Are Saved." April 16, 6.

———. 1912b. "Mercantile Marine Co.'s Loss by the S.S. *Titanic* Disaster." April 17, 7.

———. 1912c. "Loss of *Titanic* Not Expected to Change Standing of Mercantile Marine Collateral Trust 4½% Bonds." April 18, 5.

Washington Post. 1912. "Felt Sure of His Ship." April 18, 12.

8

A Possible Solution to Excessive Risk-Taking: Using Stock Ownership to Maximize Customer Loyalty

Austin Murphy

EXECUTIVE SUMMARY

This chapter explains how tying consumer price discounts to ownership of shares in the vendor can promote loyalty and trust in both buyers and sellers. The result can therefore be beneficial to both parties and can inhibit excessive risk-taking and fraud on the part of vendors.

INTRODUCTION

One of the newest developments in U.S. security trading is the right of a corporation to sell its own stock directly to the public (Murphy 2000). This new privilege has opened up a whole new set of theoretical opportunities for corporations seeking to maximize customer loyalty and better align company and customer interests.

OFFERING DISCOUNTS TO STOCKHOLDERS

In particular, it is now possible for a retail company (such as Kmart) to sell its stock out of its stores to its retail clients. In order to provide an incentive to buy its stock, the retail company could tie discounts (of 5% or so) on retail merchandise purchased by shareholders. Once customers have purchased the stock, they would have an incentive to continue to make retail purchases from the chain of stores in order to be able to obtain the discount, as well as to help the company they partially own. As such, the concept is similar to consumer cooperatives, which thrived for a time until they were overwhelmed by large discount chains (like Kmart itself), which were uninhibited by philosophical doctrines against advertising, emphasizing brand names, and allowing purchases on credit (Furlough and Strikwerda 1999).[1]

The system of selling stock to customers would also be somewhat similar to that used by warehouse chains like Sam's that require payment of an annual fee in order to be able to shop. This new sort of retail outlet, however, would allow anyone to shop, although only customers who had paid the one-time price for a share of stock would be allowed the specified discount for shareholders. The price paid for "membership" in the shareholder family would not be an expense to the customer but would instead serve as an investment that could pay dividends and go up in value.

ADVANTAGES OF CUSTOMER SHAREHOLDERS

It has long been recognized that employee morale and loyalty can be maximized through employee stock ownership plans.[2] It is hypothesized that a similar sense of customer loyalty can be achieved through a customer ownership plan. A motto of "we belong to you" might truly be justified in such circumstances. If the employees of the retailer were also offered a stock ownership plan (perhaps receiving a share of stock upon becoming employees, as well as receiving shares of stock as incentive bonuses), the customers might begin to feel themselves to be part of the same family as the employees and other shareholders.[3]

Most of these advantages also exist in consumer cooperatives (Furlough and Strikwerda 1999). However, a for-profit retail chain might be able to compete more effectively in the areas of advertising, meeting individual consumer preferences for brand names and other consumption fetishes, and offering credit (including their own credit cards, as Kmart has indeed chosen to do). In addition, a for-profit retailer may have access to greater capital resources than would a cooperative.

Moreover, for-profit retailers may not be subject to some of the negative social stigmas associated with cooperatives, the members of which are typically poor. The latter advantage may represent an especially important aspect of a for-profit retailer in the United States, where the negative stereotyping of the poor as being responsible for their own poverty is illustrated in the widespread saying, "If you're so smart, why ain't you rich?" (Loewen 1995).

The administrative costs of a customer shareholder plan might be expected to be at least as great as that incurred by warehouse chains like Sam's or a cooperative, with membership cards having to be issued in the form of shareholder cards. However, as with the warehouse chains and cooperatives, shareholder membership would provide the retailer with important information on customer preferences and demographics, as well as generating customer loyalty. Payment of dividends to the retail customers who request cash dividend payments (as opposed to dividend reinvestment) could represent an incremental administrative cost of the shareholder membership plan, although this costly task could be turned into a promotion of the retailer's products and specials with mailer inserts. The incremental administrative costs of issuing proxy and financial statements to more shareholders could similarly be offset by the marketing benefits created by annual reports designed to attract consumers to the company's products and services.[4]

While the issuance of new shares of stock might result in some dilution to existing shareholders, such dilution can easily be eliminated by the firm's buying up stock in the open market to obtain the shares offered to customers. On the other hand, such open-market purchases can be suspended when the company is in need of equity capital, so that the customer purchases of shares would provide an automatic source of funding whenever (and only if) the company needed it.

In any event, because both purchases and sales of shares of stock would require investment banking services, development of (or merger with) a brokerage firm might be synergistic. By potentially creating interest in investing for first-time investors, the system might also offer an affiliated brokerage firm with an enhanced customer base.

CONCLUSION

Promoting the purchase of stock by company customers, such as through discounts on purchases for shareholders, can better align the interests of companies and their customers.[5] Besides generating greater customer loyalty, happiness, and trust (and thereby increasing revenues while potentially lowering marketing costs), such an alignment of interests can possibly help prevent future problems associated with excessive risk-taking and outright fraud. History is full of examples of disasters that might, and should, have been prevented, including not only the tobacco scandals of today and the *Titanic* scandals of yesterday but also even the recent financial scandals in which brokerage firms recommended overpriced stock to their customers.

NOTES

1. Although some of the cooperatives attained a level of size comparable to that of the large discount chains, they generally "failed to see how they could adapt their laudable goals [of providing quality products at low prices for the benefit of an entire class of consumer owners] to the growing individualism that capitalist consumption succeeded in reaching" (Furlough and Strikwerda 1999).

2. Diamond and Verrecchia (1982) have shown that stock ownership (and stock option) plans create greater employee motivation when the employee's actions exert more effect on the stock's value—that is, when the employee is an officer with sufficient power and responsibility to carry out activities that can materially increase shareholder wealth. As a result, because spinoffs, equity carve-outs, and the issue of tracking stock that pays dividends from the earnings of specific subsidiaries create new stock over which subsidiary officers have more control, such offerings to subsidiary em-

ployees can enhance their morale, although there can also be synergy and agency problems associated with such issues (Murphy 1989). Similarly, selling customers retail stock might be more likely to be more effective in generating consumer loyalty for smaller retailers than for larger retail chains. However, both small and large retailers might be able to enhance customer loyalty by providing an annual stock dividend/bonus to customers that is proportional to the amount of purchases made by the customers (with such dividends/bonuses potentially being tax deductible as an expense).

3. This marketing technique might also be especially useful for Internet retailers seeking to improve customer interest, loyalty, and trust. For instance, Kmart itself recently initiated online direct purchases of its own stock, and there is some hope that investors in Kmart equity will also buy Kmart retail products online. However, minimum transaction amounts ($50 for existing Kmart shareholders and $250 otherwise) and fees ($2 to $10 per transaction and 5 to 12 cents per share) are required (Talaski 2000) reducing the attractiveness and potential synergy of this offering. Toyota has also just begun offering brokerage transactions online (Shirouzu 2000), although there are currently no known plans to offer direct purchases of its own securities. Although this is a purely speculative hypothesis, it is possible that Kmart could have avoided bankruptcy (and a potential future second bankruptcy as well) if it had adpted the plan described in this article (as developed for and provided to the company in the late 1990s).

4. The costs of having more shareholders could potentially be reduced by having the company offer to sell warrants or debt to its customers, but the legal and regulatory costs of such offerings might be prohibitive. In addition, such securities might not provide the same level of benefits created by direct ownership.

5. Spreading stock ownership to more stakeholders does not guarantee that management will actually act in the best interests of those owner-stakeholders, as the collapse of Enron indicates with respect to the job and investment losses of its shareholder employees. However, prior to its sinking, Enron was considered a very good place to work, and the share price was indeed maximized, if not overmaximized. Perhaps Enron's management really was trying to act in the best interests of its employees and other shareholders but was simply as ignorant as the Wall Street analysts of the excessive risks it was taking on.

REFERENCES

Diamond, D., and R. Verrecchia. 1982. "Optimal Managerial Contracts and Equilibrium Security Prices." *Journal of Finance* 37: 275–287.

Furlough, E., and C. Strikwerda. 1999. *Consumers against Capitalism.* Lanham, Md.: Rowman & Littlefield.

Loewen, J. 1995. *Lies My Teacher Told Me.* New York: New Press.

Murphy, A. 2000. *Scientific Investment Analysis.* Westport, Conn.: Quorum Books.

———. 1989. "Analyzing Sub-Classes of General Motors Common Stock." *Financial Management* 18 (Spring): 64–71.

Shirouzu, N. 2000. "Toyota Is Likely to Offer Online Stock Trading." *Wall Street Journal*, January 28, A14.

Talaski, K. 2000. "Kmart to Offer Sales of Its Stock Online." *Oakland Press*, January 29, A1.

9

A Critique of the Monday Effect: Beware of Mechanical Trading Rules Derived from Empirical Research in Financial Economics

Edwin D. Maberly and Raylene M. Pierce

EXECUTIVE SUMMARY

Inferences drawn from empirical studies in financial economics are often meaningless and counterproductive, especially when these studies suggest the existence of profitable mechanical trading rules. In many cases, more recent return data show that the anomaly is not robust over time. This study presents new research on the "Monday" seasonal as evidence that individual investors should be wary of using academic research to formulate investment decisions. Familiarity with market microstructure issues in research is shown to be just as important as familiarity with esoteric econometric techniques. In empirical finance, the two are complements, not substitutes, and ignoring one or the other can lead to erroneous investment conclusions or implications.

INTRODUCTION

Financial economists have documented in equity returns numerous anomalies that are inconsistent with the efficient-market hypothesis, which states that all relevant and ascertainable information is already reflected in security prices (Brealey and Myers 2000). Theory implies that an efficient market has no memory and that therefore in an efficient market returns should be independent of calendar time—day of the week, time of the month, month of the year, and so on.

In an apparent conflict with market efficiency, however, numerous empirical studies report that returns are a function of the day of the week. The most startling observation is that, on average, Monday returns are negative. The literature refers to this phenomenon as the "Monday effect."

This chapter finds that serious problems arise whenever calendar time anomalies like the Monday effect are extrapolated into the future without considering the fundamental causes of the anomaly. By examining more recent return data covering the period March 1990 through June 2001, this study shows that Monday's return pattern is not robust over the time period examined. In earlier time periods like the 1960s or 1970s, the lowest returns are observed on Monday, while in more recent time periods like the 1990s, the highest returns are observed on Monday. The reader is reminded of Wyckoff's (1930) famous statement:

At the time many thought that the market could be beaten by mechanical methods; that is, by some means other then human judgment. [Roger] Babson had one or more. All kinds of individuals came forward with ways of beating the stock market; each was certain his method would make a fortune. . . . Not long afterward, however, after further study, I decided once and for all that methods of this kind, which substitute mechanical plays for judgment, must fail. For the calculations on which they are based omit one fundamental fact, i.e., that the only unchangeable thing about the stock market is its tendency to change. The rigid method sooner or later will break the operator who blindly follows it. (Wyckoff 1930, 163–164)

Inferences drawn from many empirical studies in financial economics are often meaningless and counterproductive, especially when these studies suggest the existence of profitable mechanical trading rules. A number of studies strongly suggest that equity markets are inefficient, but individual investors should refrain from projecting this evidence into the future. This chapter thoroughly demonstrates this argument using more recent data investigating the Monday seasonal. In addition, studies that suggest the existence of a holiday anomaly with unusually large returns on the trading day prior to an exchange holiday (Ariel 1990) and studies claiming a significant underreaction to information contained in stock splits (Ikenberry 2002) should also be viewed with a degree of suspicion. Although not reported in this paper, the authors find no evidence of a holiday anomaly (spot or futures) or stock-split underreaction for more recent data.

The rest of this chapter is organized as follows. The first section discusses some important market microstructure issues related to interpreting day-of-the-week effects. The second section contains a literature review. Prior research findings are reexamined in the following section, in addition to more recent empirical evidence on Monday's return pattern. The last section contains a summary and conclusions. While Salbu (2002) has already admitted that deficiencies in elitist academic business education contributes to disastrous unethical behavior in the real world of U.S. business that is ruled by greed and fear (Cruver 2002), this research is important for illustrating the disastrous effects that applying the implications of elitists naïve academic research can also have in practice.

MARKET MICROSTRUCTURE ISSUES

Major studies that examine return patterns across the days of the week include French (1980), Rogalski (1984), Smirlock and Starks (1986), Connolly (1989), Kamara (1997), and Wang, Li, and Erickson (1997) to name but a few. A contention of the current paper is that Connolly, Kamara, and Wang et al. fail to recognize some important market microstructure issues associated with prior empirical studies addressing day-of-the-week effects.

High-Capitalized versus Low-Capitalized Indices

For each of the cited studies, Table 9.1 identifies by author the particular index used to calculate daily returns, the time period examined, and those studies that calculate (time-decomposed) close-to-open and open-to-close returns. Furthermore, indices are divided into two subsets based on market capitalization. The first subset includes high-capitalized indices like the S&P 500 index, the Dow Jones Industrial Average (DJIA), the Center for Research in Security Prices (CRSP) value-weighted index, the New York Stock Exchange–American Stock Exchange (NYSE–AMEX) value-weighted index, and the NASDAQ value-weighted index. These indices are representative of returns to large firms. The second subset includes low-capitalized indices, like the CRSP equally weighted index and the smallest capitalized decile of NYSE stocks. These indices are representative of returns to small firms.

For identical time periods, day-of-the-week return pattern should be similar across all five high-capitalized indices and similarly for the two low-capitalized indices. Thus, the weekend return pattern for the DJIA should mimic the weekend return pattern for all high-capitalized indices. Conversely, the weekend return pattern for the CRSP equally weighted index should mimic the weekend return pattern for all low-capitalized indices.

An important observation is that Rogalski (1984) and Smirlock and Starks (1986) examine time-decomposed returns, but only for high-capitalized indices like the DJIA and S&P 500 index (the latter of which may suffer from a stale-quote problem, associated with estimating S&P 500 index opening values, as explained in the next section). In contrast, studies by Connolly (1989) and Wang et al. (1997) examine only close–close returns; Monday's return is measured from Friday's close to Monday's close, and so forth for the other days of the week. Kamara's (1997) analysis is also based on close–close returns, but in an apparent response to a referee's comments, close–open S&P 500 spot and futures returns are reported over a shortened time period in a footnote.

Time-Decomposed Returns and Stale Quotes

S&P Corporation publishes an opening S&P 500 index price, but this price is based on the last transaction of each of the five-hundred stocks in the index as of 9:31 A.M. EST, one minute after the NYSE opens. On an average day, many stocks in multistock indices like the S&P 500 have not traded by 9:31 A.M. EST, and thus the reported opening price contains many stale quotes.[1]

The DJIA comprises thirty large capitalized stocks, and the methodology used by Dow Jones & Co. to calculate the theoretical opening value for the DJIA is unique. DJIA theoretical opening prices are reported daily in the *Wall Street Journal* and weekly in *Barron's*. The Dow's theoretical opening is based on the first reported trade for each of the thirty component stocks, which can occur at any time during the trading day but most likely before 9:45 A.M. EST. In the rare instance where a Dow stock does not trade, the previous day's closing price is used. As noted by Hiraki, Maberly, and Park (1994), the methodology adopted by Dow Jones for calculating the theoretical opening virtually eliminates the stale quote problem. In November 1997, Dow Jones instituted a policy of providing two opening values for the Dow averages, a theoretical opening and an actual opening.[2]

By selecting the DJIA for analysis, both Rogalski (1984) and Smirlock and Starks (1986) are able to determine if Monday's unusual price pattern is due to a weekend effect or a Monday trading-period effect, as measured from Monday's open to Monday's close. Terminology is often a source of confusion, which appears to be the case for some empirical studies researching Monday's return pattern. In the current study, the Monday effect is the sum of the weekend effect and Monday's trading period effect.

Although French's (1980) paper is entitled "Stock Returns and the Weekend Effect," it examines only close–close returns. Therefore, a more appropriate title is "Stock Returns and the Monday Effect." Also Connolly's (1989) paper is entitled "An Examination of the Robustness of the Weekend Effect"; like French, Connolly examines only close–close returns. Therefore, Connolly is examining the robustness of the Monday effect to alternative estimation and testing procedures, not the weekend effect. Observe from Table 9.1 that Monday's mean return over the post 1973 period is not statistically different from other days of the week. Thus, the traditional Monday effect disappears for high-capitalized indices using the "old" regression methodology. It is important to understand that Connolly's critique concerning the violation of assumptions for regression models is indeed a valid concern. However, Connolly's adjustment for these assumption violations does not explain the disappearance of the traditional Monday effect for high-capitalized indices after 1973. It disappears through natural causes—the passage of time.

The January Effect: Contaminating
Monday's Return Pattern in January

Reinganum (1983), among others, documents unusually large January returns, especially for small firms, a phenomenon known as the "January effect." Rogalski (1984) investigates the interaction between Monday's return pattern and the January effect over the period October 1974 through April 1984 and finds that in January the weekend and Monday effects disappear. In particular, both weekend and Monday effects are positive during January but negative for the rest of the year.

To examine any possible interaction between the January and Monday effects, January returns were calculated over the seventeen-year period 1975–1991. The results indicate that January returns are unusually large in 1975 and 1976, but especially for small firms. Therefore, from Rogalski (1984), the implication is for a "weak" Monday effect over the 1975–1977 subperiod, but especially for small-firm indices; in fact, this conjecture is consistent with the results presented by Connolly (1989) for the subperiod 1975–1977. Over the subperiod 1975–1977, Monday's return pattern is influenced by the unusually large returns observed in January. The proper procedure is to include a January dummy in the regression model, which isolates the impact of the January effect on Monday's return pattern.

REVIEW OF EMPIRICAL RESULTS

Pioneering Studies

French (1980) reports that Monday's S&P 500 returns over the period 1953 through 1977 are, on average, negative at –0.1681 percent, which is significant at the 1 percent level and supports the existence of a Monday effect. Rogalski (1984) examines time-decomposed returns for both the DJIA and S&P 500 index over the period October 1, 1974, through April 30, 1984, and December 29, 1978, through December 9, 1983, respectively.[3] Although Monday mean returns are negative in both cases, they are insignificant at the 5 percent level, and therefore evidence supporting a Monday effect for large firm returns is weak. In contrast, on average, weekend returns are negative and significant at the 1 percent level. Rogalski's results are interpreted as supporting the existence of a weekend effect for large firms, but not necessarily for small firms, in the post-1973 period. The study by Smirlock and Starks (1986) confirms the results of the previous two studies. In particular, large firms exhibit negative Monday returns prior to 1974, but the Monday effect disappears after 1973, at least for high-capitalized indices. Conversely, a significant weekend effect is observed for large firms, but only after 1973. These results are summarized in Table 9.1.

Financial economists should understand that seasonal patterns in equity returns are akin to well-established weather patterns. Once formed, patterns tend to persist, but then something happens. The pattern changes abruptly, and without warning. In many cases, researchers incorrectly extrapolate beyond the time period examined, which leads to incorrect inferences. There is no theoretical basis for assuming that seasonality in equity returns is immutable across time. In fact, the opposite is true. The concept of efficient markets suggests

Table 9.1
Results from Prior Studies: Weekend versus Monday Effect

	Monday returns		
Panel A: Pioneering studies	Close-Open (weekend)	Open-Close (trading)	Close-Close
French (1980)			
1953-1977			
S&P 500: Large cap	N/A	N/A	-0.1681*
Rogalski (1984)			
1974-1984			
DJIA: Large cap	-0.0804*	0.0492	-0.0312
1979-1983			
S&P 500: Large cap	-0.1315*	0.0148	-0.1167
Smirlock & Starks (1986)			
1963-1968			
DJIA: Large cap	0.0142	-0.1692*	-0.1549*
1974-1983			
DJIA: Large cap	-0.0714*	0.0551	-0.0153

*Significant at the 1 percent level. The weekend effect refers to the return pattern as measured from Friday's close to Monday's open. The Monday effect refers to the return pattern as measured from Friday's close to Monday's close. All returns are in percent. S&P 500 is the Standard & Poor's 500 index. DJIA is the Dow Jones Industrial Average. CRSP VW and CRSP EW is the Center for Research in Security Prices value-weighted and equally weighted index, respectively. NYSE and AMEX refer to New York and American Stock Exchanges.

that seasonal patterns tend to disappear or mutate after the pattern becomes widely known, as has been the case for the well-publicized January effect.[4]

Extensions of Earlier Studies

Many empirical studies test for the existence of a Monday or weekend effect using ordinary least squares (OLS), where the explanatory variables are

Table 9.1 (*continued*)

Panel B: Extensions	Monday returns		
	Close-Open (weekend)	Open-Close (trading)	Close-Close
Connolly (1989)			
1963-1965			
S&P 500: Large cap	N/A	N/A	-0.085*
CRSP VW: Large cap	N/A	N/A	-0.033*
CRSP EW: Small cap	N/A	N/A	-0.068*
1981-1983			
S&P 500: Large cap	N/A	N/A	-0.076
CRSP VW: Large cap	N/A	N/A	-0.106*
CRSP EV: Small cap	N/A	N/A	-0.080
Kamara (1997)			
1962-1993			
S&P 500: Large cap	N/A	N/A	0.033
Small-cap index	N/A	N/A	-0.146*
Wang, Li, & Erickson (1997)			
1983-1993			
NYSE-AMEX VW: Large cap	N/A	N/A	-0.0002

dummy variables representing various days of the week. For example, in the "Monday model" as described in Appendix 9.1, the intercept represents Tuesday-through-Friday daily returns where the dummy is one for Monday and zero otherwise. Therefore, Monday's return is the sum of the intercept and the slope coefficient. Connolly (1989) reports results using robust econometric methods and a generalized autoregressive conditional heteroskedasticity (GARCH) model, and the current study employs similar procedures. However, as noted previously, this study contends that the use of more advanced econometric techniques adds little to our understanding of the existence or nonexistence of the Monday seasonal effect.

Kamara (1997) examines the daily pattern of close–close returns for two indices over the 1962–1993 period, and these results are presented in panel B of Table 9.1. The S&P 500 index represents returns to large firms, while the smallest capitalized decile of NYSE stocks represents returns to small firms.

A Monday effect in S&P 500 returns does not exist, as Monday returns are numerically positive and insignificant from other days of the week. In contrast, a small-cap Monday effect is evident over the period examined. Kamara argues that the large-firm Monday seasonal is related to the ratio of institutional versus individual trading and that the disappearance of the seasonal over time is related to increased institutional trading activity, especially in the post–April 1982 period. However, increased institutional trading has no effect on the Monday seasonal for small-cap returns. Since Kamara's analysis is limited to close–close returns, inferences are only valid for the Monday effect—Friday's close to Monday's close—and these findings are not unexpected, given the empirical results presented in panel A of Table 9.1.

In a footnote, Kamara (1997) states that he finds no weekend seasonal in close–open futures and spot S&P 500 returns over a reduced time period, 1983 through 1990. However, there are two problems with these results. First, opening values for the S&P 500 index are subject to the stale-quote problem mentioned previously; second, S&P 500 index futures trade fifteen minutes after the close of the NYSE. Research by Herbst and Maberly (1992) shows that S&P 500 index futures tend to discount the occurrence of the weekend effect in spot index values. Thus, on average, S&P 500 index futures exhibit negative returns over Friday's extended trading period—4:00 to 4:15 P.M. EST. A more appropriate test of a weekend effect in both spot and index futures returns is to examine DJIA weekend returns based on the DJIA's theoretical opening and S&P 500 futures returns over the Friday open to Monday open period. The results of this analysis (see Table 9.6) support the existence of a weekend effect in both DJIA and S&P 500 index futures returns over the 1983–1990 period, and these results are discussed in the next section.

Wang et al. (1997) examine the daily return pattern for the NYSE–AMEX value-weighted index over the 1983–1993 period. Based on their findings the well-known Monday effect occurs primarily in the last two (fourth and fifth) weeks of the month. In addition, the mean Monday return for the first three weeks of the month is not different from zero. Since the data set examined is limited to close–close returns for a high-capitalized index, inferences apply only to the Monday effect, which prior studies show virtually disappears after 1973.

In the next section, robust econometric techniques and a GARCH(1,1) model are used to examine the daily pattern of DJIA time-decomposed returns to test for the robustness of the weekend effect to alternative estimation and testing procedures. These procedures are explained in more detail in the Appendix 9.1.

REEXAMINATION OF PRIOR STUDIES

Connolly (1989)

The methodology used in this section is an extension of that utilized by Connolly (1989) but applied to a different data set—theoretical opening and closing values for the DJIA over the period 1975–1991. Monday returns are compared to returns for the other days of the week as indicated by the Monday model.

The Monday Model–Least-Squares Estimators

First, the Monday model is reexamined using least-squares (LS) procedures for evidence of the weekend effect in DJIA returns for each of three subperiods 1975–1977, 1978–1980, and 1981–1983, which are identical to the subperiods examined by Connolly (1989). Results are also reported for expanded subperiods with the analysis extended through 1991. In Table 9.2, Monday's mean return is the sum of β_0 and β_1, and a significance β_1 coefficient supports a Monday seasonal.

Over identical time periods, the Monday model coefficients reported in Table 9.2 for close–close returns should be similar to those reported by Connolly (1989) for both the S&P 500 and CRSP value-weighted indices. In general, the results associated with DJIA close–close returns are similar to those reported by Connolly for the S&P 500 index. Since the DJIA and CRSP value-weighted indices are both high-capitalized indices, Monday's return pattern should be similar for identical time periods, but this is not the case. The observed discrepancy is apparently due to Connolly's mislabeling of the CRSP equally weighted index as the value-weighted index, and conversely.[5]

Consistent with prior research, the current study finds no statistical evidence of either a weekend or Monday effect over the 1975–1977 subperiod. Although negative, the mean weekend DJIA return is indistinguishable from the mean return for all other days of the week. However, the 1975–1977 subperiod appears unique, given that stock prices as measured by the S&P 500 index increased by over 55 percent from January 1975 through December 1976 and that December 1974 marks the end of a severe bear market related to supply shocks in the macro economy. The factors associated with this large increase in stock prices definitely impacts the Monday seasonal. The argument is that the subperiod 1975–1977 is atypical and shows the pitfalls of examining relatively short time periods for evidence of the Monday seasonal. Also, over the 1975–1977 subperiod the influence of the January effect potentially masks the Monday seasonal over the remaining eleven months; this interrelationship, if it exists, should be incorporated into the Monday model to avoid incorrect inferences. Note that the weekend effect in DJIA returns is significant in both of the subperiods 1978–1980 and 1981–1983. From Table 9.2, the Monday effect for DJIA returns disappears after 1983, but the weekend effect is evident after 1983.

Monday Model: Non-Normal Estimates

From Table 9.3, the magnitude of the Monday seasonal is typically lower in models based on the general error distribution (GED). Henceforth, the GED

Table 9.2
Monday Model: DJIA Least-Squares Estimates
Model: $R_t = \beta_0 + \beta_1 M_t + \epsilon_t$

Sample Period	Return Measure	β_0	β_1	σ
A. 1975-77	close-open	0.0100 (0.749)	-0.0239 (0.693)	0.3736
	close-close	0.0306 (0.986)	0.0274 (0.332)	0.8552
B. 1978-80	close-open	-0.0018 (0.103)	-0.1060** (2.533)	0.4333
	close-close	0.0505 (1.523)	-0.1615 (1.852)	0.8817
C. 1981-83	close-open	0.0471* (3.236)	-0.1199** (2.310)	0.4181
	close-close	0.0467 (1.248)	-0.0608 (0.601)	0.9792
D. 1975-83	close-open	0.0815** (2.141)	-0.0837* (3.321)	0.4095
	close-close	0.0449** (2.349)	-0.0659 (1.271)	0.9075
E. 1984-91	close-open	0.0391* (3.391)	-0.1768* (3.868)	0.6723
	close-close	0.0652* (2.778)	-0.1019 (1.054)	1.1946
F. 1975-91	close-open	0.0282* (3.998)	-0.1276* (4.857)	0.5492
	close-close	0.0544* (3.787)	-0.0829 (1.519)	1.0521

*,**Significant at the 1 and 5 percent levels, respectively.

Absolute t-statistics in parentheses. DJIA refers to the Dow Jones Industrial Average.

model with GARCH effects is denoted as the "maximum-likelihood model" (ML). These effects, however, are not systematic. The estimates of $1/v$ reported in the last column of Table 9.4 reflect deviations from normality in the return generating process, where $1/v = 0.5$ for the normal distribution and 1.0 for the Laplace distribution (see Harvey 1991). In most cases, distributions are characterized by fatter tails than the normal, though not as fat as the Laplace. However, in some cases the distribution exhibited fatter tails than the Laplace (e.g., DJIA close–open returns over the 1981–1983 subperiod, where $1/v =$

Table 9.3
Monday Model: Non-Normal Estimates
Model: $R_t = \beta_0 + \beta_1 M_t + \epsilon_t$

Sample Period	Return Measure	β_0	β_1	α_0	1/v
A. 1975-77	close-open	0.0087 (0.877)	-0.04316 (1.725)	-3.4980* (14.211)	0.8719* (18.443)
	close-close	0.0350 (1.023)	0.02248 (0.330)	-0.4583* (2.972)	0.5411* (15.739)
B. 1978-80	close-open	-0.0384* (3.456)	-0.0843* (3.269)	-4.0492* (17.267)	1.0373* (23.467)
	close-close	0.0560 (1.552)	-0.1345 (1.903)	-0.8632* (4.964)	0.6629* (16.721)
C. 1981-83	close-open	0.0321* (3.433)	-0.0728* (3.346)	-4.4620* (15.047)	1.1069* (19.008)
	close-close	0.0108 (0.297)	-0.0233 (0.282)	-0.7761* (4.400)	0.6931* (16.418)
D. 1975-83	close-open	0.0000 (0.000)	-0.0526* (3.361)	-3.846* (26.901)	0.97551* (36.713)
	close-close	0.0356 (1.752)	-0.0522 (1.246)	-0.7186* (7.256)	0.6411* (28.338)
E. 1984-91	close-open	0.0182* (4.157)	-0.0928* (12.435)	-4.612* (21.893)	1.235* (33.221)
	close-close	0.0544* (3.233)	-0.0120 (0.420)	-2.2156* (19.527)	1.0516* (54.071)
F. 1975-91	close-open	0.0087** (2.328)	-0.0692* (8.172)	-4.5478* (32.698)	1.1766* (45.263)
	close-close	0.0440* (3.497)	-0.0285 (0.984)	-1.5936* (23.34)	.8894* (89.689)

*,**Significant at the 1 and 5 percent levels, respectively. Absolute t-statistic in parentheses.

1.106). At the 10 percent level there is also weak evidence of a weekend effect in DJIA returns over the 1975–1977 subperiod. In Table 9.3, Monday's mean return is the sum of β_0 and β_1, and a significance β_1 coefficient supports the Monday seasonal.

The difference between the LS and ML findings is due to the non-normality in the distribution of daily returns. As reported in Table 9.3 for the 1981–1983 subperiod, the weekend effect in the DJIA persists, but there is no evidence of a Monday effect. Extending the data over the 1984–1991 subperiod, as reported in panel E of Table 9.3, a significant weekend effect for the DJIA is documented but no significant Monday effect. After 1983, the weekend effect persists for the DJIA, but the Monday effect disappears. These results are consistent with prior research and confirm that the timing of Monday's stock price decline is related to firm size after 1973.

Monday Model: Non-Normal Exponential GARCH(1,1)

Table 9.4 gives parameter estimates for the exponential GARCH(1,1) based on the general error distribution. Henceforth, the GED model with GARCH effects is called the "GARCH" model. Since the GARCH model may be misspecified due to serially dependent residuals, all covariance matrices are estimated using Andrews's (1991a) kernel procedures based on matrix scores to obtain consistent covariances.

In the exponential GARCH model, conditional variances can respond asymmetrically to the information content of lagged conditional disturbances. In the conditional variance model, $\alpha_1 + \alpha_2$ measures the impact of positive disturbances at lag one, while α_1 measures the impact of negative disturbances. If $_2$ is significantly different from zero, the conditional variance process is asymmetric. Table 9.4 clearly indicates that for each subperiod, conditional variances respond asymmetrically to past innovations or news. Conditional volatility rises in response to positive and negative innovations, but the response to negative innovations is larger in magnitude than to positive innovations. In this context, an innovation is synonymous with unexpected information flows or news. This implies that the symmetric GARCH procedures common to many statistical packages may inadequately capture the variance processes for financial data.

These results are consistent with least-squares and ML parameter estimates. However, the magnitudes of the coefficients are clearly influenced by the estimation procedure. The GARCH parameter estimates generally fall somewhere between the least-squares and ML estimates. Thus, the procedures used to estimate the weekend or Monday effect are potentially important factors to measurement of this anomaly. It is important to realize that inferences about weekend and Monday effects can be influenced by the time period studied and the estimation procedures used.

From Table 9.4, a significant β_1 coefficient is consistent with a weekend effect in DJIA returns, and the β_1 coefficient is significant at the 1 percent level for all subperiods except the 1975–1977 subperiod. However, after adjusting for the influence of the January seasonal, a highly significant weekend effect is documented over the 1975–1977 subperiod. This is addressed in the next section.

Interaction—Monday and January Seasonal

To investigate the potential interaction between the Monday and January seasonal, the Monday model is restated to incorporate the impact of the January seasonal, which is explained in Appendix 9.1. The results for the ML model and GARCH(1,1) model based on the general error distribution are given for each subperiod in Table 9.5. From the previous discussion, the subperiod 1975–1977 is of special interest.

Subperiod: 1975–1977

The results reported in Table 9.5 reflect an adjustment for possible interactions between the Monday and January seasonal and reveal support for a weekend effect in DJIA returns over the 1975–1977 subperiod. The corresponding coefficients β_2 and β_3 are positive and negative, respectively, and significant at the 5 percent level, with β_3 greater in magnitude than β_0. The weekend effect in January is positive and significant, but the weekend effect for the rest of the year is negative and significant. These findings are consistent with the conclusions of Rogalski (1984) regarding January and size effects on weekend and Monday returns.

Other Subperiods

No supporting evidence is found for distinct weekend or Monday effects in January for the other subperiods examined. For all other subperiods except the 1975–1977 subperiod, the results presented in Table 9.5 indicate that the results for weekend effects in DJIA returns are not impacted by the January seasonal. In summary, the results from Table 9.5 indicate that after adjusting for the interaction between the Monday and January seasonal, strong evidence exists of a weekend effect in DJIA returns in all subperiods tested over the 1975–1991 period.

Kamara (1997)

As noted in the previous section, Kamara (1997) finds no weekend seasonal in close–open futures and spot S&P 500 returns over the subperiod 1983–1990. Daily (theoretical) opening and closing DJIA values are collected for the 1983–1990 subperiod, and nontrading period returns are calculated for each day of the week. Mean returns are reported for two groups of days, Monday, and the other days of the week (Tuesday–Friday); the findings are presented in panel A of Table 9.6. The weekend return for the DJIA, on average, is negative at –0.1257 percent versus a nontrading period mean return of 0.0409 percent for Tuesday–Friday. The standard t-test for equality of means yields a p-value of 0.0000, which is highly significant.

From panel A of Table 9.6, the S&P 500 futures mean weekend return, although negative at –0.0638 percent, is insignificant from the Tuesday–Friday mean return at 0.0132 percent, which is consistent with Kamara's (1997) finding of an insignificant weekend effect for S&P index futures. However, the

Table 9.4
Monday Model: Non-Normal Exponential GARCH(1,1)
Model: $R_t = \beta_0 + \beta_1 M_t + \epsilon_t$
$$h_t = \exp(\alpha_0 + \alpha_1 \epsilon_{t-1} + \alpha_2 \epsilon^{(+)}_{t-1}) h^r_{t-1}$$

Sample Period	Return Measure	β_0	β_1
A. 1975-77	close-open	0.0033	-0.0425
		(0.336)	(1.648)
	close-close	-0.0020	0.0231
		(0.064)	(0.373)
B. 1978-80	close-open	-0.0395*	0.0943*
		(3.854)	(3.953)
	close-close	0.0588	-0.1207
		(1.699)	(1.750)
C. 1981-83	close-open	0.0315*	-0.0723*
		(3.340)	(3.360)
	close-close	0.0221	-0.0600
		(0.611)	(0.748)
D. 1975-83	close-open	0.0000	-0.0562*
		(0.000)	(4.149)
	close-close	0.0253	-0.0565
		(1.278)	(1.424)
E. 1984-91	close-open	0.0185*	-0.1179*
		(2.865)	(7.526)
	close-close	0.0540*	-0.0204
		(2.964)	(0.487)
F. 1975-91	close-open	0.0089**	-0.0786*
		(2.073)	(7.685)
	close-close	0.0398*	-0.0363
		(3.025)	(1.231)

*,**Significant at the 1 and 5 percent levels, respectively. Absolute t-statistic in parentheses.

Table 9.4 (*continued*)

α_0	α_1	α_2	γ	$1/v$
-0.1910*	-0.3255*	0.4438*	0.9566*	0.7038*
(3.105)	(3.987)	(2.616)	(74.569)	(19.937)
-0.0543**	-0.0684	0.1275**	0.9738*	0.4898*
(2.216)	(1.756)	(2.134)	(75.658)	(17.538)
-0.9831**	-0.4886**	0.9072*	0.7977*	1.0678*
(2.055)	(2.430)	(2.797)	(7.379)	(19.614)
-0.1457*	-0.1698*	0.2356**	0.9059*	0.6063*
(2.835)	(3.131)	(2.485)	(26.080)	(14.387)
-0.5478	-0.3424**	0.6012**	0.8943*	1.0765*
(1.829)	(2.177)	(2.123)	(15.159)	(16.786)
-0.1020*	-0.0939**	0.1886*	0.9465*	0.6229*
(2.752)	(2.131)	(2.744)	(44.498)	(19.328)
-0.2692*	-0.2697*	0.4732*	0.9472*	0.9585*
(6.057)	(5.211)	(5.739)	(106.161)	(36.822)
-0.0983*	-0.1141*	0.2004*	0.9502*	0.5812*
(5.101)	(5.094)	(5.129)	(86.260)	(30.127)
-1.0640*	-0.6600*	0.8662*	0.7763*	1.0450*
(6.114)	(7.432)	(5.039)	(20.545)	(39.139)
-0.1922*	-0.1569*	0.1714*	0.9176*	0.8725*
(5.238)	(10.948)	(4.138)	(58.127)	(33.857)
-0.6560*	0.4485*	0.6785*	0.8626*	1.0295*
(9.614)	(11.829)	(8.026)	(56.422)	(53.226)
-0.1444*	-0.1321*	0.1981*	0.9341*	0.7488*
(8.626)	(16.415)	(7.742)	(111.044)	(51.329)

Table 9.5
Monday Model Incorporating January Seasonal: Non-Normal Estimates
Model: $R_t = \beta_0 + \beta_1 J_t + \beta_2 J_t M_t + \beta_3 M_t + \epsilon_t$
$h_t = \exp(\alpha_0)$

Sample Period	Return Measure	β_0	β_1
A. 1975-77	close-open	0.0102	-0.0361
		(0.980)	(1.027)
	close-close	0.0171	0.2352**
		(0.475)	(2.201)
B. 1978-80	close-open	-0.0449*	0.0987**
		(4.080)	(2.562)
	close-close	0.0648	-0.1170
		(1.703)	(0.948)
C. 1981-83	close-open	0.0240*	0.0762**
		(2.622)	(2.266)
	close-close	0.0119	-0.0135
		(0.301)	(0.119)
D. 1984-91	close-open	0.0167*	0.0153
		(2.544)	(0.979)
	close-close	0.0545*	0.0392
		(3.210)	(0.501)

*,**Significant at the 1 and 5 percent levels, respectively. Absolute t-statistics in parentheses.

latter finding is potentially biased as index futures trade for fifteen minutes beyond the 4:00 P.M. EST close of the NYSE. In addition, since the Monday seasonal in spot indices is well known, one would expect that index futures would discount this phenomenon. Another test is to reexamine S&P 500 index futures over the Friday open to Monday open period; these results are reported in panel A of Table 9.6. The Friday-open to Monday-open mean return is negative at –0.0987 percent versus a mean return of 0.07531 percent for the other days of the week. The standard t-test for equality of means yields a p-value of 0.0269, which is significant at an acceptable level. After adjusting for the extended trading property of index futures, the empirical results support the existence of a modified weekend effect in S&P 500 index futures over the

Table 9.5 (*continued*)

β_2	β_3	α_0	1/v
0.2239*	-0.0527**	-3.5148*	0.8738*
(2.693)	(1.970)	(14.195)	(18.112)
0.4223**	-0.0169	-0.4091**	0.5242*
(2.295)	(0.228)	(2.549)	(12.504)
-0.0500	-0.0794*	-4.0634*	1.0381*
(0.525)	(2.918)	(17.774)	(24.008)
0.4828	-0.1688**	-0.8868*	0.6682*
(1.766)	(2.285)	(5.048)	(16.594)
0.1241	-0.0686*	-4.6106*	1.1391*
(1.336)	(3.027)	(14.829)	(18.759)
0.0767	-0.0315	-0.7762*	0.6931*
(0.319)	(0.355)	(4.401)	(16.413)
-0.0333	-0.0912*	-4.4235*	1.1963*
(1.377)	(5.865)	(22.047)	(34.565)
0.0604	-0.0176	-2.2298*	1.0548*
(0.351)	(0.435)	(19.528)	(53.608)

period 1983–1990, but in this case the seasonal is measured from Friday's open to Monday's open.

SUMMARY AND CONCLUSIONS

French (1980) published one of the first academic studies documenting a day-of-the-week effect in equity returns. Over the period 1953–1977, French reports that Monday's mean return is the lowest, at –0.1601 percent, followed by Tuesday's mean return, at 0.0157 percent. On average, S&P 500 returns are low over the first two trading days of the week. In contrast, the highest returns, on average, are observed on Wednesday and Friday, at 0.0967 and 0.0873 percent, respectively, followed by Thursday's mean return, at 0.0448 percent. Based on French's original research, the conventional wisdom is that

Table 9.6
New Evidence on the Monday Seasonal

	Friday/Monday	Other days		Friday/Monday	Other days		Friday/Monday	Other days	
	close/open	close/open	p-value	Open/open	open/open	p-value	close/close	close/close	p-value
Panel A									
1983-1990									
S&P 500 futures	-0.0638	0.0132	0.0989	-0.00987	0.07531	0.0269	N/A	N/A	N/A
DJIA: Large cap	-0.1257	0.0409	0.0000	N/A	N/A	N/A	N/A	N/A	N/A
Panel B									
March 1990-June 2001									
S&P 500 spot: Large cap	N/A	N/A	N/A	N/A	N/A	N/A	0.1201*	0.0279	0.0469

*Mean S&P 500 returns for the other days of the week are as follows: Tuesday = 0.0601, Wednesday = 0.0038, and Friday = 0.0181. All returns are in percent. The p-value is reported for the null hypothesis that the weekend or Monday mean return equals mean return for all other days of the week. S&P 500 is the Standard & Poor's 500 index. DJIA is the Dow Jones Industrial Average.

Monday's returns are related to "last-place status," and the Monday effect has generated much empirical research.

In the footnotes to Table 9.6, Tuesday, Wednesday, Thursday, and Friday S&P 500 index mean returns are reported for March 1990 through June 2001, and the reported findings are unexpected. For more recent return data, Monday returns have achieved "first-place status," followed by Tuesday returns. The Monday effect has been resurrected, but now the highest returns are observed on Mondays. Also of interest is the observation that S&P 500 Friday returns are unusually low over the 1990s. It might be appropriate to repeat Wyckoff's (1930) mantra, "The only unchangeable thing about the stock market is its tendency to change."

This chapter has attempted to remove some of the uncertainty and confusion associated with empirical research on the Monday seasonal. Familiarity with market microstructure issues is just as important as familiarity with esoteric econometric techniques. In empirical finance, the two are complements, not substitutes.

APPENDIX 9.1

Methodology

This study uses least-squares and maximum-likelihood estimation procedures to estimate the weekend and Monday effect models. Scale-invariant M-estimation is also used. Connolly (1989) used an interactively rescaled M-estimator based on weighted least squares. This method is not necessarily equivalent to scale-invariant methods and does not yield efficient parameter estimates. It is reported that the scale-invariant M-estimators based on the natural log of the hyperbolic cosine function (see Gallant 1987) are identical to the LS parameter estimates. Connolly's M-estimators were also close to LS estimates of the parameters. His conclusions about test sensitivity may have been influenced by the inefficiency of his estimators.

The computed covariance matrix and reported t-statistics for the LS procedure are robust to heteroskedasticity and autocorrelation in the disturbances without specifying a particular functional form for the process. This procedure yields similar coefficients as ordinary LS but different t-statistics. The primary advantage of this approach is the generality in the correction for nonspherical disturbances. If the return generating process is non-normal, day-of-the-week model parameter estimates from procedures admitting non-normalities will likely differ from LS parameter estimates. An argument supported by the empirical evidence is that a basic problem with the data is the non-normality in the return-generating process rather than solely heteroskedasticity. As indicated by Bollerslev, Chou, and Kroner (1992), this documented evidence of non-normality is potentially due to volatility clustering and outliers. In instances when the data generating process is suspected of being non-normal, a wider choice of distributions is necessary to obtain robust parameter estimates. One family of distributions, the general error distribution, allows for both thin and fat tails and includes the normal as a special case (see Harvey 1991; Box and Tiao 1973). Assuming sufficient regularity conditions (see Gallant 1987), ML estimators of the model parameters using the GED are consistent and asymptotically normal.

For each procedure, the asymptotic matrix is estimated from the score matrix using quadratic spectral density weights. From Andrews (1991b), the estimated covariance matrix is consistent with respect to generalized heteroskedasticity and autocorrelation in the disturbances without specifying the nature of the process. GARCH procedures, on the other hand, assume that conditional disturbances are serially uncorrelated but linearly dependent in conditional second moments. If the disturbances are serially dependent or more generally heteroskedastic than admitted by the GARCH procedure, the covariance matrix from the GARCH procedure will be biased. Therefore, even GARCH procedures should report kernel-based covariance estimates rather then covariances based on the information matrix.

Monday Model

The Monday model is expressed as follows:

$$R_t = \beta_0 + \beta_1 M_t + \epsilon_t,$$

where M_t is a dummy variable identifying Mondays, β_0 is the intercept and represents the mean return for all other days of the week, and Monday's mean return is given by $\beta_0 + \beta_1$. R_t represents the daily return for day t, and the disturbances are denoted by ϵ_t. The Monday seasonal is represented by β_1. For comparison to Connolly (1989), the Monday model examines the weekend effect hypothesis by defining R_t as the daily nontrading period return and the Monday effect hypothesis by defining R_t as the daily close–close period return.

Monday Model Incorporating January Seasonal

To investigate the potential interaction between the Monday and January seasonal, the Monday model is restated as follows:

$$R_t = \beta_0 + \beta_1 J_t + \beta_2 J_t M_t + \beta_3 M_t + \epsilon_t,$$

where J_t is a dummy variable that equals one for January and zero otherwise. $J_t M_t$ is an interaction term between the Monday and January seasonal. Weekend or Monday effects in January are measured by $\beta_1 + \beta_2 + \beta_3$, with β_3 measuring weekend or Monday effects for the rest of the year. The January seasonality is measured by β_1. As before, R_t represents the daily return for day t, and the disturbances are denoted by $_t$. The difference between Mondays in January and Mondays over the rest of the year is represented by β_2. The mean Monday return in January is given by $\beta_0 + \beta_1 + \beta_2 + \beta_3$ and for the rest of the year by $\beta_0 + \beta_3$.

NOTES

1. Rogalski (1984) obtains opening S&P 500 values from S&P Corporation for the period December 29, 1978, to December 9, 1983. In a footnote, Kamara (1997) obtains opening value for the S&P 500 index for the period 1983 through 1990. Both authors use these values to calculate time decomposed S&P 500 returns, but interpretation of such results is subject to the stale-quote problem. As suggested by one referee of this paper, a logical extension of the current research is to calculate the Friday-open to Monday-open S&P 500 index return and compare these results with the Monday-open to Tuesday-open return, and so forth for the other days of the week. However, opening S&P 500 index values are subject to the stale-quote problem, which is the main reason why this analysis is not considered fruitful and is omitted from this study. One avenue for future research is to examine open-to-open returns across the days of the week for S&P 500 depository receipts. Since this is a first trade of the day for depository receipts, in this case, the stale-quote problem does not exist. S&P 500 depository receipts began trading on the AMEX in 1993.

2. The actual Dow opening is subject to a stale-quote problem. As an example, on November 25, 1997, the DJIA closed at 7,808.95. The theoretical opening for November 26, 1997, is reported as 7,837.30, with a 10:00 A.M. EST value of 7,838.54. The actual Dow opening for November 26, 1997, is reported as 7,809.55, but the actual opening contains many stale quotes. This can be seen by comparing the Dow's value at 10:00 A.M. EST (7,838.54) to its theoretical opening (7,837.30), and the Dow's previous closing (7,808.95) to its actual opening (7,809.55).

3. Nontrading period (overnight) S&P 500 index returns should be interpreted cautiously as opening index values are subject to the stale-quote problem. In contrast to procedures for calculating (theoretical) opening values for the DJIA, S&P 500 opening values are not based on the first trade for each component stock.

4. According to the January effect, small firms earn unusually large returns over the month of January relative to large firms. This phenomenon was much publicized in the late 1970s to early 1980s. Concomitant with the introduction of index futures in 1982, the January effect greatly lessened and completely disappeared in the 1990s.

5. Connolly's (1989) paper contains over ten tables. Examination of these tables reveals the following interesting observations among reported results for the S&P 500, CRSP value-weighted, and CRSP equally weighted indices. In part C of section VI, entitled "GARCH Model Results," Connolly states, "For the 1975–1983 period, test results show the constant mean model is best for the S&P 500 and EW return measures and Model 2 is best for the VW return measure. There is no obvious explanation for this divergence of results between the return measures." However, given the nature of these three indices, the S&P 500 and the CRSP VW are most similar, but throughout Connolly reports similar results for the S&P 500 and the CRSP EW indices. To re-

solve this conundrum, Connolly's procedures are duplicated for the Monday model over an identical time period; it appears that Connolly mislabeled the CRSP VW and EW indices. Therefore, throughout Connolly's paper, reported results for the CRSP VW index are in fact for the CRSP EW index, and conversely.

REFERENCES

Andrews, D. 1991a. "Asymptotic normality of series estimators for nonparametric and semiparametric regression models." *Econometrica* 59: 307–346.

———. 1991b. "Heteroskedasticity and autocorrelation consisting covariance matrix estimation." *Econometrica* 59: 817–858.

Ariel, R. 1990. "High stock returns before holidays." *Journal of Finance* 45 (5): 1611–1626.

Connolly, R. A. 1989. "An examination of the robustness of the weekend effect." *Journal of Financial and Quantitative Analysis* 24 (2): 133–169.

Cruver, B. 2002. *Anatomy of Greed.* New York: Carroll and Graf.

Bollerslev, T., R. Chou, and K. Kroner. 1992. "ARCH modeling in finance." *Journal of Econometrics* 52: 5–59.

Box, G., and G. Tiao. 1973. *Bayesian Inference in Statistical Analysis.* Reading, Mass.: Addison-Wesley.

Brealey, R., and S. Myers. 2000. *Principles of Corporate Finance.* New York: McGraw-Hill.

French, K. 1980. "Stock returns and the weekend effect." *Journal of Financial Economics* 8 (1): 55–69.

Gallant, A. 1987. *Nonlinear Statistic Models.* New York: John Wiley & Sons.

Harvey, A. 1991. *The Econometric Analysis of Time Series.* Cambridge, Mass.: MIT Press.

Herbst, A., and E. Maberly. 1992. "The informational role of end-of-the-day returns in stock index futures." *Journal of Futures Markets* 12 (5): 595–602.

Hiraki, T., E. Maberly, and Y. Park. 1994. "Day-of-the-week mean spillover effects between New York and Tokyo: January 1976 to August 1992: A note." *Pacific-Basin Finance Journal* 2 (1): 61–71.

Ikenberry, D. 2002. "Underreaction to Self-Selected News Events: The Case of Stock Splits." *Review of Financial Studies* 15 (2): 489–526.

Kamara, Avraham. 1997. "New evidence on the Monday seasonal in stock returns." *Journal of Business* 70 (1): 63–84.

Reinganum, Marc. 1983. "The anomalous stock market behavior of small firms in January." *Journal of Financial Economics* 12 (1): 89–104.

Rogalski, R. J. 1984. "New findings regarding day-of-the-week over trading and non-trading periods: A note." *Journal of Finance* 39 (5): 1603–1614.

Salbu, S. 2002. "Foreword." In *Anatomy of Greed* (ed. by B. Cruver). New York: Caroll & Grat.

Smirlock, M., and L. Starks. 1986. "Day of the week effects in stock returns: Some intraday evidence." *Journal of Financial Economics* 17 (1): 197–210.

Wang, K., Li Y., and J. Erickson. 1997. "A new look at the Monday effect." *Journal of Finance* 52 (5): 2171–2186.

Wyckoff, Richard. 1930. *Wall Street Ventures & Adventures through Forty Years.* Burlington, Vt.: Fraser.

10

A Financial Analysis of the Economic Effects Associated with Having to Reverse Current-Account Deficits

Austin Murphy

EXECUTIVE SUMMARY

This research develops a theoretical model of current-account deficits that explains the effects of having to reverse such imbalances. The theory defines precise mathematical relationships that should exist between the balance of payments, exchange rates, interest rates, inflation, income, and ever-changing investor expectations. The model, which is consistent with both currency crises and less volatile situations, provides a very useful framework for the fundamental valuation of currencies.

The model shows the exact amount of time that a current-account deficit can be postponed with external financing, and it utilizes this information to specify precisely the effect on exchange rates. That effect is shown to be strongly influenced by the perceptions of foreign currency investors. In particular, the exact exchange rate will be determined by investor estimates as to the probability of the country utilizing a large or small devaluation (instead of a real income decline and recession) to address the current-account problem temporarily.

Given the ineffectiveness of other theories in explaining the path of exchange rates that are observed empirically, the financial model developed here is very important for explaining both currency crises and more stable situations. Perhaps most important, it is useful for understanding the current international situation, which, assuming no material change in relative protectionism worldwide, requires either a significant decline in real income in the United States or a long-term devaluation-inflation-devaluation spiral. The disastrous implications of this phenomenon on U.S. security markets was described in Chapter 1.

INTRODUCTION

One of the problems mentioned in the introductory chapter of this book for U.S. stocks and profits was related to the international trade situation of the United States. There it was mentioned that the U.S. trade situation was not particularly conducive to a positive stock market environment. This final chapter examines the crucial problem of trade imbalances in great detail and precisely models their effect on currency values, thereby showing the magnitude of the problem faced by the United States.

Trade imbalances can serve to optimize satisfaction of heterogeneous demand preferences and even make investment/output decisions more efficient, but any resulting current-account deficits generally must eventually be reversed so that the financing for the deficits can be repaid (Obstfeld and Rogoff 1995). A current-account deficit can be accompanied by high levels of productive investment (especially imported foreign investments), which may lead to a future reversal in the trade imbalance if that investment begins to create productivity improvements (and thereby enhance competitiveness in internationally traded goods and services). However, it is often the case empirically that a current-account deficit is at least partially caused by overborrowing to finance excessive consumption (or overbuilding in industries, like real estate, which do not produce goods or services that are internationally traded) and therefore cannot correct itself without having an adverse effect on other variables like exchange rates and income (McKinnon and Pill 1996). Chronic current-account deficits represent an especially serious situation that has to be addressed (Yusoff 1997).

One classical solution to reverse a current-account deficit is to allow the domestic currency to fall in value and thereby discourage imports and encourage exports to eliminate the imbalance (Afesoglu and Dutkowsky 1997). Unfortunately, this solution ignores two problems: elasticity of demand (Hufbauer and Erb 1984) and inflation induced by currency depreciation (Abuaf and Jorion 1990). Various alternative solutions designed to avoid these problems in the short term often merely postpone and magnify the negative effects of current account deficits.

The various currency crises of the 1990s have brought these issues to the forefront of relevance (Lim 1999), and attempts have been made to explain at least some of the events that represent catalysts for, or symptoms of, the crises (Miller 1998). However, existing theories have not been very successful in explaining even more stable situations (MacDonald 1990), much less the root structural causes of the currency volatility of the 1990s (Berg and Pattillo 1999).

It is true that Claessens (1991) has developed an alternative exchange-rate model that may explain at least one crisis in the 1980s (Brazil in 1986) fairly well in terms of being caused by domestic credit expansion and investor interpretations thereof. However, his model's assumption that domestic credit growth is outside the control of the domestic central bank greatly reduces the generality of it. While bank credit expansion can indeed affect future income growth, inflation, the current account, and therefore investor expectations, credit expansion is often caused by loose monetary policies of the central bank itself. In addition, whereas Claessens's (1991) model has currency crises determined strictly by the domestic credit variable, there are also many other factors that can affect currency movements through investor expectations, such as central bank statements and credibility, political policies and developments, and various economic events and situations. For instance, most central banks of Asian countries that experienced currency crises in 1997 had been fairly successful in keeping domestic credit expansion from materially changing in the years before and in the year of the crises (Aliber 2000), and concrete empirical evidence indicates that virtually no Asian currency was fundamentally overvalued with respect to monetary factors prior to the 1997 crises (Husted and MacDonald 1999).

Kane (2000) and others have hypothesized that a poor banking system (rife with corruption and politically motivated bad loans) opened up to a free market was the structural cause of the Asian currency crisis. While a banking system plagued by bad loans in an environment of deregulation can certainly lead to reduced lending and declining economic growth (Caprio and Klingebiel 1997), the case of Japan in the 1990s illustrates very well that it in no way mandates a currency crisis. In particular, Japan in the 1990s was characterized by bad loans and slow economic growth, but it had a rising currency value because of a huge current-account surplus.

Deregulation of a banking system can indeed contribute to a currency crisis, however. For instance, deregulation can increase competition in the banking industry, and this competition can reduce the profitability of existing banks and increase bank insolvencies, thereby scaring off the foreign capital needed to finance a current account deficit, as Kane (2000) himself admits.

Once a currency crisis develops, the high real interest rates imposed to defend the currency against further devaluations causes a recession, especially since the needed tight money policies restrict the central bank from providing the liquidity to the banking system to make sufficient new loans. The recession leads to further bad loans and insolvencies, especially for banks with substantial mismatched financing in foreign currencies, which rise in domestic currency value in the crisis. As a result, a currency crisis can actually cause (as well as magnify) banking problems and a recession.

There is substantial evidence against Kane's hypothesis that the Asian currency crisis of 1997 was caused by poor banking system. For instance, the Philippines did not have a banking problem prior to the 1997 currency crisis but yet experienced a sharp fall in its currency value during the period (Tanzer 1999). On the other hand, China had serious banking problems but did not suffer a devaluation in the 1997 currency crisis. Further evidence against the Kane hypothesis is provided by the empirical findings of Kho and Stulz (2000), who discovered little evidence of a crash in Asian bank stock prices prior to the Asian currency crisis in the second half of 1997. Although Thai (as well as Korean and Indonesian) bank stock prices did fall significantly from their highs just before the onset of the Thai currency collapse, they remained above their lows in existence earlier in the year. Kho and Stulz (2000) also found that Asian bank stock prices were no more adversely affected by the Asian currency crisis than other Asian stocks (such as Asian industrials). The latter findings are consistent with a theory that an initial run on the Thai currency partially related to a sell-off in Thai banking stocks was a mere catalyst to the Asian currency crisis, which then required substantially higher interest rates (to inhibit further devaluations), which in turn caused a deep recession and a bear market in stocks in general.

This research creates a model of current-account deficits that is designed to enhance comprehension of their effect on exchange rates, interest rates, inflation, and real economic growth. To illustrate the model's implications, the case of New Zealand (N.Z.) in 1999 is provided as an example. In the first section, the problems of a current account deficit and currency devaluations are modeled. Next, alternative solutions to devaluation, such as inducing a real income decline or obtaining external financing of a current-account deficit, are discussed, and a precise model of private capital inflows is developed mathematically. In the third section, the eventual effect of a current-account deficit on real income is analyzed. In the following section, the model's implications are discussed within the context of various empirical findings, such as the currency crises of the 1990s. The findings are summarized in the final section.

PROBLEMS OF USING CURRENCY DEVALUATIONS
TO SOLVE CURRENT-ACCOUNT IMBALANCES

Current-account deficits may be caused by heterogeneous time preferences for consumption and investment across different countries (Obstfeld and Rogoff 1995). Excessive current spending by domestic residents (especially on consumption goods), which can cause serious current-account deficit problems, is often spurred by government borrowings or guarantees of domestic bank/corporate liabilities (Velasco 1987). Trade imbalances may also be induced directly by temporary productivity and government spending shocks (Glick and Rogoff 1995), which have an empirical tendency to induce long-term effects on the trade balance (Rodriguez 1980). In addition, a change in the terms of trade (in the case of heterogeneous consumer risk-aversion levels) can by itself lead to different real interest rates across countries and different savings and spending patterns, which can cause current-account deficits (Stulz 1988). Moreover, current-account deficits may occur in the case of flexible as well as fixed exchange rates (Williamson 1991). Regardless of the cause or exchange rate regime, a current-account deficit must eventually reverse itself, and benign solutions, such as an improvement in the relative productivity of producing internationally traded goods and services, or an enhanced protectionist position relative to the rest of the world, are often not feasible (Murphy 2000b).

Holding all other relevant factors constant, current-account deficits increase the supply of currency relative to demand and therefore put pressure on the exchange rate to depreciate (Dooley and Isard 1982). Because a currency devaluation increases the demand for exports and reduces the demand for imports (once again assuming all other variables to be the same), many recommend this natural tendency of a currency to depreciate in the face of a current-account deficit as a solution to *correct* the imbalance (Haque, Montiel, and Symansky 1991). However, whether a currency depreciation solves a current-account imbalance (and if so, for how long) depends on the elasticity of demand for imports and for exports and on the degree (and speed) of imported inflation.

The Problem of Demand Inelasticity

While classical economic theory correctly asserts that exchange rate depreciation will encourage exports and discourage imports, imports may actually increase when measured in domestic currency, and foreign currency exports decrease, depending on the elasticity of demand for the imports and exports relative to the change in the price that is caused by devaluation (Goldstein and Khan 1978). The general Marshall (1924) and Lerner (1944) conditions required for a devaluation to improve the current-account balance is for the weighted-average elasticity of demand for imports and for exports to sum over one.

Although some evidence of low demand elasticity has been discovered empirically, such parameter values have generally been found to be caused by the famous J-curve effect, in which short-term elasticity of demand is very low but increases over time (Caves, Frankel, and Jones 1996). In particular, market participants often only slowly adjust their pricing, marketing, hedging, and production decisions to a new exchange rate levels (Dixit 1989), especially since there are costs associated with frequently changing prices in export markets to reflect new exchange rate levels (Devereux 2000). Marquez (1990) and Goldstein and Khan (1978) have reported some empirical evidence on a number of developed countries that satisfy the Marshall-Lerner condition for currency devaluation to solve a balance of payments (BOP) problem, but they were unable to find any significant evidence for developing countries. Fullerton, Sawyer, and Sprinkle (1999) have cited evidence of a serious inelasticity of demand with respect to imports into developing countries. Although the latter authors also noted some research indicating a more encouraging elasticity of demand with respect to exports out of developing countries, the latter elasticity may be much lower in the case of concurrent devaluations by an entire group of exporting countries competing with each other.

In normal circumstances, a currency depreciation does increase foreign currency export revenue. For example, N.Z. exports of sheep meat to the United States rose by 58 percent in real terms from 1997 to 1998 as a result of a 29 percent rise in the U.S. dollar against the N.Z. dollar (which made the N.Z.

sheep farmers more competitive), but this lower price caused U.S.–dollar exports to the United States to rise by only 23 percent (McManus 1999). These data imply a demand elasticity of 58/29 = 2.0 (assuming the entire increase in unit volume was caused by the currency depreciation and not other factors, such as increased incomes in the United States and changes in international freight rates). Somewhat simplistically assuming for the sake of an uncomplicated illustration that the average demand elasticity of N.Z. exports is the same as for lamb and that demand for imports is totally inelastic (because many imported manufactured goods like cars are virtual "essentials," for which there is no domestic substitute production in New Zealand), the Marshall-Lerner condition for an improvement in the current account would be met in this case (as U.S.–dollar imports would remain unchanged while U.S.–dollar exports rise).

The Problems of Importing Inflation

Even for cases where there is sufficient elasticity of demand relative to price for a currency depreciation to correct a balance of payments deficit short-term, another problem can arise. In particular, a currency devaluation may eventually cause an increase in domestic inflation that can fully neutralize the effect of the exchange-rate change.

As shown in Appendix 10.1 equations (A10.1-1) through (A10.1-6), an initial exchange-rate change can result in an increase in inflation that forces a perpetual currency depreciation to keep the current account in balance. This cycle is consistent with (but not implied by) Cassell's (1928) purchasing power parity (PPP) theory. Empirical studies indicate that PPP generally holds only over long-term intervals (Froot and Rogoff 1995), and so the amount of time T for an exchange rate change to be incorporated into inflation would normally equal about five to ten years.

For example, in early 1999, New Zealand had a current-account deficit equal to about 25 percent of exports of goods and services, so exports needed to rise by that amount to remove the deficit. Given an assumed demand elasticity of about 2.0 from the prior subsection (which once again is merely used for illustration), the trade-weighted value of foreign currencies would have to rise by 33 percent in order to bring the current account into balance (implying a 1/1.33 = 25% decline in the N.Z. dollar).[1] Although policies to be mentioned in subsequent sections could postpone the time to the devaluation, the eventual decline would cause a 33 percent rise in the domestic prices for real goods and services eventually, as shown in equation (A10.1-2). If there is no monetary loosening after the depreciation, the higher prices might be smoothed into the economy over T = 10 years, and annual inflation would increase to $[\{1 + 0\}\{1 + 0.33\}^{1/10}] - 1 = 3$ percent from its approximate 0 percent level in early 1999. Inflation would continue at that rate, since the currency would have to continue to devalue in order to keep the prior imported inflation from reigniting the BOP problem, and that inflation-induced devaluation would keep the inflation component of the cycle going.

In other situations, where no attempt is made to slow the effect of a currency depreciation on inflation, prices of real goods and services may react more quickly and powerfully. The reaction tends to be faster where there is widespread wage indexation (Obstfeld and Rogoff 1996), which is more likely to exist in countries that already have high inflation (Duca and VanHoose 1998).

At some point, exchange rate changes may result in a more immediate change in domestic prices (especially if domestic suppliers of capital and labor begin quickly to anticipate imported inflation), and imported price increases will occur over a shorter and shorter time interval. In cases of mere monthly, weekly, daily, or hourly lags in the adjustment in domestic inflation to exchange-rate changes, the inflation rate can lead to double-digit annual inflation, or even hyperinflation, with only a small exchange-rate change C.

Equations (A10.1-1) through (A10.1-9) imply that the natural tendency for a currency to depreciate in the face of a current-account deficit will lead to hyperinflation only if the full price effect of a devaluation is immediately incorporated into domestic inflation (i.e., if $T = 0$). Hyperinflation in turn can cause significant real product inefficiencies (such as by forcing suppliers of capital and labor to use expensive barter trade) and thereby exasperate the BOP problem. Although situations of $T = 0$ and hyperinflation are not typically observed cases, inflation-induced distortions in the real sector can inhibit economic productivity even in situations where only moderate inflation exists (Michalski 1972). As a result, an inflation-inducing devaluation can eventually lead to a further deterioration in the current account.

The Interaction of Demand Elasticity and Inflation Effects

Many of the same factors that cause a delay in a currency depreciation being incorporated into inflation (e.g., see footnote 16), also cause the J-curve effects that result in short-term demand for imports and exports being relatively inelastic (Caves, Frankel, and Jones 1996). In the longer term, as demand becomes more elastic, the effects of the currency depreciation work their way more strongly into higher domestic real-good prices. Thus, just as the currency depreciation starts to solve a current-account imbalance through demand elasticity, that imbalance is at least partially offset by the depreciation-induced inflation pass-through. Although the demand elasticity effects tend to work their way through the economy more quickly than inflation, the partial offset can cause chronic BOP problems that are not easy to remedy.

Thus, a devaluation tends to merely postpone a BOP problem into the future, and, in the case of very inelastic demand or devaluation-induced hyperinflation, a currency depreciation may not successfully do even that. As a result, an alternative solution must eventually be employed.

THE EFFECT OF USING ALTERNATIVE CLASSICAL
POLICIES TO CORRECT BOP IMBALANCES

Besides devaluation, standard capitalist economic theory provides several alternative methods of addressing BOP problems. These "solutions" include utilizing various forms of external financing, which postpones and magnifies the problem, and imposing on the domestic economy a real income decline, which may by itself represent an undesirable outcome. These alternatives will be evaluated in this section.

Tight Monetary and Fiscal Policies

One alternative to the dismal scenario of a continuous devaluation-inflation spiral is to utilize fiscal and monetary policies to reduce domestic demand sufficiently to cause a real decline in domestic income (Tegene 1989). Gold standards can automatically cause a monetary tightening when the current account is in deficit, through a natural outflow of gold or money to finance the deficit, which increases interest rates and thereby lowers spending and income (Marx and Engels 1988).[2] Central banks with paper currency can mimic this effect by automatically reducing the money supply in the face of a current-account deficit (Williamson 1991). Maintaining a fixed exchange rate in the face of current-account deficit pressures is a typical policy that forces a rise in real interest rates (as real interest rates must reflect an expected future real decline in the currency to reverse the current-account deficit), which in turn causes a decline in real income, as well as potentially a banking/financial crisis (Velasco 1987). In any event, the reduction in real income and resulting recession tends to cause unemployment and falling wages, so that the cost of exported goods and the amount of purchasing power available for imports are both successfully reduced (Chossudovsky 1997).

If the restrictive monetary and fiscal policies reduce real income enough (perhaps gradually over some number of periods, such as $T = 10$ years, similar to the gradual inflation adjustment previously assumed), demand can be reduced sufficiently to solve the current-account problem without an inflationary devaluation (Tegene 1989). Tight monetary policies can therefore be used to stop inflation, stabilize exchange rates, and balance the current account (Rich 1997), albeit at the cost of the lower income. Note that any actual real decline in income may be measured as a reduction in the real growth that would otherwise occur and is, in any event, underestimated by GDP figures, which include the share of national income owned by foreigners. Note also that depending on relative elasticity of demand with respect to real income and exchange rates, the real income decline (c) needed to balance the current account can actually be far less than the devaluation (C) needed to balance temporarily the current account (i.e., it is not necessary that $c = C$).

In addition, the continuous devaluation-inflation cycle explained in the first section of this article can also be broken by a real-income drop of c after an initial decline in exchange rates and the resulting one-time inflation increase. For instance, tight monetary policies utilized to reduce the real money supply (after an initial inflation shock) were widely employed in reforming Eastern European countries in the early 1990s to decrease real income greatly and generate current-account surpluses (Williamson 1991), just as they have been frequently used elsewhere in a similar fashion (Chossudovsky 1997). Because of the downward stickiness of nominal wages, it usually is politically more expedient to effect a real-income decline by using fiscal and monetary tightening after an inflationary situation has developed just to keep wages and benefits from rising with inflation, than trying to force down nominal income (Stiglitz 1993).[3]

Although the typical policy is first to initiate a devaluation, which induces inflation, and then raise interest rates sufficiently to cause a recession, which increases unemployment and lowers real wage demands (without having to lower them nominally because of the devaluation-induced inflation), there are other policy alternatives. For instance, during the 1997–1998 Asian currency crisis, there was substantial downward pressure on the N.Z. dollar (because New Zealand competed with Asia, and because the country already had an enormous current-account deficit even before the crisis). However, the very restrictive monetary policies of New Zealand prevented the devaluation from being larger (and even drove the inflation rate close to 0% despite the significant currency depreciation that did occur). This tight money, however, caused a recession that brought real incomes significantly below where they would have been (although nominal income did not fall). Though the decline in real income was not sufficient to reduce the current-account deficit in New Zealand very much, it did succeed in postponing the problem into the future (as will be explained in subsequent subsections).

IMF and International Aid Funding

It is sometimes possible to postpone a decline in the exchange rate by financing a current-account deficit with international aid or loans, such as are available from the IMF. The problem can be deferred for each year that net funding equal to the amount of the deficit is provided. However, unless there is a perpetual annual transfer equal to the current-account deficit, the aid or loans merely postpone the previously mentioned effects (which begin to occur as soon as additional new aid or loans are no longer provided).

In the case of loans that must be paid back, generally plus interest at some positive interest rate, the future delayed effect is actually larger than if the negative effects were not postponed. For instance, with a one-time loan of an amount that funds one year's current-account deficit, the debt is increased by the amount of interest that will be owed over the next year (regardless of the maturity of the loan, as longer-term debts merely compound the future interest owed). The exchange rate must therefore adjust downward not only by C to correct the original current-account imbalance, but by a further amount sufficient to create enough exports to pay off the debt (plus any interest). Thus, future inflation or real income losses (or a combination thereof) will be larger.

Some countries that qualify for IMF loans may forgo taking on such debt, because it only postpones and magnifies the problem. In addition, the infringements on sovereignty imposed by IMF lending conditions (Seib and Murray 1991), which require "responsible monetary policies" to ensure exchange rate stability (Dellas and Stockman 1993) and typically mandate other actions (such as tight fiscal policies and market reforms) that can greatly increase domestic poverty (Chossudovsky 1997), motivate some countries to avoid this solution (Henderson 1998). These reasons, as well as the negative stigma associated with IMF loans of appearing to be a beggar at the mercy of the world's richer countries (Wessel 1999), explain why New Zealand has not applied for IMF loans despite qualifying for such subsidized financing.

Financing Current-account Deficits
with Private Capital Inflows

It is also possible to postpone the negative effects of a currency depreciation with private capital inflows from foreigners. Because private investors require a real-market rate of return, they will effectively have to be paid back in future exports, the present value of which (at real market interest rates) equals the amount of needed current-account financing (Root 1990). The actual future value of these exports will exceed the value of the current-account deficit, as interest (or profit, in the case of equity capital infusions) is earned. Even if creditors reinvest their capital and interest in the country (or equity investors reinvest their profits), the effect generally is merely postponed and compounded to some future date when real payments (such as in exports) begin to be required (Obstfeld and Rogoff 1995).

Moreover, if the private financing has payments due in a foreign currency, the interest rate due on the debt will have to incorporate some premium yield for the risk of default (Murphy 2000a). As a result, private foreign currency financing will ordinarily be higher than is available on international aid financing. If the international aid were not cheaper, the countries would have no motivation to accept the economic and/or political conditions of the IMF or other organizations and countries providing foreign aid (Milverton 2000). As a result, the financing of a current-account deficit with foreign currency debt placed with private investors results in larger postponed negative effects than international aid financing (holding all else equal).

Default-risk premiums and the higher interest costs on the foreign currency financing may be avoided if foreign investors can be motivated to purchase securities with payments denominated in the domestic currency. Such a case is typically possible as long as the currency is freely convertible into other currencies. Government debt denominated in the domestic currency has no default risk, because of the ability of the foreign government to collect sufficient taxes or print sufficient money in the domestic currency to ensure payment.[4] As a result, given that uncovered interest rate parity mandates equal expected rates of return (for the same risk) when measured in the same currency (King 1998), the cost of such risk-free debt measured in foreign currency will average, over time in an efficient market, that of default-free foreign government debt in that foreign currency.[5]

Although the cost of foreign currency financing will be higher on average than the cost of domestic currency financing, foreign currency financing represents a bet on future exchange rates. As a result, borrowing in a foreign currency can end up costing less if the domestic currency value is higher than expected by the market at the time the payments on the foreign currency financing are due. Foreign currency financing can also possibly create positive announcement effects, as explained in a subsequent section on spending foreign-exchange reserves. In addition, foreign currency financing may be the only funding choice for countries with inconvertible currencies.

Regardless, private financing of a current-account deficit can continue, at the latest, only until all the capital in the country (or the time-series stream of future output) is effectively owned by foreigners and there are no more real capital goods that can be pledged for repayment (Claessens 1991). The effect of this constraint is analyzed in the next two subsections for the case of foreign financing of the current-account deficit with securities denominated in the domestic currency (i.e., that make payments in the domestic currency). The first subsection is most relevant to situations of fixed nominal exchange rates with equal inflation across all countries, or to cases with pegged real exchange rates. The second is more generally applicable, such as in situations of flexible or fixed exchange rates, and in more general situations of unequal inflation rates. A third subsection analyzes the effect of foreign currency financing and use of foreign exchange reserves.

A Simple Model of Private Capital Inflows

For a country without any government currency controls, an attempt can be made to stabilize or fix the value of the currency by attracting foreign private capital investment into domestic currency securities to fund a current-account deficit. This situation can be modeled by evaluating the maximum time that a devaluation (or currency collapse) can be postponed with such foreign financing. This boundary condition is defined in equation (A10.1-10). As shown there as an example, New Zealand could continue to hold up its currency value for thirty-four years before all the capital in the country would be owned by foreigners (after which nothing would be left to pay for imports in excess of exports).

The boundary condition (equation [A10.1-10]) reflects the fact that a current-account deficit can be financed only as long as there exists net capital stock to sell to foreigners in return for current imported consumption.[6] While some of the foreign investment can be in the form of debentures, such financing also effectively has a claim on the country's assets, albeit an unsecured one; in any event, private foreign financing of the current-account deficit is assumed to be possible only as long as the value of the country's productive assets exceeds that of its debts.

If one expects a country to postpone its devaluation for the maximum number of periods N, it is fairly easy to solve for the expected exchange rate in each period. In particular, the uncovered interest rate parity condition requires that the interest cost in the domestic currency include a premium above foreign interest rates to the extent of the expected currency devaluation (King 1998). In addition, the currency must be forecast to depreciate by an amount sufficient to eliminate the current-account deficit in N years. Also, postponing a devaluation increases its size over time, as interest must be earned by the foreigners financing the current-account deficit. As a result, the exchange rate change would be expected to be proportional to the increase in the current-account deficit caused by it growing (in domestic currency units) at the compounded domestic interest rate. This relationship is shown in equation (A10.1-12), which indicates that the interest rate on long-term N.Z. government bonds would have had to have been 9.94 percent on May 10, 1999, in order to enable the country to postpone a devaluation by thirty-four years.

The full concentration of the currency devaluation in N periods would require, assuming uncovered interest rate parity once again, that the domestic yield curve be identical to that in foreign countries, except at the maturity N, where it would be much higher. Such a situation could possibly occur if the government stated its intent to postpone the currency depreciation for N years and offered to sell special N-year bonds, the interest rate of which would be controlled to maintain a stable currency value (i.e., raising the interest rate on the N-year bonds if the currency started to fall and lowering it if it started to rise). However, such a policy is not normally observed in practice.

Instead, governments and central banks seeking to maintain a stable currency value fix short-term interest rates high enough to prevent the currency from depreciating for up to N years. To the extent they are successful, uncovered interest rate parity would not hold ex-post for all bonds with maturities less than N years. In particular, the higher short-term interest rates required to maintain the currency value would imply an overestimate of the short-term currency depreciation (Krasker 1980), given that the devaluation until period N would be zero if the central bank is completely successful. Nevertheless, the more credibility a central bank has in being able to maintain a stable currency for N years, the closer short-term interest rates would be to foreign rates and the closer the yield curve would be the same at all maturities except at period N (and the more closely uncovered interest-rate parity would hold).

For the typical cases where investors perceive that there is a chance that a country will not maintain its exchange rate for N periods, it is possible to solve mathematically for forward exchange-rate discounts and corresponding interest rate differentials. This relationship is shown in equation (A10.1-16). Given actual market interest-rate differentials (or forward rates), equation A10.1-16 can also be utilized to estimate the chance of an immediate devaluation to solve a country's balance of payments problems. For example, there was a 2.81 percent chance of a 33 percent devaluation of the N.Z. dollar on May 10, 1999.

A More General Model of Private Capital Inflows

Equations (A10.1-10) through (A10.1-16) are based on assumptions of no inflation exogenous to the model and no chance of using a gradual devaluation to resolve an existing BOP problem. It is possible to make the model more widely applicable (especially to the case of flexible exchange rates) by relaxing these assumptions, such as by explicitly allowing for a beginning inflation rate and by allowing a devaluation to occur more gradually (Connolly and Taylor 1984).

Roldos (1997) has explained cases whereby policy makers might prefer gradual currency depreciation to large, one-time devaluations. It is therefore rational to assume that the central bank will attempt to maintain a crawling peg that allows the currency to depreciate smoothly, as can be defined in equation (A10.1-17). The maximum number of years over which a country can conduct a gradual devaluation is derived in equation (A10.1-18). For instance, on May 10, 1999, New Zealand could devalue its currency gradually over an interval of sixty-seven years.

It is also useful to increase the generality of the model by allowing for the existence of some domestic and foreign inflation that is exogenous to the model. Some exogenous inflation might be expected because of existing inflation (perhaps caused by prior currency depreciation), or because of inflation expected in the future due to local monetary factors independent of the existing current-account deficit. Given that a real exchange-rate adjustment C is needed to solve the current-account deficit (which differs from a nominal exchange-rate change with nonzero exogenous inflation), the nominal exchange rate change must adjust not only for the current-account deficit but also for compounded inflation differentials. In addition, because each annual currency depreciation under the assumption of a gradual devaluation will result in an equal increase in inflation over the subsequent T years that the inflationary effects of a devaluation are incorporated into domestic prices, the nominal exchange rate must also adjust for endogenous inflation as well.[7]

Now define L as the annual probability estimated by a representative investor that the current-account deficit will be addressed with a gradual devaluation. In case of heterogeneous investor expectations, L would represent a weighted average of the subjective probability estimates of each investor, where the weights would be a function of the size of an investor's participation in the market (Murphy 1990).[8] Speculators, hedgers, and commercial bank traders, who profit more than just from the bid-ask spread of exchange rate quotations (Goodhardt 1988), all contribute to the determining of L.

Values of L less than one allow for the possibility of some other policy or solution (such as a real income decline) being forecasted to solve the problem of the current-account deficit. Drazen and Masson (1994) have modeled some of the aspects of monetary credibility that determine L. For instance, because raising interest rates would normally slow the economy and result in some real income losses, investors may revise downward their expectation of a currency depreciation when interest rates are increased. However, if the monetary authorities have no credibility, an initial rise in interest rates to support the currency could be matched with an expectation that interest rates will be lowered in the future to more than offset the initial negative effects on real income, and there may actually be a rise in L.

In any event, the new assumptions change the expected devaluation to that indicated by equation (A10.1-19). Given that uncovered interest rate parity requires the ratio of the compounded returns on risk-free bonds in two countries to equal the ratio in equation (A10.1-19), investor expectations of the probability (L) of a gradual devaluation therefore have a very important impact on interest rate differentials.

In cases where countries set their interest rates differently from those required by investors in equation (A10.1-19), exchange rates (especially the spot ones) must adjust to make the equality hold. Such situations often occur for policy reasons related to exogenous domestic inflation and unemployment. For example, a nation with a current-account deficit seeking to slow down high real economic growth in order to reduce exogenous inflationary pressures may raise interest rates to a level higher than implied by equation (A10.1-19) at existing exchange rates. The spot value of the currency may therefore rise (i.e., X_0 would fall to ensure that the equality continues to hold), even if the country has a current-account deficit that would cause its currency value to be expected to fall in the future to correct the current-account deficit (i.e., even when the currency is at a forward discount where $X'_z > X_0$). Similarly, a nation with high unemployment rates seeking to spur domestic economic growth may lower interest rates below those implied by equation (A10.1-19). The spot currency value would therefore have to fall (i.e., X_0 would rise in order to maintain the equality), even if the country had a current-account surplus (which would cause its forward or expected future exchange rate to be higher in the future).

Equation (A10.1-19) would thus be consistent with countries experiencing higher (lower) economic growth having rising (falling) currency values if those countries were raising (lowering) interest rates to reduce domestic inflationary pressures (unemployment). However, it must be emphasized that raising or lowering interest rates themselves can affect investor expectations L and therefore affect the ratio $X_{Z'}/X_0$ in equation (A10.1-19), just as many other variables can affect L and thus currency values.

For instance, if a country raised its interest rates to slow inflation in an environment of high unemployment, investors may perceive a low probability of the nation's being able to maintain sufficiently high interest rates to keep its currency value stable in the face of political pressure to raise economic growth and employment. As a result, the spot value of the currency may fall despite the interest rate increase. A recent example of this phenomena occurred in Brazil (Karp 2001). One analyst has even called it an "outdated view that if a bank raises its interest rates, its currency will strengthen." However, an alternative theory that lowering short-term rates to spark economic growth might cause yields on long-term investments to rise is "just as problematic" (Downey 2001).

It should also be mentioned that it is quite possible for a country with a current-account surplus to experience a real exchange-rate decline in spite of rising short-term interest rates, as has been observed in the first years of the euro (Barkley and Richard 2000). The fact that the increased interest rates in Europe were still less than those prevailing in the United States during this time certainly contributed to the latter phenomena. Also contributing to the euro's weakness at times has been an investor forecast of an increasing probability that the current-account deficit of the United States will be resolved with some policy variable, such as a reduction in real income, which may be politically feasible given the low unemployment rate in the United States in 2000 (Barkley 2000). Besides explaining such a readily observed phenomena, equation (A10.1-19) also indicates precisely how a significant change in investor expectations (perhaps induced by a simple catalyst) can create some of the speculative bubbles (and crashes) that sometimes characterize currency markets (Dornbusch 1982).

In addition to explaining some of the seemingly inconsistent behavior of exchange rates, equation (A10.1-19) can also be used to iterate and solve for investor expectations (L) of the probability of a gradual devaluation at any time. For example, on May 10, 1999, there was a 33.57 percent probability of a gradual devaluation of the N.Z. dollar, as shown in Appendix 10.1.

It is also possible to derive an equation for the expected currency devaluation and interest rate differential when there is a possibility of both a gradual and an immediate full devaluation. This formula is defined in equation (A10.1-22). Equation (A10.1-22) indicates, for example, that the probability of an immediate 33 percent devaluation of the N.Z. dollar was 2.02 percent, while the probability of a more gradual devaluation over sixty-seven years was 32.89 percent.

An equation can also be derived for the exchange rate discounts and interest-rate differentials that would exist after an immediate devaluation of sufficient magnitude to address fully the current-account deficit. This formula is given in equation (A10.1-23). For instance, equation (A10.1-23) indicates that the interest rate on long-term N.Z. government bonds would rise to 7.55 percent if investors did not lose confidence in the country's central bank as a result of an immediate devaluation. However, equation (A10.1-23) implies that the interest rate on long-term government bonds could easily rise much farther if there were a crisis of confidence in the N.Z. central bank resulting from a large immediate devaluation.

It is also possible to evaluate a situation where the domestic monetary authorities try to set interest rates below the level implied by equation (A10.1-23). Sometimes, because investors' perception of the probability of a subsequent immediate devaluation (B*) is so large, and/or because the amount of time (T*) they perceive that it will take for the inflationary effects of the devaluation to be incorporated into domestic prices is so small, the required interest rate specified in equation (A10.1-23) is prohibitively high for the existing economic and political situation in the country. In this situation, setting interest rates lower than given in equation (A10.1-23) would cause the currency to depreciate by more than enough to balance the current account, as net foreign capital would flee the country (as happened in the Asian currency crisis of 1997). The exact amount of any extra currency depreciation for any given interest rate is derived in equation (A10.1-24).

However, if domestic interest rates are held lower than that needed for equation (A10.1-23) to hold, it is very possible that investors might formulate an even higher expected probability of the country using a currency devaluation to solve its BOP problems and possibly even less time for inflation to be imported. In particular, market participants tend to lose further confidence in the inflation-fighting abilities of the central bank if it has not sufficiently raised interest rates in the face of devaluation-induced inflationary pressures. As a result, the values of some of the parameters in equation (A10.1-24) might change as a result of the monetary loosening, as illustrated for New Zealand in equations (A10.1-25) and (A10.1-26).

Thus, while raising interest rates merely postpones a BOP problem (and can magnify it), such a postponement can have advantages compared to an immediate devaluation because of the latter's adverse effect on investors' perception of the probability of an immediate devaluation and of the expected time for the inflationary effects of a devaluation to be incorporated into domestic prices. These two parameters are especially susceptible to change after a large devaluation, since after a devaluation there is often an expectation that future BOP problems will be addressed with further devaluations and that domestic producers will also react more quickly to such devaluations with domestic price increases. However, despite the fact that this problem can be addressed by taking actions to prevent large devaluations, it remains possible to maintain interest rates sufficiently high to attract foreign capital for only a limited time before all capital in a country is owned by foreigners (thus possibly forcing a devaluation eventually anyway).

It should also be emphasized that changes in investor perceptions of the probability of future devaluations and inflation (i.e., changes in L, B, and T in primed or starred states) modify the interest rate needed to maintain the current spot exchange rate. Interest rates are thereby determined by investor expectations in countries where the spot exchange rate is fixed. On the other hand, the spot value of the currency will decrease any time interest rates are not set as high as defined in the foregoing equations, so that a currency value in a system of flexible exchange rates can actually fall when domestic interest rates increase if the interest rates do not rise enough in a situation of changed investor expectations. In addition, the spot currency value will increase whenever interest rates are set higher than the equilibrium interest rate defined in the equations (so that it is possible for a currency with a current-account deficit to have an appreciating currency due to changes in investor perceptions, as well as due to increases in interest rates).

One possibility not often observed that also merits explanation is the existence of higher real interest rates in a country which also has a current-account surplus.[9] Such an unusual situation can occur if there is an expectation of a deterioration in the current account (perhaps due to a forecasted change in the relative level of protectionism). The model can incorporate this possibility by setting C equal to the current-account deficit that would be expected at the existing exchange rate after the changed situation (i.e., after a change in relative protectionism). The latter possibility is consistent not only with the model but also with Bernhardsen's (2000) empirical findings, which indicated that interest rate differentials are related to various macroeconomic factors (such as real income growth, unemployment, and labor cost differentials) that would affect expectations about future current-account deficits and inflation, as well as to current-account deficits and inflation directly.

The dominating effect of investors and their expectations on exchange rates in the model is consistent with the empirical observation that well over 90 percent of all currency trades are for investment purposes (Eiteman, Stonehill, and Moffett 1998). The model's implications are also consistent with the empirical finding that investor expectations of currency depreciation (e.g., as proxied by forward exchange rate discounts) tend to overestimate actual currency depreciation over most empirical investigations of short-term exchange-rate movements (Cavaglia, Verschoor, and Wolff 1993). In particular, the mere possibility (as measured by B) of an immediate devaluation sufficient to resolve temporarily a current-account deficit will result in a forward discount that will be in excess of the actual currency depreciation that would occur if a more gradual currency devaluation policy can be followed. However, the latter bias existing over most time periods will be compensated for by the rare observation of a very large and rapid currency depreciation (Krasker, 1980), which will occur with probability B according to the model.

Note that the model developed in this section has been derived under the assumption of freely convertible currencies. For countries with currencies that are not fully convertible, such as in the case of capital controls, it would be difficult to attract foreign funding of a current-account deficit via securities that make payments in the domestic currency, and so the mathematical implications of the model can be distorted. In particular, if capital controls restrict arbitrage from enforcing uncovered interest-rate parity, the implications of the model with respect to the setting of domestic interest rates can be fairly meaningless. In fact, one of the reasons countries restrict the convertibility of their currencies is to enable them to maintain interest rates below where they would otherwise have to be to maintain the same exchange rate, and so both interest rates and exchange rates may be different from what they would normally be in the case of convertible currencies.

However, even for such countries with capital controls where interest rate parity does not hold, many aspects of the model may still be valid. For instance, it is still possible to finance a current-account deficit by issuing securities denominated in a foreign currency, and it is necessary then only to modify the model's parameters so that interest-rate differentials reflect the foreign currency cost adjusted for expected exchange rate changes, as delineated in equation (A10.1-28).

Spending Foreign Exchange Reserves Issuing Securities Denominated in a Foreign Currency to Fund a Deficit

It is also possible to postpone a currency devaluation (or other adverse measures undertaken to resolve a BOP problem) by having the country's central bank sell its own investments in securities denominated in foreign currencies (i.e., use its foreign exchange reserves to buy up the domestic currency from foreigners) and thereby finance a current-account deficit from the central bank's own assets (Ben-Bassat and Gottlieb 1992). However, the expenditure of foreign exchange reserves results in a reduction in income from those foreign currency holdings, a reduction that effectively causes a further increase in the current-account deficit.[10] The expenditure of foreign-exchange reserves therefore increases the size of any needed future devaluation, as with any other financing.

On the other hand, financing a current-account deficit with central bank reserves can have peculiarly different announcement effects. In particular, the very expenditure of foreign exchange reserves might increase investor confidence in the currency (Frankel and Rose 1995), as the central bank action indicates that it is backing up its attempt to maintain the currency's value with its own money bets. As a result, the probability (L) of a gradual devaluation might thereby be reduced (i.e., investors' expectations of the probability that the BOP problem will be addressed with a currency devaluation may be decreased).

Alternatively, because the reduction in foreign currency reserves caused by their expenditure reduces the ability of the central bank to employ this solution in the future (Agenor and Masson 1999), the probabilities of a devaluation (L and B) could actually increase instead of decrease upon announcement of the fact. If too many of the reserves are used up in such open-market actions, investors may begin to believe in the inevitability of a currency depreciation to resolve a BOP crisis (implying L + B = 1.0, or even B = 1.0 in the extreme case), thus motivating them to conduct an all-out "speculative attack" on the currency (Obstfeld 1984), and forcing the country either to raise interest rates to a prohibitively high level or devalue.

Golub (1989) has explained that expending or selling foreign exchange reserves has similarities to issuing debts denominated in a foreign currency. In particular, foreign currency financing of a current-account deficit is identical to domestic currency financing with the payment obligations swapped into foreign currency (Abken 1998). In both cases, the pricing would have to reflect the default risk of the country being unable to deliver the foreign currency (i.e., in the interest rate of foreign-currency debt and in the forward or swap prices of the portfolio financing strategy). Thus, foreign currency financing has the same effect as domestic currency financing, except that a forward sale of foreign-exchange reserves is effectively conducted at the same time. Like spot foreign-exchange reserve sales, such forward sales of foreign currency can have a positive announcement effect, insofar as they represent a bet on the domestic currency having a value above the market forecast incorporated into the forward exchange rate. As a result, the probability (L) of a gradual devaluation can be reduced by the central bank issuing foreign currency debt, just as it can when the central bank sells foreign currency reserves (because investors may decide to bet with the central bank that the currency depreciation will be less than previously expected). On the other hand, the obligatory future foreign exchange payments reduces the expected value of the central bank's future foreign currency reserves and can therefore increase the perceived probabilities (B and L) of a devaluation, just as with spot sales of foreign currency reserves. In addition, as previously mentioned, the possibility of default on foreign currency debt (or on a forward foreign currency sale) increases the cost of the financing (by increasing the effective interest rate required by investors to compensate them for default risk) and may therefore result in a higher cost than the use of spot foreign exchange reserves (or pure domestic currency financing).

In the case of New Zealand in 1999, the central bank's foreign currency reserves represented only a fraction of its current-account deficit. As a result, New Zealand had very little flexibility to use this method to postpone addressing a BOP problem, even less so than Mexico in early 1994 shortly before its own crisis. However, New Zealand has been able to stabilize the exchange rate very successfully with other policies. In particular, New Zealand utilized a credible monetary tightening and temporarily higher real interest rates, which, though subsequently lowered substantially, were high enough for long enough to convince investors of the seriousness in fighting against a major devaluation in New Zealand. In addition, although the Mexican central bank in 1994 had an absolutely and relatively larger amount of reserves, New Zealand has better access to foreign currency financing at cheaper interest rates because of a higher credit rating. Its higher credit rating stems from the fact that it has never defaulted on its debts (whereas Mexico defaulted on its foreign currency debt in 1982), and investors have greater confidence in the ability and will of New Zealand to repay its obligations.

THE EVENTUAL EFFECT OF CURRENT-ACCOUNT DEFICITS ON INCOME

The foregoing analysis indicates that neither the use of currency devaluations nor any type of financing of a current-account deficit can solve BOP problems. Instead, such policies merely postpone the day of reckoning when there must occur a real decline in domestic income that can sufficiently reduce the demand for imports, or when some protectionist solution to a BOP problem, such as that described in Murphy (1992), can be implemented.

It is interesting to observe that funding a current-account deficit with private domestic currency financing naturally creates its own real income decline solution. In particular, the higher domestic interest rates needed to attract foreign investors automatically slow economic growth and thereby create a reduction in the demand for imports. If there is sufficient investor confidence that the central bank will eventually employ some solution other than a devaluation (such as a real income reduction), then B and L can both be fairly low, real interest rates can be minimized according to equation (A10.1-22), and the slightly slower economic growth can gradually solve the BOP problem over time.

If it is assumed that a reduction in real income of c will be used to solve the BOP problem but that the actual reduction in real income will actually be spread evenly over the same number of years as the needed devaluation, it is possible to adapt equation (A10.1-19) to estimate the exact extent of the needed annual decline in real income growth.

While equation (A10.1-29) is similar to equation (A10.1-19), the differences in the two equations are likely to cause the real income decline to be far less than the currency depreciation needed to solve a BOP problem. For instance, the real income decline is not compounded by the devaluation-induced inflation over time. In addition, if the elasticity of demand for imports relative to real income changes is much higher than the elasticity of demand relative to exchange rate changes, it is possible that c is less than C by a very large amount. Regardless, solving a BOP problem by gradually reducing real income, instead of by initiating a deep depression that solves the problem immediately, magnifies the cumulative negative effects on income, because the failure to solve the current-account deficit problem immediately would result in some continued foreign financing being required. The additional interest paid to foreigners on that financing would contribute to future current-account deficits, which would eventually have to be addressed, with further decreases in domestic income.

For example, for New Zealand, investors currently do not perceive a large likelihood of the devaluation solution (especially not an immediate large one), and so real interest rates in New Zealand do not have to be excessively high to prevent an immediate currency depreciation. As a result, the necessary real income decline (or, alternatively, a less likely devaluation solution) can be made gradually. Assuming $c = C = 0.33$, equation (A10.1-29) indicates that the exact estimate is a $W = 0.69$ percent annual decrease in real income for N' $= 67$ years for New Zealand. With compounding, this annual decrease implies that real income will be $\{1/1.0069\}^{67} = 63$ percent of what it would otherwise have been in sixty-seven years.

On the other hand, if there is little investor confidence in the ability of the central bank to use anything but a devaluation to solve the BOP problem, perceived probabilities of devaluation (B and/or L) will have very large values, real interest rates will have to be very high, and the required real income decline of c will effectively be forced over just a few years. If the entire real income decline were realized over the course of just one year (as might be the case with extremely high real-interest rates persisting over that time interval), real income would be perpetually $1/1.33 = 75$ percent of what it would otherwise have been (and so eventually the country would be better off than with a more gradual devaluation).

Prohibitively high real-interest rates forcing large declines in real income are often the case after a large devaluation, where interest rates are determined by equation (A10.1-23), which may reflect much higher probabilities of future devaluation than the parameters in equation (A10.1-22). However, extremely high real-interest rates can be forced on any country any time investor confidence in the ability and will of the central bank to maintain its currency's value is lost. For instance, a decline in investor confidence in the N.Z. central bank can cause a very large increase in B and L in equation (A10.1-22), which in turn would increase real interest rates in New Zealand that would force the needed real income losses to be concentrated more quickly, possibly causing a major economic depression. Alternatively, if New Zealand did not have the political will to maintain a depression long and deep enough to solve the BOP problem, it might choose a devaluation alternative, which itself might result in such high real-interest rates, according to equation (A10.1-23), that a depression would have to occur anyway.

Nonetheless, it should be emphasized that the eventual solution to a BOP problem does not necessarily have to involve a real income decline, even though it typically does empirically. For instance, a continuation of the slow reduction in worldwide trade barriers over future decades might benefit New Zealand more than its trading partners, which are characterized by greater protectionism (Murphy 2000b). Such an improvement in relative protectionism for the country would reduce its current-account deficit and would therefore decrease the size of the needed gradual income losses (and/or devaluation) needed to solve the BOP problem. As mentioned in the introduction to this research, improved domestic productivity can also represent a solution to a current-account deficit, but such a solution tends to require some sort of protectionist subsidy that focuses the productivity increase on the export or import-competing sector to be effective in solving a BOP problem (Murphy 2000b). New Zealand could in fact implement a productive protectionist plan, such as that proposed by Murphy (1992), since the size of its current-account deficit would certainly permit some level of increased protectionism according to WTO rules (Edlin 1999).

GENERAL MODEL IMPLICATIONS

This research has shown that if a country cannot (or will not) initiate protectionist policies that would improve its relative competitive position with limited or no negative side effects, that country's BOP problems will eventually result in a real income decline or a devaluation-inflation-devaluation spiral (the latter of which can lead to unstable hyperinflation). The model also demonstrates how the needed income decline can be spread (and magnified) over many years. As the N.Z. example illustrates, the model is consistent with stable currency situations, even in cases of extremely high current-account deficits.

In addition, the theory provides a mathematical framework for understanding currency crises. In particular, countries that suffer currency crises tend to start out with large current-account deficits (Frankel and Rose 1996), which they have been able to finance with high domestic real interest rates (Velasco 1987). Equation (A10.1-22) of this research specifies the exact level of interest rates needed to prevent a currency crisis from evolving.

The model developed in this study is especially useful because it is consistent with various general empirical findings, including some that are not easily explainable by other theories. For instance, the empirical evidence presented by Edison and Pauls (1993) that time-series real exchange rates and real interest rates are not cointegrated is explainable by the model developed here. In particular, the model predicts that high real interest rates will attract capital and raise currency values, all else being equal. However, the model also implies that higher real interest rates will typically exist in countries with current-account deficits, whose currency values are very likely to fall in the future, despite any short-term rise in their values caused by high real interest rates attracting investment in the currency. The higher interest rates may therefore only slow or delay a real currency depreciation over time (as opposed to causing a permanent real exchange rate rise), thereby leading to the empirical finding of little correlation between real exchange rates and real interest rates. This modeling sequence of events is supported by the empirical findings reported by Murphy (1996), who discovered that after adjusting for PPP effects, relative interest rate differentials by themselves have only a short-term, temporary impact on exchange rates.

More generally, the model is consistent with the widespread empirical findings that interest rate differentials are directly and positively related to inflation differentials and the size of current-account deficits (Bernhardsen 2000). It is also consistent with empirical evidence on currency crises. For instance, in an empirical analysis that evaluated twenty-six currency crises over the period 1970–1995, Kaminsky and Reinhart (1999) found that 85 percent were preceded by a decline in export growth (causing or intensifying a current-account problem), and 89 percent were preceded by an increase in real domestic interest rates (as the countries may have initially tried to meet the resulting investor requirements of higher returns in this environment of a rising C). In an even broader study, Frankel and Rose (1996) provided data indicating that current-account deficits for 117 countries experiencing currency crashes between 1971 and 1992 averaged 8 percent of GDP (and in most cases ranged between 6% and 12%).

One especially interesting empirical finding of the latter authors, Frankel and Rose (1996), was that real economic growth typically dropped significantly prior to the currency crashes they investigated (perhaps at least partially because of a rise in real interest rates). As would be consistent with the model developed in this research, lower economic growth may cause investors to forecast that the high real interest rates needed to maintain the currency value are not likely to be maintained because of the politically unattractive environment of lower income and employment growth. As a result, at some point, a catalyst scares investors into perceiving an increased chance of a devaluation, with herding behavior among investors magnifying initial fears (Calvo and Mendoza 1996). Sometimes the panic spreads to other similar countries (Kaminsky and Reinhardt 2000), especially ones with more privatized capital markets and low foreign-exchange reserve levels (Miyakoshi 2000). In any case, the catalyst-induced rise in the required interest rate needed for currency stability under these circumstances (because investors are expecting a very high probability of devaluation) is considered by the affected countries to be too high to maintain (especially in the face of declining employment and income growth), and the currency collapses.

Some illustrations of catalysts that apparently increased investors' probability estimates of devaluation to a prohibitively high level are provided by the major currency crises of the 1990s. In particular, the removal of currency controls greatly increased the currency devaluation needed to balance Russia's current account (C) in 1991 and made investors believe that a large currency devaluation (B) was inevitable (Murphy 2000b). An outflow of mafia capital related to government attempts to crack down on organized crime drastically reduced foreign exchange reserves in Mexico and greatly reduced the country's ability to finance its current-account deficit by drawing on those reserves in late 1994 (Murphy 1995), thereby increasing investors' expectations of a large immediate devaluation (B). In Southeast Asia in 1997, banking problems reduced potential economic growth (Miller 1998), thereby reducing the amount of time that a full devaluation could be postponed (N') as well as increasing investors' perception of the probability of devaluation (L and B) because of the resulting reduced tolerance for a BOP solution that would decrease real income growth further. Fears that Russia would have to abandon its tight monetary policies in order to pay back wages to workers caused investors' forecasts of the probability of devaluation (L and B) to rise so far in 1998 that real interest rates of over 100 percent could not prevent a devaluation of the Russian ruble by over 60 percent (Murphy 2000b). The default of a local government on its debts in Brazil greatly increased the cost of foreign currency borrowing and reduced the ability of that country to continue to use such funding to finance its large current-account deficit in early 1999 (Katz and Cohn 1999), thereby increasing investor perceptions of the probability of an immediate large devaluation (B). Political uncertainty about the removal of government ministers accused of corruption and anti-IMF policies raised investor forecasts of an immediate devaluation (B) so high that despite real interest rates of over 5,000 percent, Turkey was forced to abandon its fixed exchange rate in early 2001 and allow its currency to devalue by about 30 percent (Pope 2001).

In all these cases, an increase in C, L, and/or B (and/or a reduction in N') raised the interest rate required to continue to be able to postpone a devaluation, as per equation (A10.1-21). The countries' decision to allow a devaluation under such circumstances may have been partially motivated by the fact that the increasing of interest rates can itself cause investors to raise their expectations of a devaluation (as they may not believe the country can maintain such rates for very long). Such further increases in the probabilities (L and B) of a devaluation thereby force rates ever higher.

Some of the aforementioned devaluations have resulted in contagion and reverse contagion, sometimes years after the initial crisis. For instance, the collapse of the Brazilian currency in 1999 was followed in 2001 with a far worse collapse of the currency of its neighbor, Argentina. In particular, the decline in Brazil's currency value was large enough to cause Argentina, its major trading partner, to suffer a severe recession (Karp and Druckerman 2000), as Argentina became relatively less competitive against Brazil. Exports out of Argentina fell, while imports into Argentina rose, thereby slowing its own economic growth at the same time that it was also forced to raise interest rates to maintain its own currency value (and the interest rate increase further slowed the Argentinian economy). Argentina finally had to abandon its 1:1 peg to the U.S. dollar late in 2001, with its currency value falling by over 60 percent in a very short period of time, despite the country having long been held up as a "star student" in following capitalist advice and pressure (Druckerman 2002a). The collapse of the Argentinian peso was then followed by a second collapse of the Brazilian currency in 2002 (Druckerman 2002b).

After each devaluation, interest rates had to remain fairly high, as given in equation (A10.1-23), to prevent further devaluations. Where it was not politically possible to maintain such high interest rates, the currency fell farther (as in Indonesia in 1997). In any event, the high interest rates caused major recessions that helped the current accounts and currency values to recover.

The theory developed in this article yields many other insights on international finance, especially with respect to the overwhelming importance of ever-changing investor expectations. In addition, having been designed with rather unrestrictive assumptions,[11] it can be useful for investors, economists, and policy makers alike in almost any variety of situations.[12] For instance, it is robust to cases where currency changes are incorporated into inflation over long or short periods. It is also consistent with unidirectional and reversal currency moves. (With respect to the latter, the model is consistent with significant currency-value declines after significant rises in prior years resulting in no net effect on inflation, as the deflationary effect of the earlier rise in the currency value, smoothed into prices over a long period of time, is offset by the inflationary effect of the later fall, which is smoothed into prices over an overlapping long period of time.) The model can be applied to developed as well as less developed countries, and it is even applicable to international reserve currencies such as the euro. (In particular, the foreign central bank reserve currency holdings represent merely the effect of another set of investors whose expectations affect exchange rates.)

Even the virtually omnipotent United States itself is not immune to the implications of the model developed here. In particular, its huge current-account deficit, which now approaches 5 percent of GDP (Phillips 2000) must eventually be reversed. As a result, the United States, like other countries that consume more than they produce, may be forced to choose between a large reduction in real income, a gradual reduction in real income, a devaluation-inflation-devaluation spiral, or some combination of the three. Even though most U.S. debts held by foreigners are denominated in its domestic currency (i.e., the U.S. dollar), the value of c or C (the size of the real income or currency decline needed to solve the country's current-account problem) might be higher than in New Zealand (despite the slightly lower current-account deficit), because the elasticities of demand with respect to exchange rates and real income may be lower in the United States. For instance, Coy (2002) reports that it would take a 43 percent depreciation of the U.S. dollar to increase exports by 30 percent and cut the current-account deficit in half (and it would take a 23% increase in real foreign demand to increase exports by the same amount).

Nevertheless, while the United States may not be able to change the mathematical laws of global capitalism described in this research, it may be able to employ more forcefully some of the alternative treatments for the problem described in Murphy (2000b). In particular, it could bring down its current-account deficit by increasing its own protectionist policies at the same time that it forces other countries to open up their markets more to its imports. Unlike other countries, the United States may be able to do so (without fear of economic retaliation from the rest of the world) because of its enormous military, political, and propaganda power, as explained in Murphy (2000b). In that way, the United States might be able to maintain its leading economic position in the world. In contrast, nineteenth-century Britain, which successfully imposed a very exploitative free trade on its own massive colonies (Smith 2000), lost its overwhelming dominance in income and wealth by the early twentieth century to independent countries, like the United States itself, which successfully exercised much more protectionist trade policies to develop rapidly (Bairoch 1993).

CONCLUSION

This research develops theoretical relationships that should exist between current-account deficits and other variables like inflation, exchange rates, interest rates, income, and investor expectations. For example, it is shown that although a current-account deficit can be temporarily solved with a devaluation, such a currency depreciation will eventually lead to domestic inflation and the need for further devaluations. As a result, a currency depreciation by itself does not represent a long-term solution. On the other hand, attempts to postpone devaluation by obtaining outside funding for the current-account deficit are demonstrated mathematically to merely magnify the problem later by increasing the size of the real income decline needed to prevent the alternative choice of a devaluation-inflation-devaluation cycle.

Within the context of an external financing of a current-account deficit, boundary conditions are developed for determining the maximum number of years that a balance of payments problem can be deferred into the future with the outside funding. These boundary conditions imply various equations for the currency depreciation that will eventually occur. The equations are then combined with investor estimates of the probability of an immediate devaluation and of a gradual devaluation to compute an expected exchange rate change over any number of periods. The model is important for defining precisely how investor expectations affect exchange rates for a given interest rate (or affect interest rates for a fixed exchange rate).

The model of investor expectations focuses on the case of free exchange-rate markets (i.e., convertible currencies that can be traded without government restrictions) in which investors have the dominating influence. In such markets, uncovered interest-rate parity must hold, and it is possible to use the interest rate differentials in two countries to solve for investors' probability estimates of a devaluation. Because a devaluation can be either large and immediate or more gradual, there will be a distinct probability of each type of devaluation, with the sum of both those probabilities generally equaling less than one, due to the possibility of using some other method of solving a BOP problem (such as a real income decline). This conceptual framework is used to define how changes in investor perceptions on the resolution of current-account deficits cause currency movements of various magnitudes and direction (as well as provide precise estimates of two extreme forms of devaluation).[13]

The implications of the theory are illustrated using as an example the contemporary situation in New Zealand. New Zealand had an enormous current-account deficit in the late 1990s but nevertheless managed to avoid an immediate large decline in its income or currency value.[14] The mathematical model is also explained to be consistent with currency crises (such as those in Mexico in 1994, in Southeast Asia in 1997, in Russia in 1998, in Brazil in 1999, and in Turkey in 2001) as well as with more stable situations and events.

Besides being important for analyzing investor perceptions and their effects, the theory can be employed to evaluate economic policy alternatives (and to show that many traditional policies undertaken to resolve a BOP problem merely magnify the negative effects). The model can also be very useful to financial market participants, especially for those investing in less developed countries, where current-account deficits and currency crises are so chronic and have such an enormous impact on investor returns. However, rigorous empirical testing of the full implications of the theory is left to future research.

APPENDIX 10.1

Assume the exchange rate X of domestic currency units per foreign currency units must be expected to increase by C in order to correct a domestic current-account deficit. Then,

$$\underline{X}_u = X_0(1 + C), \qquad (A10.1\text{-}1)$$

where the subscripts denote the time period, with u being the amount of time before the currency devaluation occurs (e.g., u = 0 in the case of an instantaneous devaluation), and where an underlined variable denotes an expected value. For simplicity, assume that inflation is 0 percent worldwide to begin (with this assumption being relaxed later), but assume that domestic inflation eventually will fully reflect an exchange rate devaluation over a subsequent period,[15] so that

$$\underline{P}_{u:T+u} = \underline{X}_u/X_0 - 1, \qquad (A10.1\text{-}2)$$

where P denotes the domestic inflation rate between the subscripted time periods separated by a colon, and T is the number of years for a devaluation to fully induce an equal amount of domestic inflation.[16] Equation (A10.1-2) is consistent with the empirical evidence that exchange-rate changes lead or cause inflation (Abuaf and Jorion 1990).

In addition, assume that future exchange-rate changes must reflect contemporaneous future inflation differentials in order to maintain the current account in balance, so that

$$\underline{X}_{u+T} = \underline{X}_u(1 + \underline{P}_{u:\,T+u}). \qquad (A10.1\text{-}3)$$

Substituting A10.1-1 and A10.1-2 into A10.1-3 yields

$$\begin{aligned}\underline{X}_{u+T} &= X_0(1 + C)\,(\underline{X}_u/X_0)\\ &= \underline{X}_u(1 + C).\end{aligned} \qquad (A10.1\text{-}4)$$

A similar relationship as in A10.1-2 and A10.1-4 would also hold between future exchange rates and inflation rates, so that

$$\underline{P}_{t-T:t} = \underline{X}_{t-T}/\underline{X}_{t-2T} - 1 = C, \text{ and} \qquad (A10.1\text{-}5)$$

$$\underline{X}_t = \underline{X}_{t-T}(1 + C). \qquad (A10.1\text{-}6)$$

If an exchange rate change is incorporated immediately into prices (i.e., T = 0), such as in cases of where prices are set in a foreign currency multiplied by the current market exchange rate (as has sometimes occurred in the past in countries with hyperinflation, such as in some Latin American nations previously), equation (A10.1-2) implies)

$$\underline{P}_{0:u} = \underline{X}_u/X_0 - 1 \text{ if T} = 0. \qquad (A10.1\text{-}7)$$

Since the exchange rate change at period u must reflect both C and the contemporaneous inflation rate to keep the current account in balance,

$$\begin{aligned}\underline{X}_u &= X_0(1 + C)(1 + \underline{P}_{0:u})\\ &= X_0(1 + C)(1 + \{\underline{X}_u/X_0\} - 1)\\ &= \underline{X}_u(1 + C) \qquad\qquad \text{if T} = 0,\end{aligned} \qquad (A10.1\text{-}8)$$

as follows by inserting for $\underline{P}_{0:u}$ in the equality from equation (A10.1-7), and as is consistent with equation (A10.1-4) at T = 0. Because no exchange rate can make equation (A10.1-8) hold (except when C = 0), it implies that a devaluation cannot be used to correct a current-account deficit in the case of T = 0, just as structural inflationists claim (Kindleberger 1968). Similarly, inserting T = 0 into equation (A10.1-6) indicates

$$\underline{X}_t = \underline{X}_t(1 + C) \text{ if T} = 0. \qquad (A10.1\text{-}9)$$

Model 1: Exchange Rates with Maximum Postponement of a One-Time Devaluation

Now assume that domestic capital and the current-account deficit grow proportionally with GDP. Given that a devaluation would be required at the latest when all the domestic capital has been used up to finance past current-account deficits, the number of years that the current-account deficit is postponed cannot exceed a value that causes a violation of the boundary condition

$$M(1 + g)^u - F - A \sum_{n=1}^{u}(1 + g)^n\,(1 + i_d)^{u-n+1} \geq 0. \qquad (A10.1\text{-}10)$$

where u represents the number of years that a resolution of a current-account deficit is postponed, M is the country's current capital stock (net of foreign capital holdings) as a percentage of GDP, g is the forecasted growth rate in nominal GDP, F is the percentage of GDP currently owned by foreigners, A is the current-account deficit as a percentage of GDP, and i_d is the domestic interest rate (on domestic government bonds) owed annually on the amount of the current-account deficit financed (so that the current-account deficit, measured in the domestic currency, increases its size each year by the amount of that interest). All the terms in boundary condition (A10.1-10) have been normalized by effectively dividing through by current GDP for simplicity. The third term of the boundary condition (i.e., the last multivariable one on the left-hand side) essentially represents the amount of additional foreign capital given to foreigners in return for their continuing to finance each year's current-account deficit (which grows at the rate g with GDP) and in return for an assumed reinvestment of all earnings on the financing (which compound at the rate i_d). N is the highest value of u that satisfies the boundary condition (A10.1-10).

For example, the IMF's *International Financial Statistics*, the *Wall Street Journal*, the local N.Z. press (such as the May 11, 1999, *Palmerston North Evening Post*), and Kelsey (1999) permit estimation of A = .07, M = 5, F = .95, g = .03, and i_d = .0639 for New Zealand for one particular day in the first half of 1999 (May 10).[17] Boundary condition A10.1-10 therefore indicates the maximum N = 34 (where i_d should theoretically reflect the domestic interest rate on bonds maturing just before u = N = 34, such as at N − 1 = 33, but the rate is proxied here by the longest-term N.Z. government bond available because there are no N.Z. bonds in existence with such long maturities).

Because C is defined to be a percentage of GDP, it is necessary to adjust for GDP growth g, so the annual geometric increase in the current-account deficit resulting from using domestic currency financing to fund it equals

$$I = \{1 + g + i_d\}/\{1 + g\}. \qquad (A10.1-11)$$

Assuming that the elasticity of demand related to exchange rates is constant,

$$\underline{X}_N/X_u = 1 + CI^N \quad \text{if } u = N. \qquad (A10.1-12)$$

Uncovered interest rate parity implies that one plus the annualized domestic interest rate on N-year bonds would be higher than one plus the N-period foreign interest rate i_f by the factor of $[\underline{X}_N/X_0]^{1/N}$. On the other hand, uncovered interest rate parity would require that interest rates on bonds maturing in N − 1 periods equal foreign interest rates (i.e., $i_d = i_f$ for each maturity less than N) if there is no chance of a devaluation before u = N.

For instance, if New Zealand wanted to maintain its current exchange rate as long as possible, the required annual yield on its N-period bonds would be determined by I, C, N, and i_f. On the particular day in 1999 being examined, I = {1 + .03 + .0639}/{1 + .03} = 1.0620, while C = .33 and N = 34 as before. As a result, equation (A10.1-12) implies that yields on thirty-four-year N.Z.

government bonds would have to be $[1 + \{.33(1.0620)^{34}\}]^{1/34} = 1.0393$ times one plus the interest rate on thirty-four-year foreign risk-free government bonds. For the day in question, the *Wall Street Journal* reported $i_f = 5.78$ percent as the yield on the longest-term U.S. Treasury bond (which serves as a proxy for an N-period foreign government bond). As a result, the interest rate on thirty-four-year (N-period) N.Z. bonds would have to be $\{1.0578 \times 1.0393\} - 1 = 9.94$ percent to postpone the devaluation needed to solve the country's BOP problem for thirty-four years (i.e., if u = N).

Model 2: Exchange Rates When Investors Perceive an Uncertain Fixed Exchange Rate

On the other hand, if the central bank is unwilling, or lacks sufficient credibility, to maintain a stable exchange rate for N periods, equations (A10.1-1) and (A10.1-6) imply that a forecasted imminent devaluation would cause the exchange rate to be expected to depreciate over any Z years by

$$
\begin{aligned}
\underline{X}_Z/X_0 &= (\underline{X}_Z/\underline{X}_T)(\underline{X}_T/\underline{X}_u)(\underline{X}_u/\underline{X}_0) \\
&= (1 + C)^{\{Z/T\} - 1}(1 + C)(1 + C) \qquad \text{(A10.1-13)} \\
&= (1 + C)^{1 + \{Z/T\}} \qquad \text{if } u = 0.
\end{aligned}
$$

Immediately after the devaluation of C,

$$
\underline{X}_Z/\underline{X}_u = (1 + C)^{\{Z/T\}} \text{ if } u = 0, \qquad \text{(A10.1-14)}
$$

assuming a continuous need to devalue in order to offset the future inflation caused by the initial devaluation. Uncovered interest rate parity implies that equations (A10.1-13) and (A10.1-14) would also represent the ratio between compounded returns on domestic and foreign government bonds making payments in their respective currencies before and after devaluation, respectively.

For example, if a devaluation were imminent in New Zealand, its interest rates on short-term one-year debt prior to the devaluation would, from equation (A10.1-13), have to be $[1.33^{1 + \{1/10\}}]^{1/1} = 1.3685$ times one plus the short-term foreign U.S. interest rate of .0512, less one, or 43.86 percent. After devaluation, interest rates would be only $[1.33^{\{Z/10\}}]^{1/Z} = 1.33^{\{1/10\}} = 1.0289$ times the sum of one plus the foreign interest rate at any maturity, or $[1.0289 \times 1.0512] - 1 = 8.16$ percent short term and $[1.0289 \times 1.0578] - 1 = 8.84$ percent long term.

In actual fact, prior to period u, expected exchange rates and interest rates might be somewhere between those implied by equations (A10.1-12) and (A10.1-13), depending on how much credibility the central bank has with investors. In particular, if investors believe an immediate devaluation is more likely, currency depreciation and interest rates might be closer to those implied by equation (A10.1-13), but nearer to those implied by equation (A10.1-12) otherwise.

Since a devaluation could actually occur at any time between u = 0 and u = N, investors may formulate some probability f_u of devaluation in each possible period u. The exchange rate in period Z if there is a devaluation in period u can be defined as $\underline{X}_Z\{u\}$. Given a devaluation of CI^u in period u, from generalizing equation (A10.1-12), and given the same devaluation every T periods thereafter as inflation is imported, from equation (A10.1-2),

$$\begin{aligned} \underline{X}_Z\{u\}/X_0 &= (\underline{X}_Z/\underline{X}_u)(\underline{X}_u/\underline{X}_0) \\ &= (1 + CI^u)^{\{Z-u\}/T}(1 + CI^u) \qquad (A10.1\text{-}15) \\ &= (1 + CI^u)^{1+[\{Z-u\}/T]}. \end{aligned}$$

Weighting each possible $\underline{X}_Z\{u\}$ by the probability f_u of the devaluation occurring in period u, and allowing for a possibility of no devaluation until after period Z, it is possible to compute the expected exchange rate in any period Z as

$$\underline{X}_Z = \sum_{u=0}^{Z} f_u \, \underline{X}_Z\{u\} + X_0(1 - \sum_{u=0}^{Z} f_u). \qquad (A10.1\text{-}16)$$

Note that there is no requirement that the f_u terms sum to 1.00 over any time interval Z; nor is there even a requirement that they sum to 1.00 over the maximum interval N, as it is always possible that a country will solve its BOP problem with a real-income decline (or some other policy) instead of with a currency devaluation.

The actual forward exchange rate discount and interest-rate premium at each maturity would therefore be determined by the ratio $\underline{X}_Z/X_0$, where $\underline{X}_Z$ is determined by equation (A10.1-16). With a complete list of forward exchange rates across all maturities 1 to Z (or with a complete spectrum of interest rates in both currencies that can be used to derive implied forward exchange rates using interest rate parity), it would be possible to solve equation (A10.1-16) for the probability f_u of devaluation in each period u. Note that equations (A10.1-12) and (A10.1-13) merely represent special cases of equation (A10.1-16), where $f_N = 1.00$ and $f_0 = 1.00$, respectively.

Whether higher probabilities for devaluations sooner or later cause forward exchange-rate discounts (and interest rate premiums) to be higher or lower at different time periods depends on the values of all the variables in the complex function given in equation (A10.1-16), but the values of T (i.e., the time for currency devaluation to be incorporated into domestic inflation and thus require a further devaluation) and i_d (i.e., the rate at which the current-account deficit grows over time if a devaluation solution is postponed) have particularly strong effects. In any event, the model's implications remain generally consistent with the purchasing power parity (PPP) theory, insofar as exchange rates will adjust at some point for deviations from absolute purchasing power parity that are causing the current-account deficit and then follow relative purchasing power parity thereafter, with the exchange rate following the depreciation-induced inflation (Manzur 1990).

It should be emphasized that the foregoing equations are based on an assumption of 0 percent exogenous inflation in both countries. Because boundary condition (A10.1-10) incorporates inflation in the nominal growth rate g, and because equal domestic inflation and foreign inflation would cancel out their effects on C, this assumption distorts the analysis only if inflation exogenous to the model is different domestically than elsewhere.

Even if there is a beginning domestic inflation rate that is not the same as in foreign countries (and is expected to persist exogenously to the model), the implications of the model are still applicable for exogenously real variables. In particular, in the case of different exogenous inflation rates, application of the equations is still relevant for measuring real exchange-rate changes and differences in real interest rates up through period u. Beyond period u, equations (A10.1-10) through (A10.1-16) remain applicable in an exogenously real sense (i.e., for measuring the nominal exchange rate change less the amount of the change explained by differential exogenous inflation rates, and for estimating nominal interest rates less exogenous inflation, so that f_u can still be measured by specifying $\underline{X}_Z/\underline{X}_u$ to equal one plus the current real domestic interest rate divided by one plus the current real foreign interest rate, raised to the Z power).

For instance, assume that one wanted to estimate the probability of a complete 33 percent devaluation of the N.Z. dollar over the next year on the particular day being examined in early 1999. At that time, nominal one-year government interest rates were 4.91 percent in New Zealand and 5.14 percent in the United States, while inflation was 0.3 percent in New Zealand and 1.5 percent in the United States. These data imply real one-year interest rates were $\{1.0491/1.003\} - 1 = 4.60$ percent in New Zealand and $\{1.0514/1.015\} - 1 = 3.59$ percent in the United States. Assuming $f_0 = 0$ (which can be ascertained from overnight interest rates), $\underline{X}_Z/\underline{X}_0 = 1.0460/1.0359 = 1.0097$ for $Z = 1$. Given that $I = \{1 + .03 + .0491\}/1.03 = 1.0477$ for the one-year horizon being studied, equation (A10.1-16) implies that $1.0097 = f_1[1 + \{.33(1 + .0477)^1\}] + [1 - f_1]$. Solving for the unknown in the latter equation, it follows that $f_1 = .0281$. Thus, equation (A10.1-16) indicates that there is a 2.81 percent chance of a 33 percent devaluation of the N.Z. dollar over the next year.

Model 3: Exchange Rates with Exogenous Inflation and Investor Perceptions of Different Devaluation Possibilities

The prior models have assumed a complete devaluation needed to eliminate temporarily the current-account deficit over the course of one year. However, it may be more realistic to assume that any devaluation may occur over N' years, so that there is a gradual reduction of the current-account deficit as specified by the function

$$A_n = A_{n-1}[1 - \{n/N'\}], \tag{A10.1-17}$$

where a variable primed (') denotes a value that is different from that in the simpler model, and where the subscripts on the current-account deficit (A) denote future time periods.[18] Then, the maximum number of years the complete devaluation could be postponed would be the maximum value of N' that satisfies the boundary condition

$$M(1 + g)^{N'} - F - A_0 \sum_{n=1}^{N'}(1 + g)^n (1 + i_d)^{N'-n+1} \prod_{q=1}^{n}[1 - (q/N')] \geq 0. \qquad (A10.1\text{-}18)$$

Boundary condition (A10.1-18) is the same as boundary condition A10.1-10, except that the current-account deficit declines over time with the gradual devaluation, and so the additional amount of capital given to foreigners (i.e., the third term on the left-hand side of the inequality) incorporates this reduction via the compounding of the term $[1 - (q/N')]$.

Boundary condition (A10.1-18) indicates the maximum $N' = 67$ for New Zealand. Thus, by gradually allowing the currency to depreciate (to $1/67 = 1.5\%$ of the needed devaluation annually) in order to address slowly the current-account imbalance, the full depreciation can be postponed for sixty-seven years in New Zealand.

Assuming some exogenous domestic and foreign inflation rates $\underline{P}_d$ and $\underline{P}_f$, respectively, and defining L as the probability of using a gradual devaluation to solve the current-account deficit problem, the devaluation expected over any Z periods changes to

$$\underline{X}'_Z/X_0 = [1 + P'_{0:Z}][1 + \{LC \sum_{n=1}^{Z} (n/N')]^{n-1} \prod_{q=1}^{n-1}\{1 - (q/N')\}\}]$$

$$[(1 + \underline{P}_d)/(1 + \underline{P}_f)]^Z \qquad\qquad \text{if } u = N', \qquad (A10.1\text{-}19)$$

where

$$P'_{0:Z} = \{\prod_{j=1}^{Z}[1 + \{LC \sum_{n=1}^{j-1} (n/N')]^{n-1} \prod_{q=1}^{n-1}\{1 - (q/N')\}\}]^{(Z-j)/T}\} - 1 \qquad (A10.1\text{-}20)$$

equals the currency depreciation over Z years that must occur in order to compensate for each gradual devaluation being incorporated into inflation over T years (as $P'_{0:N'}$ represents the compounded endogenous inflation over N' periods).

For instance, using 1998 inflation rates of 0.3 percent in New Zealand and 1.5 percent in the United States as the estimated exogenous inflation rates, and using interest rate spreads on the longest-term government bonds in New Zealand and the United States as proxies for the sixty-seven-year yield spreads, equation (A10.1-19) implies that $X_{N'}/X_0 = (1.0639/1.0578)^{67} = 1.4700$. The value of L that solves equation (A10.1-19) for N' is .3357 for New Zealand. This result implies investors must believe that there is a long-term 33.57 percent likelihood that New Zealand will use a gradual currency depreciation to solve its BOP problems (otherwise, if the probability were higher, domestic interest rates would have to be higher). Naturally, the 33.57 percent figure is dependent on the estimate of C, $\underline{P}_d$, $\underline{P}_f$, and other parameters used in the equation (such as the use of the longest-term bond yields as a proxy for the yield on sixty-seven-year bonds), but it does seem to indicate that investors perceive a very large probability of New Zealand's using some policy other than a devaluation to solve its BOP problem.

Equation (A10.1-19) can also lead to meaningful implications concerning the exchange-rate change over a number of years less than N'. For instance, equation (A10.1-19) implies one-year returns on risk-free government bonds in New Zealand should be $[1 + \{(.3357 \times .33)/67\}][1.003/1.015] = .9905$ of the return to one-year risk-free foreign bond investments. Since nominal one-year interest rates on risk-free government bonds are 4.91 percent in New Zealand and 5.14 percent in the United States, the equation A10.1-19 ratio (of 0.9905) approximates the actual $1.0491/1.0514 = .9978$ ratio between short-term bond returns in New Zealand and the United States. The small difference in the two ratios may exist because the parameters like C, $\underline{P}_d$, and $\underline{P}_f$ are estimated with error. For example, $\underline{P}_d$ might be underestimated given professional bank forecasts of an increase in N.Z. inflation to over 1 percent in 1999.

The possibility of a devaluation of another magnitude in a different time period can also be explicitly incorporated into the model. For instance, it is possible to allow for an immediate devaluation sufficient to resolve completely the BOP problem now, as in much prior research (Obstfeld 1986). In that case, the exchange rate will reflect a weighted average of the exchange-rate change under each possibility, with the weights determined by B, which is defined as investors' estimate of the probability of an immediate devaluation, and $1 - B$, which represents the probability of the alternative case defined in equation (A10.1-19) holding true.

Under simpler conditions, equation (A10.1-13) provided an estimate of the expected currency depreciation prior to an immediate devaluation. However, with the new assumptions about exogenous inflation and the possibility of a gradual devaluation, the equation must be adjusted. In particular, define a starred variable (*) as one with a value if an existing BOP problem is temporarily resolved with an immediate devaluation of C under the new set of assumptions, and assume that $1 - B^*$ is the probability that future BOP problems caused by endogenous inflation resulting from an initial immediate devaluation will be solved via some policy other than a devaluation (such as tight monetary and fiscal policies that can reduce real incomes). Then, the expected nominal exchange rate change over any Z periods is

$$\underline{X}^*_Z/X_0 = (1 + C)(1 + B^*C)^{\{Z/T^*\}}[(1 + \underline{P}_d)/(1 + \underline{P}_f)]^Z \text{ if } u = 0. \qquad (A10.1\text{-}21)$$

Combining equations (A10.1-18) and (A10.1-20) and multiplying by their respective probabilities,

$$\underline{X}_{\sim Z}/X_0 = (1 - B)(\underline{X}'_Z/\underline{X}_0) + B(\underline{X}^*_Z/\underline{X}_0), \qquad (A10.1\text{-}22)$$

where $\underline{X}_{\sim Z}$ represents the expected exchange rate under the assumption of a possibility of both a gradual devaluation (with an implied probability of L{1 –

B} in this adapted model) and an immediate and full devaluation (with probability B). The earlier equation (A10.1-19) is identical to the more general equation (A10.1-22) in the case of B = 0, and equation (A10.1-21) is identical to equation (A10.1-22) in the case of B = 1.

It is fairly simple to solve for B using equation (A10.1-22). For instance, assume that investors predict T* = 10 and B* = 1 after an immediate devaluation in New Zealand, then equation (A10.1-21) implies $\underline{X}^*_Z/\underline{X}$ = 1.3523 for Z = 1. It was earlier found that $(\underline{X}'_Z/\underline{X}_0)$ = .9905 for Z = 1 for New Zealand from equation (A10.1-19), and relative one-year interest rates indicated $\underline{X}\sim_Z/\underline{X}_0$ = .9978, so that equation (A10.1-22) implies .9978 = [(1 – B)(.9905)] + 1.3523B. Solving for the unknown, B = 2.02 percent. Thus, investors may perceive a very small (2.02%) chance over the next year of an immediate devaluation of the N.Z. dollar sufficient in size (C = .33) to bring its current account back into balance, but they forecast a much larger chance of .9798 × .3357 = 32.89 percent for a more gradual devaluation.[19]

After an immediate devaluation of C, equation (A10.1-21) implies that

$$\underline{X}^*_Z/X_u = (1 + B^*C)^{\{Z/T^*\}}[(1 + \underline{P}_d)/(1 + \underline{P}_f)]^Z \text{ if } u = 0. \qquad \text{(A10.1-23)}$$

For instance, for New Zealand, if it is again assumed that B* = 1.0 (i.e., assuming that the immediate depreciation of the currency causes investors to lose confidence completely in the country's willingness to use methods other than immediate devaluations to combat future BOP problems), and that T* = T = 10 (i.e., it will take ten years for currency declines to be incorporated into domestic inflation), equation (A10.1-23) indicates that an immediate devaluation would cause the long-term bond yield in New Zealand to rise to [{1 + (1.0 × .33)}$^{67/10}$(1.003/1.015)^{67}]$^{1/67}$[1.0578] – 1 = 7.55 percent. If the loss in confidence in the country's will to defend its currency's value causes market participants to also lose some confidence in the inflation-fighting powers of the central bank, T* might fall to just five years, and long-term interest rates would rise to 10.66 percent. Similarly, if B* = 1.0 and T* = 10, short-term interest rates would rise to only (1.0168)(1.0514) – 1 = 6.90 percent after a full devaluation of C = .33, whereas the one-year interest rate would rise much farther, to 10.00 percent, if B* = 1 and T* = 5.

If interest rates are set differently than those given in equation (A10.1-23), it is possible to derive the new equilibrium spot exchange rate. In particular, assuming that subsequent upward pressure on the exchange rate caused by the resulting current-account surplus would eventually offset any extra inflation induced by the larger devaluation, the value of the future expected exchange rate $(\underline{X}^*_Z)$ would remain unchanged. In order for uncovered interest-rate parity to continue to hold in this case of the artificially low domestic interest rates, the spot currency value would have to decline by an extra amount, so that the new spot exchange rate would be

$$X\#_u = X_u[\{\underline{X}^*_Z/X_u\}^{1/Z}(1 + i_f)/\{1 + i_d\#\}]^Z, \qquad \text{(A10.1-24)}$$

where # denotes a variable value when interest rates are set differently from those required to maintain a given spot exchange rate implied by equations (A10.1-18) through (A10.1-23). In equation (A10.1-24), setting interest rates below the level needed to maintain the spot exchange rate X_u (which would balance a current account) would cause the spot exchange rate to fall to $X\#_u$. After a larger fall in the currency value, the additional decline in the spot exchange rate needed to bring the current account into balance after the subsequent endogenous inflation would be less than otherwise because it would have already fallen part of the way to $\underline{X}^*_z$. It should be emphasized, however, that $\underline{X}^*_z$ itself might change, as B^* and T^*, which determine the value of $\underline{X}^*_z$ in equation (A10.1-32), might be different in this case of looser monetary policy.

For example, if New Zealand tried to set the one-year interest rate at 6 percent after a devaluation when $B^* = 1.0$ and $T^* = 10$ would normally require $i_d = 6.90$ percent (as previously computed), the currency would fall by an extra $(1.06/1.0690)^1 - 1 = -0.84$ percent below X_u if B^* and T^* continued to equal 1.0 and 10, respectively. This additional immediate decline would mean that the currency would have to fall only 99.16 percent as far in the future to reach the same level ($\underline{X}^*_z$) that would also be reached in period $Z = 1$ if interest rates were determined by equation (A10.1-23).

On the other hand, B^* and T^* might very well be adversely affected by an easy monetary policy that set the interest rate at 6 percent, and the exchange rate might fall much farther initially and in the longer term. For example, if $B^* = 1$ as before but $T^* = 5$ when $i_d\# = .06$, then equation (A10.1-23) yields a new value for $\underline{X}^*_1$ which can be inserted into equation (A10.1-24), so that

$$X\#_u = X_u[\{X_u(1 + .33)^{1/5}/X_u\}^{1/1}(1 + .0514)/\{1 + .06\}]^1, \qquad (A10.1-25)$$

implying $X\#_u$ equals $1.0501X_u$. The spot foreign currencies would therefore appreciate by an extra 5.01 percent above where they would have been if interest rates had been set at 6.90 percent (compared to a mere 0.84% additional appreciation if T^* had stayed equal to 10). Although the future expected one-year appreciation of the foreign currencies thereafter would continue to be reduced by the $(1.06/1.0690)^1 - 1 = -0.84$ percent that reflects the interest-rate-parity effect of lower interest rates on future expected future currency changes, $\underline{X}^*_1$ would remain over 4 percent above where it would have been if one-year interest rates had been set at 6.90 percent.

If T^* is reduced to a very small value, the effect on the foreign currency appreciation is much larger. For instance, in the prior New Zealand example, where interest rates are set at 6 percent instead of 6.90 percent, the spot foreign currency values would rise to

$$X\#_u = X_u[\{X_u(1 + .33)^{1/5}/X_u\}^{1/1}(1 + .0514)/\{1 + .06\}]^1$$
$$= 4.1278X_u \qquad (A10.1-26)$$

if $T^* = .2$ (i.e., if some sort of almost immediate imported inflation pass-through within one-fifth of a year were expected). This spot currency value would represent an additional appreciation of 312.78 percent above where it would have been if interest rates had been set at 6.90 percent (and would likely cause hyperinflation).

In any event, whenever interest rates are set differently than implied by equations (A10.1-18) through (A10.1-23), some form of equation (A10.1-24) applies. For instance, except in cases after a major devaluation, $\underline{X}$~$_Z$ would effectively have to be substituted for $\underline{X}^*_Z$ in equation (A10.1-24), so that

$$X\#_Z = X_0[\{X\text{~}_Z/X_0\}^{1/Z}(1 + i_f)/\{1 + i_d\#\}]^Z. \qquad (A10.1\text{-}27)$$

For example, if New Zealand lowered its current one-year interest rate from 4.91 percent to 4.5 percent (without any prior full devaluation to X_u), and if all the other variables remained the same, the N.Z. dollar would fall in value by $(1.045/1.0491)^1 - 1 = 0.39$ percent. It must be emphasized again, however, that varying the interest rate from that determined by equations (A10.1-18) through (A10.1-23) can result in a change in B, L, and T and thereby change the value of $\underline{X}$~$_Z$ to be plugged into equation (A10.1-27), just as setting the interest rate below that determined by equation (A10.1-23) can change the value of $\underline{X}^*_Z$ to be plugged into equation (A10.1-24).

For countries with capital controls, i_d must reflect the foreign currency cost adjusted for expected exchange rate changes

$$i_d = \{1 + i_f\}\{\underline{X}_Z/X_0\}^{1/Z} - 1 \qquad (A10.1\text{-}28)$$

for government bonds with the maturity of Z, where $\underline{X}_Z$ must be estimated econometrically (or by increasing an estimate of the country's current trade-weighted cost of earning foreign currency by inflation differentials, as per purchasing power parity), instead of being computed directly from interest rate differentials observable in the market under the assumption of interest-rate parity. Using the estimate of i_d in equation (A10.1-28) to compute I in equation (A10.1-11), and in all the other equations as well, boundary conditions (A10.1-10) and (A10.1-18) could still be employed to measure the amount of time a current-account deficit can be postponed via foreign financing. In addition, the remaining equations could still be utilized to estimate the probability of devaluation (under the assumption, however, that the subjective exchange rate forecast is representative of investors' forecasts).

By replacing C with c, by setting $P_d = P_f = P'_{0:N'} = 0$, and by assuming L in equation (A10.1-19) represents the probability of a real income decline with a value of one, a modified equation (A10.1-19) can be employed to measure the total decline in real income required over N' years to eliminate a current-account deficit. Raising the resulting right-hand side to the 1/N' power provides an estimate of the lower annual economic growth W that would persist for N' years.

$$W = [1 + \{c \sum_{n=1}^{N'} (n/N')]^{n-1} \prod_{q=1}^{n-1} \{1 - (q/N')\}\}]^{1/N'} - 1. \qquad (A10.1\text{-}29)$$

NOTES

1. To compute this value, complex econometric procedures should really be used to estimate aggregate demand elasticity across all industries for all trading partners (not just for exports to the United States of sheep meat, which represents only a small portion of N.Z. trade), but the simple example here provides an illustration of the analysis. Note that using the United States as the proxy for the foreign world outside New Zealand also biases the results, as the U.S. dollar itself may be expected to depreciate somewhat against other foreign currencies in order to correct its own current-account deficit. Regardless, any parameter estimate for C should incorporate qualitative information, such as the fact that the United States is threatening to impose protectionist barriers against lamb imports from New Zealand as a result of the large N.Z. market share increase in 1998 (de Lacy 1999), and so further increases in N.Z. sheep meat exports to the United States may not be possible regardless of any exchange rate depreciation. In addition, the extent to which the income component of the current account is affected by an exchange rate change should also be considered. For instance, if there is a large negative income balance in the current account that derives from debt denominated in the domestic currency, a currency devaluation may decrease this amount in terms of foreign currency values. However, any income earned by foreigners on debt denominated in a foreign currency would be unchanged by a devaluation (as would generally any income from foreign holdings of domestic equities, since domestic currency profits tend to grow with currency depreciation, inflation, and nominal GDP long-term). Indeed, Calvo and Mendoza (1996) have found empirical evidence indicating that the large increase in dollar-linked debt in Mexico just before its devaluation in 1994 may have contributed to the need for a larger devaluation of the Mexican peso than otherwise would have been required.

2. In cases of paper money backed by gold, the currency of the country with the current-account deficit first suffers a deterioration in its exchange rate against the currencies of other countries with gold standards, thereby causing its importers to pay in gold (instead of depreciated currency) because the effective cost is lower (even after considering the transaction costs of shipping the gold), and thereby resulting in the decline in both the supply of gold and the domestic money supply that sends up domestic interest rates (Marx and Engels 1988). In these circumstances, the currency of the country with the current-account deficit would then have to rise in value as a result of the interest rate increase drawing in more capital, and in order for uncovered interest rate parity (King 1998) to hold under these conditions, the appreciation would continue up to a point where the currency of the country with the current-account deficit is at a premium to the other gold-backed currencies that have lower interest rates (as long as the country with the current-account deficit is expected to maintain the gold standard). The rise in interest rates and related currency appreciation is often high enough to even cause an inflow of gold into the country with the current-account deficit, until the high interest rates and currency value can slow the economy sufficiently to reverse the current-account deficit (Marx and Engels 1988).

3. Declines in income can cause more mobile resources, such as skilled workers and capital, to leave the country, and the loss of such valuable resources can greatly damage a developing economy (Bhagwati 1977). Serious brain drain can also occur in developed industrialized countries (Brenner 1999), as can capital flight (Lindsey 1999). While these problems can be mitigated, respectively, with capital controls (Giovannini

1992) and with an exit tax, as in China (Wong 1997), a more typical solution employed (and usually recommended by the IMF) is to have the income reductions concentrated among the less mobile and less valuable resources among the poor (Chossudovsky 1997). For instance, "necessary belt-tightening" often is just another phrase for reductions in social spending. In addition, Mauro and Spilimbego (1999) have empirically found that recessions by themselves tend to increase the unemployment rate more among unskilled workers, whereas laid-off skilled workers have a much greater ability to move to a job in another country.

4. To the extent that there is a possibility of the country being unwilling (or unable) to make repayments on its domestic currency debts (or a chance of expropriation and/or higher tax rates in the case of foreign equity capital), there may be some default risk, and a higher return premium would have to be offered even on domestic currency financing. However, in most cases, the risk of a country defaulting on its domestic debts is negligible; even in the notorious case of Russia in 1998, it was not the ninety-day payment postponement on some of its domestic government debt but the large currency decline that caused enormous losses for investors (and such losses would have occurred with a currency devaluation any time). As a result, this risk can be assumed to be incorporated into the expected currency depreciation for domestic debt (although a special risk premium may indeed be required on foreign equity investments to compensate for the risk of expropriation and/or higher tax rates that may be more likely to occur in countries with large current-account deficits and extensive foreign ownership of capital). Note that such an assumption in no way removes the potentially enormous currency depreciation risk that exists with some government bonds denominated in their own currencies, especially in countries with high inflation rates, as it merely assumes that investors are compensated for such risk with higher interest rates.

5. While a higher return could be required on some currency debts (and a corresponding lower one on others) because of systematic investor preferences for assets of specific countries (Frankel 1988), tests of such phenomena have "found no significant empirical evidence of risk premia" (Hooper and Morton 1982). Although some researchers have hypothesized that the empirical tendency of interest rate differentials to exceed exchange rate changes over most time periods to be caused by a bizarre currency risk premium (Bansal and Dahlquist 2000), that empirical tendency can be more rationally explained by the small probability of a large but seldom-observed currency devaluation (Krasker 1980). As a result, premiums for systematic currency preferences are assumed to be insignificant in this model (at least relative to the premium required for expected currency changes). In any event, adjusting for such premiums would add only a residual yield term that would not materially affect the conclusions of this research.

6. Obstfeld and Rogoff (1996) have indicated that it could be theoretically feasible to postpone a resolution to a current-account deficit indefinitely, as is mathematically possible in boundary condition A10.1-10 if M and g are sufficiently large and A and i_d are sufficiently small. However, such a possibility is very remote. In particular, even if the long-term domestic interest rate were 0 percent (as is extremely unlikely for a country with a current-account deficit), solving inequality A10.1-10 for an infinite time horizon requires that $M > A + \{A/g\}$, or that the domestic capital in the country exceed the current-account deficit by a factor of more than the inverse of the economic growth rate. Although the latter condition is feasible (especially for a nation with a reasonably high economic growth rate and a very low current-account deficit),

the former is not (especially for a country with a reasonably high economic growth rate). More typically, the interest rate will equal or exceed the economic growth rate (Clements 2001), in which case boundary condition A10.1-10 cannot hold at a value of u equal to infinity. Even when the interest rate is less than the growth rate, most observable cases would result in N being less than infinity. (Even in any rare situations where the boundary condition held at a value of u equal to infinity, the possibility of a shock that would change some of the values in the inequality to cause it to no longer hold would generally be high enough to make the subsequent analysis explained in the text relevant for some sets of feasible scenarios that would affect the exchange rate.)

7. It is being assumed that only devaluation induces inflation endogenously and that any expected domestic inflation caused by importing foreign inflation is incorporated into exogenous domestic inflation P_d.

8. L could also represent the percentage of the BOP problem expected to be resolved with a currency depreciation, where this expected percentage itself would be a function of the weighted-average probability estimates of investors (with the weights again being determined by investor wealth). Alternatively, L could incorporate estimates of different devaluations (including an immediate and full devaluation of C) each year (and probabilities thereof) if it is assumed that L is some complex weighted average of such devaluation sizes (and probabilities).

9. As Bernhardsen (2000) has demonstrated empirically, relative interest rate differentials tend to be related directly and positively to the size of current-account deficits and inflation differentials.

10. Note that the foreign currency reserves themselves may be built up via open market purchases of foreign currencies or via the sale of foreign currency debt. Dellas and Galor (1992) have explained why countries would raise more foreign currency financing than is actually needed currently, insofar as the excess foreign currency reserves can be used to make amortization payments on the debt and thereby maintain a good credit rating until it is possible to pay off the debt in full.

11. The model could be broadened to allow for additional probability estimates for the path of devaluation (such as a higher probability of a large devaluation in two years than at any other time). However, adding additional probability variables would unduly complicate the mathematics of the model (which would be underidentified, given far more unknown variable values than equations), and a myriad of probability estimates for different times and degrees of devaluation might not yield meaningful information (even if they could be empirically estimated). Note that various possible devaluation paths (in terms of timing and degree) can probably be adequately parameterized by combinations of the two extremes (B and L) of the existing model, especially given the fact that L can be alternatively specified to equal investors' forecast of the percentage of a BOP problem that is to be solved with a devaluation (e.g., see footnote 8). Note also that an equation for estimating the probability in each period of a full devaluation solution to a current-account deficit was provided in equation (A10.1-16). Whereas equation (A10.1-22) is generally applicable to cases of both fixed and floating exchange rates, equation (A10.1-16) can usually only be applied to cases of fixed exchange rates with similar inflation rates across countries. Equation (A10.1-16) can also be applied to situations of targeted fixed real exchange rates (such as a crawling peg, or even a general unofficial tendency of central banks to maintain a specified real exchange rate via open market operations and interest rate policies) as long as it is realized that the model is then measuring exogenous real exchange rate changes (with

corresponding implications on real interest rate differentials, as explained earlier in the text).

12. While the model (or an adaptation thereof) can be readily programmed using the equations of this article, commercial software utilizing the theory is available and sold relatively inexpensively by SIA (www.scianalysis.com). The software comes bundled with programs that also conduct more general investment analysis such as state-of-the-art valuation of stocks and complex debts (including callable and convertible bonds and mortgage-backed securities), as well as sophisticated portfolio and financial planning evaluations, as described in more detail in Murphy (2000a).

13. There is some evidence that the short-term currency trading decisions of large investors are heavily affected by technical factors that cause investor sentiment to move in short-term trends that tend to be unrelated to fundamentals but that eventually reverse themselves to reflect fundamental currency values more accurately (Froot and Ramadorai 2002). Since currency changes affect relative inflation and fundamental values (as shown in this research itself), investor perceptions (and any trending or herding thereof unrelated to fundamentals) can indeed represent self-fulfilling prophecies.

14. The N.Z. dollar did eventually decline by over 20 percent in 2000, but the country did not have to raise interest rates to a very high level thereafter as its central bank was able to maintain investor confidence that the devaluation would increase inflation only very slowly and that other solutions to the nation's BOP problems would be found.

15. Although prices in foreign countries might fall as a result of the appreciation of their currencies against the currency of the country with the BOP problem (and thus partially offset the devaluation-induced inflation in the country with the BOP problem), one country's devaluation has only a partial (and generally negligible) effect on the larger world economy (Kindleberger 1968). Where that partial effect is relatively larger (as with economically more significant countries), it will generally take a larger C to get the BOP to balance (since the price decline in the foreign countries lowers foreign costs and allows their exporters to lower prices in their currency to partially offset the effect of the currency appreciation). In addition, the downward stickiness of nominal wages (Stiglitz 1993), typically inhibits actual deflation in countries with rising currencies (and some downward stickiness in real wages actually restricts the fall in any positive inflation rate in countries with rising currency values). As a result, this factor often does not materially affect the analysis.

16. Inflationary effects are likely over shorter time periods for internationally traded goods, including for exports as well as goods that compete against potential imports, and so T tends to be shorter for countries more dependent on international trade. However, it should be mentioned that order backlogs, fixed contracts existing before devaluation, and hedging can prevent the inflationary effect from being immediate even for internationally traded items, as can lags in adjustments in production and distribution, so that the effect often phases in over a year or more (Caves, Frankel, and Jones 1996). For products and services that are not easily traded across borders, the effects are more gradual, as the cost of labor and other input factors might only slowly increase with the cost of internationally traded goods and generally only to the extent of domestic inflation, which itself might only fully rise to the level of the currency depreciation after many years, as the domestic input factors continue to raise their prices to reflect the delayed effect on inflation of their own past increases (Soedersten and Reed 1994).

17. Note that the numbers employed here are strictly for illustration and so are estimated somewhat roughly. For instance, the longest-term N.Z. government bond

reported in the May 11, 1999, *Evening Post* had a maturity of only fourteen years, and the spread between the yield on this bond and a U.S. government bond with the same maturity was added to the yield on a thirty-year U.S. government bond (as reported in the May 11, 1999, *Wall Street Journal*) to estimate the yield on a very long-term N.Z. government bond. Similar rough estimates are used subsequently, such as having yields on N.Z. government bonds with a maturity of between one and two years proxy for the yield on a one-year bond because there were no listed N.Z. government bonds with an exact one-year maturity.

18. This assumed path for the devaluation-induced resolution of the current-account deficit has the characteristic of an orderly currency depreciation that central banks often attempt to implement with various monetary, interest rate, and intervention policies in order to minimize the effects of large shocks to the system, but it is by no means the only reasonable function. Other paths for a gradual depreciation could be assumed, but the subsequent results and implications of the model would generally not be greatly affected, just as modifying other simple mathematical assumptions of the model, such as altering the form of the positive relationship between currency depreciation and inflation defined in equation (A10.1-3), would not impact the general findings of the model. However, since potentially more accurate paths and assumptions (which might better reflect the effect of the complex relationships between central bank designs and investor expectations and actions) would increase the precision of the exact numerical estimates for many of the variables of the model, there may be significant use for subsequent research that would attempt to solve for the most realistic functions from empirical data.

19. Short-term interest rates have actually declined dramatically from their highs in 1998, implying that B and L may have earlier been much higher. The past official policy of New Zealand automatically increasing its interest rates 1 percent for every 2 percent decline in its trade-weighted currency value (Hosking 1999) may have contributed to N.Z.'s ability to keep B and L relatively low and thereby enabled the country to postpone the much larger needed currency or real income decline with far lower interest rates than was possible for many countries in Southeast Asia. Although the N.Z. central bank no longer formally uses this decision criteria, its statements still imply some inverse relationship between the currency value and interest rates (Weir 1999).

REFERENCES

Abken, P. 1998. "Beyond Plain Vanilla: A Taxonomy of Swaps." In *Financial Derivatives* (ed. by R. Kolb). Blackwell: Oxford.

Abuaf, N., and P. Jorion. 1990. "Purchasing Power Parity in the Long Run." *Journal of Finance* 45: 157–174.

Afesoglu, S., and D. Dutkowsky. 1997. "On the Dynamics of Balance of Payments Constrained Growth." *Applied Economics* 29: 1343–1351.

Agenor, P., and P. Masson. 1999. "Credibility, Reputation, and the Mexican Peso Crisis." *Journal of Money, Credit, and Banking* 31: 70–84.

Aliber, R. 2000. "Credit Expansion in the Trouble Asian Economies: Domestic vs. Foreign Causes." Paper presented at the American Economic Association Meeting.

Bairoch, P. 1993. *Economics and World History*. Chicago: University of Chicago Press.

Bansal, R., and M. Dahlquist. 2000. "The Forward Premium Puzzle: Different Tales from Developed and Emerging Economies." *Journal of International Economics* 51: 115–144.

Barkley, T. 2000. "Dollar Stands Tall on Shaky Ground over Uncertainty of Presidential Election." *Wall Street Journal*, November 24, B13.

Barkley, T., and C. Richard. 2000. "Short-Covering Rally Boosts the Euro, Lifting It from Near Its Record Low." *Wall Street Journal*, August 31, C13.

Ben-Bassat, A., and D. Gottlieb. 1992. "Optimal International Reserves and Sovereign Risk." *Journal of International Economics* 33: 345–362.

Berg, A., and C. Pattillo. 1999. "Are Currency Crises Predictable? A Test." *IMF Staff Papers*, 107–138.

Bernhardsen, T. 2000. "The Relationship between Interest Rate Differentials and Macroeconomic Variables: A Panel Data Study for European Countries." *Journal of International Money and Finance* 19: 289–308.

Bhagwati, J. (ed.). 1977. *The New International Economic Order: The North–South Debate*. Cambridge: MIT Press.

Brenner, R. 1999. "Currencies Don't Lie." *Forbes Global Business & Finance*, March 8, 59.

Calvo, G., and E. Mendoza. 1996. "Mexico's Balance-of-Payments Crisis: A Chronicle of a Death Foretold." *Journal of International Economics* 41: 235–264.

Caprio, G., and D. Klingebiel. 1997. "Bank Insolvency: Bad Luck, Bad Policy, or Bad Banking?" *Annual World Bank Conference on Development Economics, 1996*. Washington, D.C.: World Bank.

Cassell, G. 1928. *Post-War Monetary Stabilization*. New York: Columbia University Press.

Cavaglia, S., W. Verschoor, and C. Wolff. 1993. "Further Evidence on Exchange Rate Expectations." *Journal of International Money and Finance* 12: 78–98.

Caves, R., J. Frankel, and R. Jones. 1996. *World Trade and Payments*. New York: HarperCollins.

Chossudovsky, M. 1997. *The Globalization of Poverty: Impacts of IMF and World Bank Reforms*. Penang: Third World Network.

Claessens, S. 1991. "Balance of Payments Crises in an Optimal Portfolio Model." *European Economic Review* 35: 81–101.

Clements, J. 2001. "Stocks over Bonds: A Holow Victory?" *Wall Street Journal*, May 8, C1.

Connolly, M., and D. Taylor. 1984. "The Exact Timing of the Collapse of an Exchange Rate Regime and Its Impact on the Relative Price of Traded Goods." *Journal of Money, Credit, and Banking* 16: 194–207.

Coy, P. 2002. "Deeper Debt for Uncle Sam." *Business Week*, March 18, 28.

De Lacy, H. 1999. "How N.Z. Ruined a Good Market." *Press*, May 1, 10.

Dellas, H., and O. Galor. 1992. "Growth Via External Public Debt and Capital Controls." *International Economic Review* 33: 269–281.

Dellas, H., and A. Stockman. 1993. "Self-Fulfilling Expectations, Speculative Attack, and Capital Controls." *Journal of Money, Credit, and Banking* 25: 721–730.

Devereux, M. 2000. "How Does a Devaluation Affect the Current Account?" *Journal of International Money and Finance* 19: 833–851.

Dixit, A. 1989. "Hysteresis, Import Penetration, and Exchange Rate Pass-Through." *Quarterly Journal of Economics* 104: 205–228.

Dooley, M., and P. Isard. 1982. "The Role of the Current Account in Exchange-Rate Determination: A Comment on Rodriguez." *Journal of Political Economy* 90: 1291–1294.

Dornbusch, R. 1982. "Equilibrium and Disequilibrium Exchange Rates." *Zeitschrift fuer Wirtschafts und Sozialwissenschaften* 102.

Downey, J. 2001. "Euro Hits a Low for 2001 against the Dollar." *Wall Street Journal*, March 30, C9.

Drazen, A., and P. Masson. 1994. "Credibility of Policies versus Credibility of Policymakers." *Quarterly Journal of Economics* 104: 735–754.

Druckerman, P. 2002a. "As Argentina Defaults, Will IMF Be a Victim?" *Wall Street Journal*, January 4, A5.

———. 2002b. "Candidate Gomes's Popularity Is Contest for Brazil's Markets." *Wall Street Journal*, July 8, A12.

Duca, J., and D. VanHoose. 1998. "The Rise of Goods-Market Competition and the Decline in Wage Indexation: A Macroeconomic Approach." *Journal of Macroeconomics* 20: 579–598.

Edison, H., and D. Pauls. 1993. "A Re-Assessment of the Relationship between Real Exchange Rates and Real Interest Rates: 1970–1990." *Journal of Monetary Economics* 31: 165–187.

Edlin, B. 1999. "Central Bank Does Not Absolve Govt.'s Duty to Manage Monetary Policy." *Independent*, March 31, 34.

Eiteman, D., A. Stonehill, and M. Moffett. 1998. *Multinational Business Finance*. Reading: Addison-Wesley.

Frankel, J. 1988. "Recent Estimates of Time-Variation in the Conditional Variance and in the Exchange Risk Premium." *Journal of International Money and Finance* 7: 115–125.

Frankel, J., and A. Rose. 1995. "Empirical Research on Nominal Exchange Rates." *Handbook of International Economics* 3: 1689–1730.

———. 1996. "Currency Crashes in Emerging Markets: An Empirical Treatment." *Journal of International Economics* 41: 351–366.

Froot, K., and K. Rogoff. 1995. "Perspectives on PPP and Long-Run Real Exchange Rates." *Handbook of International Economics* 3: 1647–1688.

Froot, K., and T. Ramadorai. 2002. "Currency Returns, Institutional Investor Flows and Exchange Rate Fundamentals." Harvard NOM Working Paper 02–21 (July).

Fullerton, T., C. Sawyer, and R. Sprinkle. 1999. "Latin American Trade Elasticities." *Journal of Economics and Finance* 23: 143–156.

Giovannini, A. 1992. "Capital Controls and International Trade Finance." *Journal of International Economics* 33: 285–304.

Glick, R., and K. Rogoff. 1995. "Global versus Country-Specific Productivity Shocks and the Current Account." *Journal of Monetary Economics* 35: 159–192.

Goldstein, M., and M. Khan. 1978. "The Supply and Demand for Exports: A Simultaneous Approach." *Review of Economics and Statistics* 60: 275–286.

Golub, S. 1989. "Foreign-Currency Government Debt, Asset Markets, and the Balance of Payments." *Journal of International Money and Finance*, 285–294.

Goodhardt, C. 1988. "The Foreign Exchange Market: A Random Walk with a Dragging Anchor." *Economica* 55: 437–460.

Haque, N., P. Montiel, and S. Symansky. 1991. "A Forward Looking Macroeconomic Simulation Model for a Developing Country." *Journal of Policy Modeling* 13: 41–65.

Henderson, C. 1998. *Asia Falling?* New York: McGraw-Hill.

Hooper, P., and J. Morton. 1982. "Fluctuations in the Dollar: A Model of Nominal and Real Exchange Rate Determination." *Journal of International Money and Finance* 1: 39–56.

Hosking, R. 1999. "Market Divided over 'Quiet' Ditching of Unpopular Monetary Conditions Index." *National Business Review*, February 12, 8.

Hufbauer, G., and J. Erb. 1984. *Subsidies in International Trade*. Washington, D.C.: Institute for International Economics.

Husted, S., and R. MacDonald. 1999. "The Asian Currency Crash: Were Badly Driven Fundamentals to Blame?" *Journal of Asian Economcs* 10: 537–550.

Kamin, S. 1999. "The Current International Financial Crisis: How Much Is New?" *Journal of International Money and Finance* 18: 501–514.

Kaminsky, G., and C. Reinhart. 1999. "The Twin Crises: The Causes of Banking and Balance-of-Payments Problems." *American Economic Review* 89: 473–500.

———. 2000. "On Crises, Contagion, and Confusion." *Journal of International Economics* 51: 145–168.

Kane, E. 2000. "Capital Movements, Banking Insolvency, and Silent Runs in the Asian Financial Crisis." *Pacific-Basin Finance Journal* 8: 153–175.

Karp, J. 2001. "Brazil Central-Bank Chief Faces Biggest Challenge." *Wall Street Journal*, March 26, A16.

Karp, J., and P. Druckerman. 2000. "Big Latin Customs Union Mercosur Reaches a Crossroads." *Wall Street Journal*, December 15, A15.

Katz, I., and L. Cohn. 1999. "Pulling Brazil Back from the Brink." *Business Week*, Asian Edition, May 10, 64–65.

Kelsey, J. 1999. *Reclaiming the Future*. Toronto: University of Toronto Press.

Kho, B., and R. Stulz. 2000. "Banks, the IMF, and the Asian Crisis." *Pacific-Basin Finance Journal* 8: 177–216.

Kindleberger, C. 1968. *International Economics*. Homewood: Irwin.

King, A. 1998. "Uncovered Interest Parity: New Zealand's Post-Deregulation Experience." *Applied Financial Economics* 8: 495–503.

Krasker, W. 1980. "The 'Peso Problem' in Testing the Efficiency of Forward Exchange Rate Markets." *Journal of Monetary Economics* 6: 269–276.

Lerner, A. 1944. *The Economics of Control*. New York: Macmillan.

Lim, L. 1999. "An Overview of the Asian Financial Crisis." *Journal of Asian Business* 15: 79–81.

Lindsey, L. 1999. "Arranged Marriage." *Forbes Global Business & Finance*, March 8, 69.

MacDonald, R. 1990. "Empirical Studies of Exchange Rate Determination." In *Current Issues in Monetary Economics* (ed. D. Lewellyn and C. Milner). London: Macmillan.

Manzur, M. 1990. "An International Comparison of Prices and Exchange Rates: A New Test of Purchasing Power Parity." *Journal of International Money and Finance* 9: 75–91.

Marquez, J. 1990. "Bilateral Trade Elasticities." *Review of Economics and Statistics* 72: 75–86.

Marshall, A. 1924. *Money, Credit, and Commerce*. New York: Macmillan.

Marx, K., and F. Engels. 1988. *Das Kapital*. Berlin: Dietz Verlag.

Mauro, P., and A. Spilimbergo. 1999. "How Do the Skilled and the Unskilled Respond to Regional Shocks?" *IMF Staff Papers* 47: 1–17.

McKinnon, R., and H. Pill. 1996. "Credible Liberalizations and International Capital Flows: The 'Overborrowing Syndrome.'" In *Financial Deregulation and Integration in East Asia* (ed. T. Ito and A. Krueger). Chicago: University of Chicago Press.

McManus, J. 1999. "US Retaliates on NZ Lamb." *Independent*, February 17, 1–4.
Michalski, W. 1972. *Export Trade and Economic Growth*. Hamburg: Verlag Weltarchiv.
Miller, M. 1998. "The Current Southeast Asia Financial Crisis." *Pacific-Basin Finance Journal* 6: 225–233.
Milverton, D. 2000. "IMF Overhauls Loan Plan, a Win for U.S." *Wall Street Journal*, September 18, A26.
Miyakoshi, T. 2000. "The Causes of the Asian Currency Crisis: Empirical Observations." *Japan and the World Economy* 12: 245–253.
Moran, P. 1999. "NZ Farmers Guarded over Reforms in Europe." *Dominion*, March 13, 2.
Murphy, A. 1990. "Using the CAPM as a General Framework for Asset Pricing Analysis." *Journal of Financial Research* 13: 233–241.
———. 1992. "An Analysis of Terms of Trade Problems." *Economic Systems* 16: 149–160.
———. 1995. "Parallels between Eastern Europe and Mexico." *International Economic Newsletter* 40: 1–3.
———. 1996. "The Determinants of Exchange Rates between Two Major Currencies." *Multinational Business Review* 4: 107–111.
———. 1998. "A Note on Economic Growth in Eastern Europe." *Journal of Economic Issues* 32: 1150–1152.
———. 2000a. *Scientific Investment Analysis*. Westport, Conn.: Quorum Books.
———. 2000b. *The Triumphy of Evil: The Reality of the USA's Cold War Victory*. Fucecchio, Italy: European Press Academic.
Obstfeld, M. 1984. "Balance-of-Payments Crises and Devaluation." *Journal of Money, Credit, and Banking* 16: 208–217.
———. 1986. "Rational and Self-Fulfilling Balance-of-Payments Crises." *American Economic Review* 76: 72–81.
Obstfeld, M., and K. Rogoff. 1995. "The Intertemporal Approach to the Current Account." *Handbook of International Economics* 3: 1731–1800.
———. 1996. *Foundations of International Macroeconomics*. Cambridge, Mass.: MIT Press.
Phillips, M. 2000. "Key Trade Deficit Measure Sets Record." *Wall Street Journal*, March 16, A2.
Pope, H. 2001. "Central Bank Throws Lifeline to Turkey Markets." *Wall Street Journal*, February 27, A17.
Rich, G. 1997. "Monetary Targets as a Policy Rule: Lessons from the Swiss Experience." *Journal of Monetary Economics* 39: 113–141.
Rodriguez, C. 1980. "The Role of Trade Flows in Exchange Rage Determination: A Rational Expectations Approach." *Journal of Political Economy* 88: 1148–1158.
Roldos, J. 1997. "On Gradual Disinflation, the Real Exchange Rate, and the Current Account." *Journal of International Money and Finance* 16: 37–54.
Root, F. 1990. *International Trade and Investment*. Cincinnati: South-Western.
Seib, G., and A. Murray. 1991. "IMF Effort to Reform Soviet Economy Runs Many Daunting Risks." *Wall Street Journal*, October 15, A1.
Smellie, P. 1999. "Winbox-Style Tax Schemes Reappear." *Star Times*, June 13, A1–A2.
Smith, J. 2000. *Economic Democracy: The Political Struggle of the 21st Century*. Armonk, N.Y.: Sharpe.

Soedersten, B., and G. Reed. 1994. *International Economics*. New York: St. Martin's Press.

Stiglitz, J. 1993. *Economics*. New York: W. W. Norton.

Stulz, R. 1988. "Capital Mobility and the Current Account." *Journal of International Money and Finance* 7: 167–180.

Tanzer, A. 1999. "The Ronald Reagan of the Pacific." *Forbes Global*, May 31, 25–26.

Tegene, A. 1989. "On the Effects of Relative Prices and Exchange Rates on Trade Flows of LDCs." *Applied Economics* 21: 1447–1463.

Velasco, A. 1987. "Financial Crises and Balance of Payments Crises." *Journal of Development Economics* 27: 263–283.

Weir, J. 1999. "No Tears in Exporters' Lager." *Dominion*, June 12, 11.

Wessel, D. 1999. "More Group Therapy Awaits Global Finance." *Wall Street Journal*, December 13, A1.

Williamson, J. 1991. *The Economic Opening of Eastern Europe*. Washington, D.C.: Institute for International Economics.

Wong, K. 1997. *International Trade in Goods and Factor Mobility*. Cambridge, Mass.: MIT Press.

Yusoff, M. 1997. "Economic Performance and Policy Adjustments of the Southeast Asian Nations." *Journal of Asian Business* 13: 5–26.

Index

About the Editor and Contributors

Don Bloomquist is president of SIA in Sterling, Illinois.

Dejan Joksimovic is employed by IBISCO Ltd.

Edwin D. Maberly is professor at the University of Canterbury in Christchurch, New Zealand.

Elton McGoun is on the faculty of Bucknell University, Lewisburg, Pennsylvania.

Cynthia Miree is assistant professor of management at Oakland University in Rochester, Michigan.

Dusan Mramor is on the faculty of the University of Ljubljana, in Slovenia.

Austin Murphy is professor of finance at Oakland University in Rochester, Michigan.

Raylene M. Pierce is lecturer at the University of Canterbury in Christchurch, New Zealand.

Arline Savage is assistant professor of accounting at Oakland University in Rochester, Michigan.

Usamah A. Uthman is professor of petroleum and minerals at King Fahd University in Dhahran, Saudi Arabia.